THE LANDLORD'S LEGAL GUIDE IN TEXAS

Traci Truly
Attorney at Law

SPHINX® PUBLISHING
AN IMPRINT OF SOURCEBOOKS, INC.®
NAPERVILLE, ILLINOIS
www.SphinxLegal.com

First Edition, 2003

Published by: **Sphinx® Publishing, An Imprint of Sourcebooks, Inc.®**

<u>Naperville Office</u>
P.O. Box 4410
Naperville, Illinois 60567-4410
630-961-3900
Fax: 630-961-2168
www.sourcebooks.com
www.SphinxLegal.com

This publication is designed to provide accurate and authoritative information in regard to the subject matter covered. It is sold with the understanding that the publisher is not engaged in rendering legal, accounting, or other professional service. If legal advice or other expert assistance is required, the services of a competent professional person should be sought.

From a Declaration of Principles Jointly Adopted by a Committee of the
American Bar Association and a Committee of Publishers and Associations

This product is not a substitute for legal advice.

Disclaimer required by Texas statutes.

Library of Congress Cataloging-in-Publication Data
Truly, Traci.
    The landlord's legal guide in Texas / by Traci Truly.-- 1st ed.
       p. cm.
    ISBN 1-57248-355-5
    1. Landlord and tenant--Texas--Popular works. I. Title.

KFT1317.Z9 T78 2003
346.76404'34--dc22

                                        2003016479

Printed and bound in the United States of America.
VHG Paperback — 10 9 8 7 6 5 4 3 2 1

CONTENTS

VI ◆ *the landlord's legal guide in texas*

Chapter 17: Evictions 85
    Public Hearing
    Possible Tenant Defenses

Chapter 18: Hiring an Attorney. 93

Chapter 19: Recovering Possession. 95
    Abandonment
    Agreeing to End the Tenancy
    Acceptance of Past Due Rent
    Tenant's Bankruptcy

Chapter 20: Other Liabilities. 99
    Personal Injuries
    Criminal Acts of Third Parties
    Tenant's Criminal Activity

Chapter 21: Conclusion 103

Glossary 105

Appendix A: Texas Landlord and Tenant Statutes 113

Appendix B: Texas Forcible Entry and Detainer Statutes. . . . 145

Appendix C: Texas Rules of Civil Procedure Relating to
            Forcible Entry and Detainer. 149

Appendix D: Blank Forms 155

Index 197

Using Self-Help Law Books

Before using a self-help law book, you should realize the advantages and disadvantages of doing your own legal work and understand the challenges and diligence that this requires.

The Growing Trend

Rest assured that you won't be the first or only person handling your own legal matter. For example, in some states, more than seventy-five percent of the people in divorces and other cases represent themselves. Because of the high cost of legal services, this is a major trend and many courts are struggling to make it easier for people to represent themselves. However, some courts are not happy with people who do not use attorneys and refuse to help them in any way. For some, the attitude is, "Go to the law library and figure it out for yourself."

We write and publish self-help law books to give people an alternative to the often complicated and confusing legal books found in most law libraries. We have made the explanations of the law as simple and easy to understand as possible. Of course, unlike an attorney advising an individual client, we cannot cover every conceivable possibility.

Cost/Value Analysis

Whenever you shop for a product or service, you are faced with various levels of quality and price. In deciding what product or service to buy, you make a cost/value analysis on the basis of your willingness to pay and the quality you desire.

When buying a car, you decide whether you want transportation, comfort, status, or sex appeal. Accordingly, you decide among such choices as a Neon, a Lincoln, a Rolls Royce, or a Porsche. Before making a decision, you usually weigh the merits of each option against the cost.

When you get a headache, you can take a pain reliever (such as aspirin) or visit a medical specialist for a neurological examination. Given this choice, most people, of course, take a pain reliever, since it costs only pennies; whereas a medical examination costs hundreds of dollars and takes a lot of time. This is usually a logical choice because it is rare to need anything more than a pain reliever for a headache. But in some cases, a headache may indicate a brain tumor and failing to see a specialist right away can result in complications. Should everyone with a headache go to a specialist? Of course not, but people treating their own illnesses must realize that they are betting on the basis of their cost/value analysis of the situation. They are taking the most logical option.

The same cost/value analysis must be made when deciding to do one's own legal work. Many legal situations are very straight forward, requiring a simple form and no complicated analysis. Anyone with a little intelligence and a book of instructions can handle the matter without outside help.

But there is always the chance that complications are involved that only an attorney would notice. To simplify the law into a book like this, several legal cases often must be condensed into a single sentence or paragraph. Otherwise, the book would be several hundred pages long and too complicated for most people. However, this simplification necessarily leaves out many details and nuances that would apply to special or unusual situations. Also, there are many ways to interpret most legal questions. Your case may come before a judge who disagrees with the analysis of our authors.

Therefore, in deciding to use a self-help law book and to do your own legal work, you must realize that you are making a cost/value analysis. You have decided that the money you will save in doing it yourself outweighs the chance that your case will not turn out to your satisfaction. Most people handling their own simple legal matters never have a problem, but occasionally people find that it ended up costing them more to have an attorney straighten out the situation than it would have if they had hired an attorney in the beginning. Keep this in mind while handling your case, and be sure to consult an attorney if you feel you might need further guidance.

Local Rules

The next thing to remember is that a book which covers the law for the entire nation, or even for an entire state, cannot possibly include every procedural difference of every jurisdiction. Whenever possible, we provide the exact form needed; however, in some areas, each county, or even each judge, may require unique forms and procedures. In our state books, our forms usually cover the majority of counties in the state, or provide examples of the type of form which will be required. In our national books, our forms are sometimes even more general in nature but are designed to give a good idea of the type of form that will be needed in most locations. Nonetheless, keep in mind that your state, county, or judge may have a requirement, or use a form, that is not included in this book.

You should not necessarily expect to be able to get all of the information and resources you need solely from within the pages of this book. This book will serve as your guide, giving you specific information whenever possible and helping you to find out what else you will need to know. This is just like if you decided to build your own backyard deck. You might purchase a book on how to build decks. However, such a book would not include the building codes and permit requirements of every city, town, county, and township in the nation; nor would it include the lumber, nails, saws, hammers, and other materials and tools you would need to actually build the deck. You would use the book as your guide, and then do some work and research involving such matters as whether you need a permit of some kind, what type and grade of wood are available in your area, whether to use hand tools or power tools, and how to use those tools.

Before using the forms in a book like this, you should check with your court clerk to see if there are any local rules of which you should be aware, or local forms you will need to use. Often, such forms will require the same information as the forms in the book but are merely laid out differently or use slightly different language. They will sometimes require additional information.

Changes in the Law

Besides being subject to local rules and practices, the law is subject to change at any time. The courts and the legislatures of all fifty states are constantly revising the laws. It is possible that while you are reading this book, some aspect of the law is being changed.

In most cases, the change will be of minimal significance. A form will be redesigned, additional information will be required, or a waiting period will be extended. As a result, you might need to revise a form, file an extra form, or wait out a longer time period; these types of changes will not usually affect the outcome of your case. On the other hand, sometimes a major part of the law is changed, the entire law in a particular area is rewritten, or a case that was the basis of a central legal point is overruled. In such instances, your entire ability to pursue your case may be impaired.

To help you with local requirements and changes in the law, be sure to read Chapter 2 on *Legal Research*.

Again, you should weigh the value of your case against the cost of an attorney and make a decision as to what you believe is in your best interest.

INTRODUCTION

This book is designed to help Texas landlords and tenants understand their rights and responsibilities. There are specific laws, both state and federal, that apply to the relationship between landlords and their tenants. It is important to know these laws. A landlord who faithfully follows the law, will find it much easier to have a successful business venture. On the other hand, a landlord who either does not know the rules or does not follow them, will potentially be faced with the loss of rental income, a fine owed to a tenant, and the expense of attorney's fees and court costs.

There are two primary types of landlord-tenant relationships—*residential* and *commercial*. In this book, parts of the law that apply equally to both types will be discussed and you will find information specific to each.

Chapter 1 discusses laws that apply to all landlords with an emphasis on discrimination statutes. Basic legal research tools are explained in Chapter 2 if you need assistance beyond this text.

Chapter 3 explores selecting a tenant, while the different types of tenancies available are discussed in Chapter 4. Chapter 5 addresses the lease document and the issues surrounding it.

Chapters 6–10 deal with problems and concerns during a tenancy including security deposits, repairs, security devices, smoke detectors, and utilities. Chapter 11 discusses problems between the landlord and tenant and Chapter 12 addresses some ways to remedy those problems.

Chapter 13 looks specifically to manufactured housing, while Chapters 14 and 25 address specific issues of commercial leases. Chapters 16 through 18 discuss ending the tenancy, using eviction as a tool, and whether to hire an attorney. Chapter 19 looks at the property after the tenancy has ended and Chapter 20 addresses additional liabilities a landlord faces. In addition, there are numerous appendices containing Texas laws and blank forms to use.

I | LAWS THAT APPLY TO ALL LANDLORDS

Most of the state laws that govern the landlord-tenant relationship are found in *The Texas Property Code*. Chapter 91 of the *Property Code* contains some provisions that apply to all landlords and tenants, though this is not an exhaustive list. Chapter 92 focuses on the provisions for residential tenancies, while commercial tenancies are covered in Chapter 93. Special rules for manufactured homes can be found in Chapter 94. (See Appendix A for a copy of the Property Code.) In Texas, the procedure for *eviction* is called a *forcible entry and detainer*, and is covered in Chapter 24 of the Property Code. (See Appendix B for a copy of Chapter 24.) Chapter 2 discusses how to find some of these laws as well as other legal resources.

In addition to the Code Chapter discussed above, there are other federal and state laws that every landlord should know.

Discrimination

Texas state law has provisions that ban *discrimination* by landlords regarding renting to a particular tenant. Specifically, landlords cannot discriminate based on race, religion, sex, national origin, handicap, or familial status. *Familial sta-*

tus refers, in a residential tenancy situation, to whether the prospective tenant has minor children. This law is similar to federal anti-discrimination laws, and may be found in Chapter 301 of the Property Code. It is commonly referred to as the *Texas Fair Housing Act.*

Chapter 121 of the Human Resources Code requires landlords to rent to disabled persons with an *assistance animal.* Landlords cannot use a *no pets* rule to bar the assistance animal, nor can the landlord charge additional rent because of the assistance animal. A pet deposit may be charged.

Civil Rights Act of 1968

In addition to these state laws, there are some federal laws that apply to the landlord-tenant relationship. *The Civil Rights Act of 1968* bars any policy that has a discriminatory effect. (42 U.S.C. Secs. 3601-3617.) (See Chapter 2 for an explanation of references.) Penalties for violating this law include *actual damages* and *punitive damages* of up to $1,000. Actual damages refers to monetary losses sustained by the victim of the discrimination. Punitive damages are assessed strictly as *punishment* for the wrong-doing, somewhat like a fine.

Claims for violations of this law are pursued either by filing a civil suit (generally in federal district court), by filing a complaint with the *Department of Housing and Urban Development (HUD),* or by filing a complaint with the United States Attorney General. If you are served with a notice of a complaint against you under any of these methods, it is very important that you respond to the notice, appear for all scheduled hearings, and provide all records requested. If you fail to do so, the law provides that you can be fined up to $1,000 and, more importantly, you can be sent to prison for up to one year.

There are some situations in which this law does not apply. An owner of three or fewer *single-family dwellings* is not subject to this law if there is no more than one sale of a unit within the preceding twenty-four month period, and if no real estate agent or discriminatory advertisement is used. An owner who lives in the building is also exempt as long as there are four or fewer units.

Complaints under this law must generally be made within 180 days of the act of discrimination. However, if *coercion* or intimidation is used, this time limit does not apply.

Section 1982

Although a person must prove that a policy of discrimination exists in order to have a valid complaint under this law, there is another law that allows for punishment of discrimination any time a person has an intent to discriminate. This law is also a *Civil Rights Act*, commonly referred to as *section 1982*. (42 U.S.C. Sec. 1982.)

The 1988 Amendment

There is a third Civil Rights law that applies to landlords. It is the *1988 Amendment to the Civil Rights Act of 1968*. This law added discrimination against the handicapped and against families with children. This means that landlords cannot refuse to rent to handicapped persons and to families with children. A landlord must allow a disabled person to make modifications to the rented premises to accommodate his or her specific needs. However, if modifications are made, the disabled person must remove the modifications and return the property to its original condition when he or she leaves.

If you are constructing a new building and it has four or more units, to be in compliance with this law, the building must provide electrical facilities and common areas that are accessible to the handicapped.

Complaints regarding violations of this law must be filed within two years of the violation. There are no limits on the amount of punitive damages that can be awarded. If the government files against the landlord, the landlord can be fined up to $10,000 for the first offense, $25,000 for the second violation within a five-year period, $50,000 for the third violation, and $50,000 for each additional violation within a seven-year period.

The same exemptions that are available under the original version of the Civil Rights Act are available under this amendment. As before, it does not apply to single- family residences when the owner owns three or fewer, if there is no more than one sale within twenty-four months, and if no real estate agent or discriminatory advertising is used.

Retirement Communities. The 1988 amendment created some additional exemptions to allow *retirement communities* and *assisted living facilities* to continue to operate. Dwellings in state and federal programs for the elderly are exempt. Private properties in which the units are all rented by persons sixty-two or older are exempt, as are properties in which at least eighty percent of the units are rented to persons fifty- five and older. Religious housing and private clubs are also exempt.

ADA

In commercial buildings, there is another federal law that landlords must obey. It is the *Americans with Disabilities Act* (ADA). (42 U.S.C. Sec. 12101.) This law may seem fairly simple on the surface, but it has generated quite a bit of litigation. Many of the requirements are not specifically defined by the statute. Instead, this law says that *reasonable accommodations* must be made so that persons with *disabilities* have access to the facilities. If a building is not accessible, then it must be modified if access is *readily achievable* without *undue burden* or *undue hardship*. These words come from the statute, but are not defined in it. There remains much room for question as to what each of these terms actually requires of a building owner and what persons are actually covered by the law.

Reasonable Accommodations. What changes are necessary and what is meant by accessible, will vary based on the circumstances. Access will include things like being able to get into the building and make use of the facilities. The size of the business, the nature of the business, and how people use the facilities, are all factors to be considered. For example, a small business located in a historic building is likely to have features of its premises that are not in compliance with the law. But, if the necessary modifications cost more than a million dollars and the business grosses $200,000 dollars a year, those owners might reasonably argue that the modifications would cause an undue hardship. Also, the historic nature of the building may mean that the changes are not readily achievable. However, if that same small business can make its facilities accessible by spending $5000 to widen a doorway or add a ramp, then the situation is different, and they will need to make those changes. The larger the business, more things will be included in what is considered *reasonable*.

Small Business. For small businesses with fewer than thirty employees and less than one million dollars in sales, the government has provisions for tax credits to offset some of the costs of modifications required by the ADA. For more information, talk to a tax preparer or accountant. You will need IRS forms 8826 and 3800 to claim these credits.

Applicability. Since this law applies to businesses, it is not just the landlord that can have *liability* under it. The commercial tenant can also be punished for failing to be in premises that comply with the ADA. This is an area that landlords and tenants should consider addressing in the lease so that each party knows his or her obligations and rights in regard to modifications to the premises.

Exemptions. The only exemptions under this law are for religious organizations and private clubs.

Penalties. The penalties for violating this law are fairly substantial. Fines for the first violation can be up to $50,000, while subsequent violations can cost up to

$100,000 for each offense. The courts can also issue injunctions. These are court orders that require you to do certain things or to refrain from doing certain things. These orders would relate to the conducting of your business until the needed modifications are made.

Local Law

In addition to all of the state and federal laws discussed thus far, you will also need to determine if there are any local laws that apply. You can do this by checking your local *ordinances*. Contact the city or county offices where the property is located to find out if any ordinances apply to the property. If you have other questions, some larger cities may have a *tenants' association* that can provide you with information.

Assumed Name

A final area to address, is that of the landlord's business organization. If you are using any name other than your legal name, you must register the name of your business with the county in which you are doing business. This is called an *assumed name*. If you are incorporated or registered as a *limited liability company (LLC)* and using any name other than the exact name of the corporation or limited liability company as it is listed with the Texas Secretary of State, then you must file an assumed name registration. A *corporation*, LLC, as well as a *partnership* must register with the Secretary of State and the counties where it is doing business under the assumed name.

In regards to landlord-tenant situations, the requirement applies to landlords using the apartment building name, a management company name, or any other name not their own. These must be registered as assumed names.

If you are doing business or own the rental property in any name other than your own, please pay careful attention to the disclosure of ownership and management provisions found in subchapter E of Chapter 92 of the Property Code. Information about the owner of the property, the agent for rent collection, and any management company used by the owner must be given to the tenant.

2 LEGAL RESEARCH

The need for legal research is a distinct possibility if the time comes that you need to use the court system in your landlord-tenant relationship. This book gives you the fundamental knowledge you need to accomplish your goal and answer your questions, but you may find yourself needing more detailed information in a specific topic area. Finding the legal authority you need and understanding how statutes, court cases, and the law is recorded is the subject of this chapter.

Statutes

Laws are found in two places. The first place is *statutes*. Statutes are laws passed on the federal level by Congress, and in Texas, by the state legislature. Texas state laws are found in a set of books called, *Vernon's Revised Statutes Annotated* and *Vernon's Revised Codes Annotated*. *Revised* simply means that the books have been updated with changes in the laws. *Annotated* means that the books also contain a listing of some court cases that have been decided based on the statutes. These books are referred to as the *Black* statutes because the books are black in color. The laws related to the relationship between landlords and their tenants are found primarily in the *Property Code*. Therefore, if you need to look up these laws yourself, you would go to the Black statutes section and look for the book titled *Vernon's Property Code Annotated*.

Court Cases

The second place in which laws are found are the cases decided by the courts. Courts interpret the statutes and codes as applied to a particular set of facts. Each state has a federal court system and a state court system. In the federal court system, the case is initially heard by a trial court called the federal district court. Sometimes the decisions made by these courts are written out in detail and published. This is called a *reported decision* or an *opinion*. These can be found in a set of books called *The Federal Supplement*.

The next level in the federal system is the *Court of Appeals*. In Texas, the *Fifth Circuit* Court of Appeals hears these cases. This court's decisions are reported in a set of books called the *Federal Reporter*. Cases are next appealed to the United States Supreme Court. Their decisions are found in two different books—*The Supreme Court Reporter* and *The Lawyer's Edition*. If you are doing your own legal research, the law library you are using should have at least one of these sets of books.

Cases in the state court system also begin at the *trial court level*. Depending on the type of case it is, a case may be heard in a state *district court*, a *county court* (sometimes called *county court at law*) or a *justice court*. There are specific state laws that determine which court your case should use, although many landlord cases begin in the justice court. Unless the statute under which you are filing suit indicates otherwise, you should generally file landlord-tenant relationship suits in the justice court. Also, it should be in the county and precinct where the leased property is located.

A case that begins in a justice court is appealed next to the county court. Cases from district and county courts are appealed to the state court of appeals and then to the Texas Supreme Court. In Texas, trial court decisions are not reported in any sets of books. When you get to the court of appeals levels, decisions are written out and published. You will find the decisions of both the state appeals court and the Texas Supreme Court in *The Southwestern Reporter*. After the Texas Supreme Court, the final stop in the appeals process is the United States Supreme Court.

If you are representing yourself in court, you need to know the specific statutes and codes that apply to your case and any case decisions that interpret those laws. While every attempt is made to have the information in this book be as current as possible, you will still need to update the information since laws are constantly changing. Every time the state legislature meets, there is a possibility that statutes or code provisions will be changed.

Additionally, courts hear cases throughout the year, and a court decision that affects your case could by made at any time. You will also need to remember that this book is, by definition, general and cannot cover every situation that might arise in a landlord-tenant relationship. Therefore, you need to be sure you know what the most current case decisions are, and that you are reading the most current version of the statutes and codes.

In the statute and code books, you will need to check the main part of the book, and also look for any *supplements*. These supplements are usually found in the front or back of the book. This is called a *pocket part*. Other times, the supplement will be in a separate, soft-cover book kept next to the main volume in the statute section.

Case Citation Examples

As you read through this book and do legal research on your own, you will see specific cases cited as follows: Smith v. Jones, 876 S.W.2d 299 (Tex. 1995). This is just an example, and not a real landlord-tenant case. However, if it were a real case, you would find the court's decision in volume 876 of the Southwestern Reporter. It is very important to note the number (2d) that comes after the reporter's name abbreviation. There are three sets of Southwestern Reporters (called *series*). Series one and two both have volumes numbered 1 through 999. The third series is numbered the same way, but has not yet reached volume number 999. In the example above, you need to make sure you are looking in the second series, volume 876, for the case. The case is on page 299 of that book. The information in parentheses tells which court made the decision, and the date that it was made. In this example, it is a Texas Supreme Court decision from 1995.

United States Code In this book, there will be some references to federal laws. Where possible, you will be given the common name of the law and the formal citation, so that you can look it up for yourself. For example, in the previous chapter, anti-discrimination laws were discussed. One of those laws is the Civil Rights Act of 1968. Its citation is 42 U.S.C. Sec. 3601-3617. The federal laws passed by Congress are found in a set of books called *The United States Code*, which is abbreviated U.S.C. Therefore, you would find the Civil Rights Act of 1968 in the volume of the United States Code books that contains title 42. Then, look for Sections 3601-3617.

Legal Encyclopedias

While doing legal research, you will find some other materials that may be helpful to you. If you want to read an overview of the laws in a particular area, you can look up that topic in a legal encyclopedia. There are legal encyclopedias that cover the law on a national basis. Two of these are *Corpus Juris Secundum* and *American Jurisprudence*. Texas has its own set of legal encyclopedias called *Texas Jurisprudence* or *Tex Jur*. Since these books concentrate on Texas law, you should focus on reading these books, rather than the national sets.

Digest

If you need to locate cases that apply to your situation, one place to find them is in the *annotations* that follow the text of the law in the Black statutes. Another place is a set of books called a *digest*. These books contain lists of cases grouped together by topic, and will have the name and citation of the case and a brief summary of the decision under each topical listing.

Practice Manuals

Most law libraries also contain books that are generally referred to as *practice manuals*. These books will contain summaries of the law, with forms that you can use for your case. Of course, you may have to adapt the form to fit your particular situation.

Procedural Rules

If you are filing your own court case, familiarize yourself with the *procedural rules* that apply to court cases. These rules can be found in *The Texas Rules of Civil Procedure*. The rules about what you can and cannot use as evidence in court are found in the *Texas Rules of Civil Evidence*. A law library will have copies of these laws, and you will usually find them near or as a part of the Black statutes.

Local Rules

Courts in different counties may also have some rules that apply just in that court. These are called *local rules*. You should ask the clerk of the court your case will be in, if there are any specific local rules that apply to that court. A particular court may also have specific forms they want you to use, so you should remember to ask about any such forms before you file your case. The forms contained in this book are designed to follow Texas law and are adaptable to your given situation. However, if the local court you are in has preferred forms, you should use those forms. Do not use ones that you either drafted yourself, got from this book, or got from another form book.

Doing your own legal research can be a difficult job. The information contained in this book will make that job easier. However, if your situation involves a complex legal question, you may want to consider whether the money you save in representing yourself is worth it, or whether you would be better off to hire an attorney or at least invest in a consultation with one. (If you think an attorney is required for your situation, Chapter 18 discusses hiring and working with lawyers in greater detail.)

3 | SELECTING A TENANT

A landlord has the freedom to decide whether or not to rent to a particular person, assuming that the landlord is in compliance with all of the anti-discrimination laws previously discussed. The landlord should follow a number of steps in making this decision.

Screening Prospective Tenants

The first step should be to *screen* the prospective tenant. Every landlord should require each prospective tenant to complete a written application. Although there is no one form landlords are required to use, certain basic information should always be obtained. That information includes:

✪   names;

✪   current addresses;

✪   current phone numbers;

✪   employer's names and contact information;

✪   driver's license number;

✪   date of birth; and,

✪   social security number.

Tenant Application

This information should be obtained for each person who will be living in, or renting the property, to adequately screen tenants. A landlord should also ask for the names, addresses, and phone numbers for two or three previous landlords, so that the prospective tenant's references can be accurately verified. It is also wise to ask for bank references and any history of litigation or previous eviction proceedings on the application. A sample **TENANT APPLICATION** is in Appendix D (form 1, p.157.)

As a landlord, you should review the prospective tenant's credit history. Although the law allows you to do so, you must obtain the person's written authorization before accessing the credit report. A good place to get this permission is on the rental application. You should also obtain authorization to verify previous rental information, employment information, and bank reference information. All you need to do is include a sentence that states:

By signing the application, the prospective tenant authorizes the landlord to obtain a copy of their credit history, previous rental information, employment information, verification and bank reference.

While a landlord has great latitude in asking questions of a prospective tenant, there are some questions that should never be asked. Any questions that are targeted toward determining the ethnicity of the prospective tenant should not appear on the application. Asking these types of questions violates the law and sets the landlord up for a discrimination claim by any prospective tenant to whom a landlord decides not to rent. Therefore, do not ask tenants to identify their race or ask any questions about nationality.

Now that you have this information, use it to learn as much as possible about your prospective tenant. Call the previous landlords for references. If you do not recognize the name of the previous landlords, you should consider verifying that they are, in fact, actual landlords engaged in the business of renting property. That way, you can ensure the accuracy of the information the prospective tenant has supplied and gauge the credibility of the information supplied by the reference.

Internet   There is a great deal of data publicly available on the Internet. You might want to consider doing a search for information about your prospective tenant using a service such as **www.publicdata.com**. This site contains information regarding criminal records, sex offender registrations, and, for those of you seeking information from Dallas County, information about civil court matters, criminal court records, and eviction records. There are also services that will do these investigations for you, as well as obtain credit histories. Although there is a charge for this service, it is generally money well spent. Also, the landlord can charge an *application fee* to offset the cost. There are a number of companies that provide this service and you can locate them by searching under *tenant screening* online. Here is a partial listing:

- ✪   www.tenantchk.com

- ✪   www.amerusa-tenantscreening.com

- ✪   www.americandatabank.com

- ✪   www.anewtenant.com

- ✪   www.detectfraud.com

- ✪   www.tenantscreening.com

- ✪   www.tsci.com

You can also use a service such as *CBI/Equifax Tenant Apartment Protection Service* (800-388-0456).

Credit Reporting Agencies   There are three main credit reporting agencies. They are *Equifax*, *Experian* and *TransUnion*. If you wish to contact the main credit reporting agencies directly, the website addresses are **www.equifax.com**, **www.experian.com**, and **www.transunion.com**. (In Texas, Equifax uses a company called *CSCS, Inc.* in Houston to manage and maintain the database of credit histories.)

Basically, the three reporting agencies offer the same types of services. They generally collect and maintain information about consumer's credit histories. Different companies report to different agencies, so it is important to check a prospective tenant's history with all three. They will each offer various services designed to help their business customers as well as providing consumers and businesses with copies of credit reports.

Equifax says it helps businesses find and market to the right consumer. *Experian* says it provides the knowledge, creativity, and expertise to help implement effective customer relationship management, marketing, and risk management. *Transunion* claims to have products and services to help you build your business through any stage of the account cycle, acquisition, management, collections, in many industries, including real estate.

Application Deposits

If a prospective tenant completes and returns an application, the law allows landlords to collect an *application deposit*. An application deposit is defined as the sum of money given to the landlord in connection with a rental application and that is refundable to the applicant if the applicant is rejected as a tenant.

However, if you decide to charge an application deposit for a residential lease, you must be familiar with the provisions of section 92.351, and the sections following regarding the refunding of the deposit. A landlord who, in bad faith, fails to refund the application deposit, can be fined an amount equal to the sum of $100, three times the application deposit, and the applicant's reasonable attorney's fees. Also, note that the law says that a landlord is deemed to have rejected an applicant if the landlord does not give notice of acceptance to the prospective tenant on or before the seventh day after the applicant either submits the completed rental application to the landlord or, if there is no written application, the date the landlord accepts the application deposit.

Once you have selected your tenant, the next step is deciding what kind of tenancy you will have. Then, you will need to prepare the lease.

4 TYPES OF TENANCIES

In preparing to lease your property, the next step is to determine what type of *tenancy* your lease will include. There are four different types. The differences between them relate to the length of the lease period.

Fixed Term Tenancies

The most common type of tenancy is a *fixed term*. This simply means that your lease will be for a specific period of time, beginning and ending on a certain date. Of course, the parties can agree to renew the lease so that it continues beyond the ending date. A fixed term tenancy terminates *automatically* at the end of the term. The sample **RESIDENTIAL LEASE** (form 2, p.159) is a fixed term lease, with a period of one year.

Periodic Tenancies

The second type of tenancy is the *periodic tenancy*. This type of tenancy covers a certain period of time, and renews automatically if rent is paid and no notice of termination given. A *year-to-year* tenancy is created when the parties agree to an annual amount of rent, and do not set a specific ending date for the lease. The lease renews for another year when the annual rent is paid by the tenant.

Common periodic tenancies are *month-to-month*. It is created in the same way as the year-to-year, except the parties agree on a monthly rent amount and the lease renews for a one month period upon each rental payment. A periodic tenancy requires *notice* for termination. The length of time required for the notice depends on the length of the tenancy. A sample **Periodic Tenancy Lease** (form 3, p.163) and a **Landlord's Notice to Terminate Lease** (form 4, p.167) are found in Appendix D.

Holdover Tenancies

A periodic tenancy can also be created when a tenant, under a fixed term lease, holds over. A *holdover tenant* is one who remains in the premises after the end of the lease term. If the written lease does not address the holdover and the landlord accepts rental payments under the same terms as in the written lease, then the law deems that the parties have agreed to a new lease under the same terms as the existing written lease. A party can change this provision by giving written notice to the other party, declaring that a holdover creates only a month-to-month-lease. Therefore, from the landlord's perspective, the written lease should contain a provision that, in the event of a holdover, the landlord consents only to a month-to-month lease.

Tenancies at Will

A third type of tenancy is the *tenancy at will*. This type of tenancy is created when the agreement between the landlord and the tenant does not establish a specific term. An agreement of this type allows the tenant to occupy the premises so long as rent is paid. Tenancies at will are terminable at *any time*, by *either party*. Generally, tenancies at will are created through an oral agreement between a landlord and tenant.

Tenancies at Sufferance

The fourth type of tenancy is called the *tenancy at sufferance*. A tenancy at sufferance is created when a tenant holds over after the term of the lease, but the landlord does not accept rent payments. Once the landlord accepts rent payments, a periodic tenancy has been created. The landlord, in a tenancy at sufferance, can terminate the tenancy at *any time*.

5 THE LEASE

Section 92.001 of the Property Code defines a *lease* as any written or oral agreement between a landlord and a tenant that establishes or modifies terms, conditions, rules, or other provisions regarding the use and occupancy of a dwelling. *Dwelling* is defined as one or more rooms rented as a permanent residence to one or more tenants. There is no specific form that is required to have a valid, binding lease, but there are certain things that should always be included.

Lease Requirements

The case of *National Convenience Stores, Inc. v. Martinez*, 784 S.W. 2d 468 (Tex. Ct. App.-Texarkana, 1989) lists the minimum requirements for a lease. Those requirements include:

- ✪ the names of the parties to the agreement;

- ✪ a description of the property being leased;

- ✪ the time period covered by the lease;

- ✪ provisions allowing the tenant to be in possession of the premises;

- ✪ the amount of the rent;

- ✪ the terms of payment; and,

- ✪ a signature by both the landlord and the tenant.

While these are the minimum requirements, most landlords and tenants choose to include additional provisions to further define the relationship between the parties and their respective rights and obligations.

Oral Leases   Although the definition of lease clearly shows that it is possible to have an *oral lease*, it is always better to have a written agreement. Additionally, you should be aware of a legal doctrine called the *statute of frauds*. While a complete discussion of this rule is beyond the scope of this book, it requires any lease agreement, with a term longer than one year, to be in writing, and signed by the party against whom enforcement is sought. This means that the lease must be signed by both parties to be enforceable. If only signed by one party, it is only enforceable against the party who signed it. This is a general rule, but both the landlord and tenant must know that there are certain duties imposed by the Property Code that are binding, regardless of the status of the lease.

Statutory Obligations

Section 92.006 of the Property Code lists obligations imposed by law on landlords and tenants. The obligations themselves are addressed in subchapters C, D, E, and G. These requirements control certain provisions, in spite of the general rule that parties can agree to whatever provisions they wish to put in the lease. (These obligations will be discussed in greater detail in the following chapters.)

Some of these obligations cannot be waived, even if it says they are waived in the lease and both parties have signed it. The landlord's duties and the tenant's remedies relating to security deposits, security devices, and utility cutoffs cannot be waived. Neither can the landlord's duty to disclose ownership and management to the tenant. The requirement of the landlord to install a smoke detector and the tenant's remedy for failure to install one, cannot be waived. However, the parties can agree in the written lease to waive the landlord's duty to inspect and repair the smoke detector. If there are conditions on the premises that affect the physical health or safety of the tenant, the landlord's duty to repair these conditions cannot be waived unless certain conditions are met (see Chapter 7).

Lead Paint Disclosure

If the dwelling was built before 1978, federal law requires an additional obligation of the landlord. This applies whether or not there is a written lease. Also, it applies to all rental units except those specifically for the elderly or zero bedroom units, such as efficiencies. The tenant must be given what is called the **LEAD PAINT DISCLOSURE** (form 5, p.168),and it must be accompanied by a pamphlet called *Protect Your Family From Lead in Your Home.*

The landlord has a duty, as a part of this warning, to disclose any known information regarding lead based paint or paint hazards. Information, such as the location of the lead based paint and the condition of the surface, are covered by this requirement. The landlord must also provide any records or reports relating to lead based paint to the tenant. There must also be an attachment to the lease that states that the landlord has complied with all these legal requirements. This attachment must be signed and dated by the landlord and the tenant. More information about the lead paint warnings, as well as copies of the disclosure and the pamphlet, are available from the Federal Department of Housing and Urban Development (HUD). These documents can be found on HUD's website, **www.hud.gov**. The disclosure form is available in both English and Spanish, while the pamphlet is available in English, Spanish, and Vietnamese

Landlords must keep copies of the disclosures provided to their tenants for at least three years from the date of the beginning of the leasing period.

The regulations themselves are found in the Code of Federal Regulations (C.F.R.) Chapter 24, part 35, subpart A, and 61 Federal Register 9065. Both the C.F.R. and the Federal Register are available at most law libraries and online legal research cites such as **www.findlaw.com**.

Optional Provisions

While not required for an agreement to qualify as a lease, there are other provisions that should always be included in a written lease. If the landlord intends to require a *security* or *damage deposit*, the terms of that deposit should always be included in the lease. It is also a good idea to include provisions setting out which party is responsible for *maintenance* of specific items and areas.

Pets

The lease should contain a clause about whether or not *pets* will be allowed. The numbers of pets and types of pets not permitted should also be addressed in this section. While not as much of a concern in single-family rentals, a limit on the number of pets is often appropriate, and should contain provisions for time limits for keeping new litters if the pets give birth. A **PET ADDENDUM** (form 6, p.170) is included in Appendix D.

From the landlord's perspective, a failure to include a clause on pets means that you cannot control the number and types of pets your tenants keep in the property. Obviously, failure to control this issue may mean that your property suffers damages far in excess of the security deposit.

Late Fees

Provisions for *late fees* and returned *check fees* should be included in the lease if the landlord intends to charge for these things. It is important to include a specific due date in the lease for rental payments, as well as the specific dollar amount of the rent. If the lease is for one year and the rent will be paid in one installment, the rent amount should be stated as an annual amount. If the rent will be paid monthly, the rent is shown as the monthly amount. Landlords using late fees usually give the tenant a few days, normally five, as a grace period. This time period should be contained in the lease.

Failure to include a provision for late fees may cause you to have problems getting your rent money at the first of the month when it is really due.

Options to Renew

If the parties want to include an option to renew the lease, this provision should be specifically included in the written lease. If the rent will be increased for the option period, this should be included in the original lease. Otherwise, the renewal will be on the same terms as the original lease.

Rent Changes

Once a lease is signed, the landlord cannot raise the tenant's rent unless this right is contained in the written lease. At the end of the lease term, the rent can be changed and a new agreement entered into between the landlord and the tenant.

Insurance

Any requirements for the tenant to have insurance should be contained in the lease. If you fail to include such a provision and a significant loss occurs, that according to the lease is the tenant's responsibility, you, as the landlord, may end up having to pay to correct the problem yourself and then sue the tenant to get your money back. There is not an insurance provision in the sample **RESIDENTIAL LEASE** (form 1). However, if you want to include one, you can add a sentence to that part of the lease that deals with the tenant's repair obligations setting out what kind of insurance the tenant must have and what the coverage amount requirements are.

Subletting   The lease should also contain provisions for *subletting* if the landlord intends to allow the tenant to sublet. This is necessary because Section 91.005 states that the tenant may not sublet unless the landlord agrees in writing.

Payments   If the landlord does not want to accept cash payments, then there must be a specific clause in the lease requiring the tenant to pay by check, money order, or other negotiable instrument. If this clause is not included in the lease, then the landlord must accept cash payments. This rule is found in Section 92.011 of the Property Code. The landlord is also required to give the tenant a receipt for the payment, and to maintain a record of the payments and payment dates in a record book.

This provisions is important because it is more difficult to track cash payments and many landlords, especially those who do not personally collect each month's rent, often prefer the greater protection offered by checks and money orders.

Attorney's Fees   Most landlords also want to be able to get their *attorney's fees* reimbursed by the tenant if they have to go to court. This provision should be included in the lease. (see Chapter 7).

Even if, at the time the lease is negotiated, you do not think you would hire an attorney to represent you, you should include this provision in the lease anyway. If it's not there, there may be some instances in which you will not get those fees back in court. It is hard to know at the beginning of a lease what complications may arise, and it may turn out that you want to hire an attorney after all. The sample leases included in Appendix D contain many of these provisions.

Problem Clauses

There are, however, some things that should not be part of a lease agreement. For example, a landlord should never include a clause prohibiting the tenant from changing the locks. In the event of a burglary or damage to property from vandalism during a break-in, the landlord could be held financially responsible for a tenant's losses.

If there are any provisions in the lease that place extra burdens on the tenant, or if the tenant is waiving any of their rights, these clauses should be specifically *initialed* by the tenant. The landlord should not make any attempt to hide these types of clauses or locate them in places in the lease where they are unlikely to be noticed by the tenant. Taking these actions means that the clause will probably not be enforced against the tenant in court. However, if the tenant has initialed the problem clause, and there are no laws that prohibit its enforcement, then the terms of the lease contract will probably be upheld by a court.

Number of Occupants   While the parties are generally free to set the terms of the lease themselves, Section 92.010 limits the number of occupants in a leased residential dwelling to no more than three adults per bedroom, unless the landlord is required by law to allow a higher occupancy, or the adult is seeking *temporary* refuge from domestic violence. Temporary is defined as no longer than one month.

Implied leases   As a landlord, you should not give a tenant keys to the property being leased or allow them to take possession of it until the lease has been negotiated and signed. If the tenant is in possession of the premises with the landlord's consent, a judge could rule that there was an *implied lease*. This would allow the tenant to stay even without the tenant's agreement to pay rent. While the courts will not generally allow a tenant to occupy premises without the payment of some rent, this situation creates many additional problems for the landlord and should always be avoided.

Unconscionable Provisions   There may be other provisions in a lease that a judge may refuse to enforce. These are provisions that put an undue burden on one party, or waive a party's rights. In this case, the provision is considered unconscionable. There is no hard and fast rule in the Property Code as to what is *unconscionable*. Basically, that decision will be made by a judge based on the facts of each situation. If you are negotiating a lease provision that is not standard, or one that you have any question about, you can do some legal research on your own to see if you can find any cases that have ruled on that particular type of provision. As a landlord in this situation, you might want to consult with an attorney, or actually hire a lawyer to draft the lease provisions for you.

Signing the Lease

If there are changes made to the lease after it has been prepared, but before it is signed, all parties will need to initial the change and sign the lease. Every adult who will be occupying the dwelling should sign the lease. However, the lease is not invalid if all occupants have not signed it. It is sufficient if just one has signed the lease.

The landlord must also sign the lease. If the property is owned by an individual, then that individual should sign the lease. If the property is owned by a corporation, then a person authorized by the corporation should sign. For properties owned by partnerships, any partner can sign. Additionally, the partnership can authorize an agent to sign for the partnership.

The signatures to a lease do not need to be notarized or witnessed.

NOTE: *You will find many sample lease forms available for sale in stores and online. Before you use any of these forms, read them carefully. Many of these forms are not appropriate for use in Texas. If you use one of these forms, you could end up violating Texas law because of some of the provisions contained in the form. You could also end up owing a lot of money in damages and attorney's fees if you end up in court over one of these forms.*

Commercial v. Residential Leases

On occasion, you may run into a question of whether the lease is *residential* or *commercial*. This situation will occur when the tenant is both living in the premises and operating his or her business out of the premises. In that situation, it is wise to operate under the residential rules.

Example: In the case of *Warehouse Partners v. Gardner*, 910 S.W.2d 19 (CAS 1995), the tenant told the landlord about his plan to live and work in one unit. The tenant had several meetings with the landlord's agent, and the agent approved construction plans. The court found that this was sufficient to put the landlord on notice that the premises were being used as a residence. The court went on to construe the rights and obligations of the parties under the residential rules.

This case is also an example of how complex a fight between a landlord and a tenant can become. The tenant filed two suits against the landlord. Both were appealed, and the tenant alone spent at least $43,000 in attorney's fees.

6 | SECURITY DEPOSITS

The laws about security deposits on residential leases are found in sections 92.101 through 92.109 of the Property Code. The code defines a *security deposit* as any advance of money paid by a tenant to a landlord, other than a rental application deposit or advance payment of rent, that is intended primarily to secure performance under a lease of a dwelling. There is no legal limit to the amount of the security deposit.

Return of Security Deposits

An area of conflict often occurs between tenants and landlords over the retention of the security deposit. Basically, the landlord has the obligation to refund the security deposit unless one of the provisions in the Property Code allows the deposit to be kept. Section 92.103 requires the landlord to return the deposit on or before the 30th day after the date the tenant surrenders the premises. In other words, the landlord has no more than *30 days* after the tenant leaves to refund the deposit

Many landlords have tried to get around this requirement by requiring the tenant to give advance notice that he or she is leaving, in order to get the deposit back. That way, in the absence of the notice by the tenant, the landlord would have the right to keep the deposit. If the landlord intends to use this requirement, there must be a clause in the written lease that gives the tenant the duty to notify the landlord in advance that the tenant is surrendering the premises. While there is nothing illegal about the use of such a clause, section 92.103 requires that this clause either be underlined or printed in conspicuous bold print in the lease.

The fact that there is a specific provision requiring a landlord to emphasize this clause and call it to the tenant's attention demonstrates that the court system does not particularly look with favor on these types of clauses. Therefore, if the landlord does not comply with the provisions of this law and tries to withhold the security deposit based on lack of notice of surrender by the tenant, the landlord can expect to be penalized in court for withholding the deposit.

Holding Security
Deposits

The landlord cannot spend the security deposit, and then claim lack of money as an excuse for not refunding the deposit. The law says that the tenant's right to the security deposits take priority over all of the landlord's other creditors, even the bankruptcy trustee if the landlord files for bankruptcy.

Texas does not have any specific laws about what kind of bank account a landlord must use for security deposits, but landlords would be wise to keep the security deposits in an account separate from their personal or regular business accounts. This helps to avoid the temptation to use the money for other purposes and then replace it by the time the tenant leaves. The landlord should always be in the position to refund all tenant's security deposits at any time, since there are financial penalties for failing to refund the security deposit in a timely fashion. Every landlord should also have some sort of accounting and record keeping system in place. Section 92.106 requires a landlord to maintain accurate records on security deposits.

Without Taking
Possession

If the tenant backs out of the lease without ever taking possession of the premises, landlords may think this gives them the right to automatically keep the security deposit. However, Section 92.031 states that if the tenant finds a replacement tenant that is acceptable to the landlord, and the replacement tenant occupies the dwelling by the time the original lease was to begin, then the landlord must refund the original tenant's security deposit. Any prepayments of rent by the tenant must also be refunded.

If the landlord is the one who finds the replacement tenant, the landlord is permitted to deduct certain fees from the security deposit or any rent prepayments. The amount that can be deducted is either an amount set out in the lease as a lease cancellation fee or the landlord's actual expenses incurred in finding the replacement tenant. The landlord is allowed to include a reasonable amount in those expenses, to compensate for the time the landlord spends looking for a new tenant.

If a landlord has a lease with a tenant who backs out and that tenant presents a proposed replacement tenant, the landlord should screen the proposed tenant just like any other applicant. If the applicant would otherwise be acceptable, a landlord cannot just refuse to accept the proposed replacement tenant, and use the lack of a new tenant to justify keeping the security deposit.

Mitigation

Section 91.006 requires a landlord to *mitigate* their damages. Mitigate means the landlord has a legal obligation to do everything they reasonably can to limit any losses they may suffer when a tenant breaches a lease. That means that, in the replacement tenant situation, a landlord who declines to accept a replacement tenant without a valid reason for doing so, will not be in compliance with the duty to mitigate damages, and could later be punished by a court for wrongfully withholding the security deposit.

Deductions from Security Deposits

There are some expenses that may be deducted from the security deposit. If the tenant *damages* the property, the landlord may deduct the costs of repairing those damages from the deposit. Also, if there are damage clauses in the lease that set amounts for which a tenant is liable if they breach the lease, and the tenant has in fact breached the lease, then those amounts can also be withheld. The landlord may not withhold any amounts that are for normal *wear and tear* of the premises.

Accounting

If the landlord is going to keep any part of the security deposit, a specific accounting must be given to the tenant. This means that the tenant must be given a detailed, *itemized list* of the reasons for each deduction and the amount of money withheld under each item. This accounting should be given to the tenant at the same time the security deposit is returned. A sample **LANDLORD'S NOTICE TO TENANT OF RETENTION OF SECURITY DEPOSIT** (form 7, p.171) can be used for this accounting. If additional specific items are damaged or repaired that are not contained in the sample, be sure to add them as well.

Failure to give this accounting will trigger financial penalties to the landlord under Section 92.109. This section states that a landlord who, in bad faith, fails to provide a written description, and itemized list of all damages and charges, forfeits the right to keep any of the security deposit. A landlord also loses the right to file suit against the tenant in court to collect money for the damages to the premises. Additionally, the landlord may be required to pay the tenant's attorney's fees if the tenant sues to collect the security deposit.

If the tenant still owes unpaid rent after leaving and there is no dispute between the landlord and the tenant about the amount of unpaid rent, then the landlord does not have to supply the tenant with the itemized accounting in order to withhold the security deposit.

Bad Faith   Landlords also face liability under Section 92.109, if they withhold any portion of the security deposit in *bad faith*. In that event, the landlord can be ordered to pay money to the tenant in an amount equal to the sum of $100, three times the amount of the security deposit wrongfully withheld, and the tenant's reasonable attorney's fees incurred in a suit to recover the deposit.

There is a provision in this section of the code to which landlords should give careful attention. If the landlord fails to return a security deposit or give the tenant a written description and itemized list of the deductions on or before the 30th day after the tenant surrenders possession of the premises (i.e. leaves), then the law *presumes* that the landlord is acting in bad faith. Therefore, it is critically important for landlords to carefully comply with the provisions on the itemized list of deductions and to do so in a timely manner.

Burden of Proof   Another factor for the landlord to consider is *burden of proof*. In normal cases, the person who files the lawsuit has the legal responsibility of proving his or her case. For instance, if the landlord sues the tenant for unpaid rent, it is the landlord's obligation to prove to the judge what the amount of the rent is, how much the tenant has paid, and how much is still owed. Based on that general rule, the landlord might be tempted to think that it would be up to the tenant to sue them for the security deposit and prove to the judge that the landlord did something wrong when all of the deposit was not returned. This is a serious mistake on the landlord's part. Section 92.109 (c) says that if a tenant files suit against a landlord to get a security deposit back, the landlord has the burden of proving to the judge that he or she acted properly in keeping some or all of the security deposit. To assist the landlord with this burden have the tenant complete a **PROPERTY REPORT** (form 8, p.173) upon moving into the premises. This will help show the condition when the tenant took possession of the property. The landlord will still need to demonstrate to the court the condition in which it was returned, but at least this will help prevent a tenant from claiming something was broken or needing repair when he or she took possession.

Forwarding Address

Landlords do not have to return the security deposit or provide a written itemization of deductions until the tenant has provided a forwarding address to the landlord. However, the tenant does not lose the right to the deposit just because he or she failed to give the landlord the forwarding address. That means that the landlord must keep the security deposit and itemization available for the tenant and cannot just spend the money because there is no forwarding address.

Sale of Premises

Another condition, other than the tenant surrendering the premises, affects the return of the security deposit is a *change in ownership*. Any time ownership of a leased premises changes, the new owner becomes liable for return of the security deposits from the date the new owner acquires legal title to the premises. The original owner remains liable for the security deposits until the new owner gives the tenant a signed statement acknowledging that the new owner is responsible for the security deposits. Section 92.105 requires this notice to the tenant to be in writing, and signed by the new owner. It must state that the new owner is responsible for the security deposit and state the amount of the deposit. These rules apply to all new owners, except the mortgage holder of the rental premises if they acquire title to the property as the result of a foreclosure. This means that if you are a landlord and you either sell your property, or file for bankruptcy, or the property is placed in receivership, you should make sure that the new owner gives all of your tenants for whom you were holding security deposits this notice. Otherwise, you could be liable to the tenants for the security deposits, even if you had turned them over to the new owner.

Lease Provisions and Security Deposit Deductions

A case that illustrates the importance of interpreting your lease provisions correctly is that of *Miro v. Garner*, 52 S.W.3d 407 (App. 13th Dist., 2001). In that case, the written lease required the tenant to surrender the premises in as good a condition as when the lease began. The landlord was allowed, under the lease ,to make deductions from the security deposit for any damage done to the premises except wear and tear. The lease was ending and the landlord had a contract to sell the house. The night before the closing on the sale of the house, the pipes broke, causing significant flooding damage and resulting in the sale price being reduced by $5200. The landlord then retained the security deposit, giving the tenant the required itemize list, and filed suit against him for the amount of the reduction in the sale price not covered by the security deposit. The court interpreted the lease to make the tenant liable for only those damages caused by the negligence or intentional acts of the tenant, meaning that the tenant was not liable for the flood damage. That meant that although the landlord complied with the provisions of the law for withholding the deposit, she was found to have acted in bad faith, because the retention of the deposit was not authorized by the lease. The actions a landlord takes regarding security deposits are controlled by law and by the lease provisions.

Last Month's Rent

A final note about security deposits. Many tenants think that they do not need to pay the last month's rent because the landlord has the security deposit and can use it to cover that rent. Section 92.108 states that a tenant who takes this action is presumed to have acted in bad faith and, if sued by the landlord, can be ordered to pay the landlord three times the amount of the rent wrongfully withheld, plus the landlord's attorney fees. Therefore, tenants should always pay all of the rent owed and wait for the landlord to return the security deposit.

7 | REPAIRS

One issue that frequently arises in the landlord-tenant relationship is that of repairs to the rented premises.

Duty to Repair

Section 92.052 requires the landlord to make a *diligent effort* to repair or remedy a condition that materially affects the physical health or safety of an ordinary tenant, if the tenant gives the landlord notice of the problem. The notice of the problem should be given to the person or place where rent is normally paid. At the time the notice is given, the tenant must be current on rent in order for the landlord's duty to repair to be triggered. A **TENANT'S REPAIR NOTICE TO LANDLORD** (form 10, p.176) can be used to notify a landlord of needed repairs.

What is required by the phrase *diligent effort* is something that is not specifically defined, and will vary from case to case based on the facts in each particular situation. You will also note that the code limits the landlord's duty to repairing those conditions that *materially affect an ordinary tenant*. A problem that bothers a particular tenant, but would not be a problem for most tenants, is not one that materially affects an ordinary tenant. The landlord would not have a duty to repair under this section of the code for that one, particular tenant.

ADA   A condition or problem adversely affecting a tenant that is related to a disability of the tenant's, may impose a duty to repair on the landlord. The *Americans with Disabilities Act (ADA)* punishes a landlord that discriminates in any way against a disabled tenant.

Causation   Another important factor in determining the landlord's duty to repair the premises is how the problem or condition was caused. While landlords do have the duty to repair conditions caused by normal *wear and tear,* other problems caused by a tenant or a tenant's guest do not have to be repaired by the landlord.

Notice to Tenant   Any time the landlord enters the leased premises, even for things like required repairs, the landlord must:

  ✪   tell the tenant that the landlord will be entering the premises;

  ✪   tell the tenant when the entry will occur; and,

  ✪   give the tenant the reason for the entry.

A **LANDLORD'S NOTICE OF INTENT TO ENTER PREMISES** (form 9, p.175) is included in the appendix.

Timeliness   The law requires the landlord to make the required repairs within a reasonable amount of time. Once again, this is something that will vary depending on the facts of each case. The more complex a particular repair, the longer the amount of time that will be considered reasonable for the landlord to make the repairs. However, Section 92.056(d) creates a rebuttable presumption that *seven days* is reasonable. If the landlord is unable to complete the repairs within the seven day period, he or she will need to prove that the nature and severity of the problem was such that the repairs could not be made within the seven day period, or that the labor, materials, and utilities needed to make the repairs, were not reasonably available to permit the repairs in that time frame.

The date that the landlord received the tenant's notice is also a factor that can be considered in determining whether or not the time it took to complete the repairs was reasonable. The law says that the landlord has received the notice when it is either actually received by the landlord, his or her agent, employee, or when the United States Postal Service has attempted to deliver the notice to the landlord.

If the landlord fails to make the repairs within a reasonable time after a tenant gives notice, then the tenant is required by Section 92.056 to give the landlord a subsequent notice, unless the original notice was given by certified mail, return receipt requested, or by registered mail. The **TENANT'S REPAIR NOTICE TO LANDLORD** (form 10, p.176) can be used for both the first and second notice.

Once the notice has either been given by certified mail or registered mail, or given a second time, and the landlord has still refused to repair, then the tenant has four options under Section 92.056(e). The tenant can:

❂ have the condition repaired;

❂ deduct the amount of the repairs from the rent;

❂ terminate the lease; or,

❂ file suit against the landlord.

If the tenant elects to terminate the lease, then the tenant is entitled to a *pro rata refund* of rent from the date of the termination or the date the tenant moves out, whichever is later. The tenant may also deduct the amount of the security deposit from the rent, without the need to file a lawsuit. The tenant is also entitled to get the security deposit refunded using the standard measures discussed in Chapter 6.

Tenant Makes Repairs
If the tenant chooses to make the repairs him or herself, then the provisions of Section 92.0561 control. This section limits the amount of the deduction from the rent a tenant can take to no more than the amount of one month's rent under the lease or $500, whichever is greater. If the tenant's rent is subsidized by the government, then the deduction limitation amount is determined by the fair market rent for the premises, as determined by the governmental agency subsidizing the rent, and not the amount of rent actually being paid by the tenant. Repairs may be made as often as necessary as long as the total repairs and deductions in any one month do not exceed this limitation.

The law sets some limits on the tenant's right to choose this option. At least one of the notices to the landlord must state that the tenant intends to have the condition repaired, and give the landlord a description of what the tenant intends to have done to repair the problem.

Additionally, not every problem with a property allows the tenant to exercise this option. At least one of the following things must have occurred before the tenant is entitled to relief under this section. The landlord has failed to remedy:

- ✪ a backup or overflow of raw sewage inside the dwelling;

- ✪ flooding from broken pipes;

- ✪ natural drainage inside the dwelling;

- ✪ the water service after it had been completely ceased (and the lease imposed a duty on the landlord to provide potable water); or,

- ✪ a heating and/or air conditioning unit that is not working properly.

Where the heating and/or air conditioning equipment is not working properly, the landlord must have been notified in writing by either the appropriate local housing, building, or health official that the lack of heating or cooling materially affects the health or safety of an ordinary tenant.

The landlord has some time under each one of these conditions to make the needed repairs. With a sewage backup problem or interior flooding issue, the repair must be made immediately. For conditions related to potable water and qualifying heating and air conditioning problems, the landlord has three days to make the repairs. For other conditions, the landlord has seven days. If the landlord does not make the repairs within the appropriate time period, then the *repair and deduct remedy* becomes available to the tenant.

The landlord has a method to delay the repair and deduct remedy by sending the tenant an affidavit under Section 92.0562. Either the landlord or an authorized agent of the landlord must sign the affidavit and swear under oath to its information. The reasons for the delay and the diligent efforts made by the landlord to get the problem fixed must be in the affidavit. The affidavit must also contain the names, addresses, and telephone numbers of contractors, suppliers, and repairmen contacted by the owner, and the dates of each contact.

Once the landlord complies with the requirements of this section, the repair deadline is extended for fifteen days. Failure to repair must be caused by a delay in getting the necessary parts, and the landlord must not be responsible for the delay. If the failure to repair is caused by a shortage of labor or materials after a natural disaster, such as a tornado, hurricane, or flood, the repair deadline is extended for thirty days.

It is important that the landlord be acting in good faith when he or she signs this affidavit. A landlord who signs an affidavit for repair delays in bad faith is subject to being fined the sum of one month's rent, plus $1,000, in addition to the judicial remedies discussed later in this chapter.

Exceptions

There is an exception to these deadlines contained in Section 92.054 for losses from insured casualties like fire or hail. In this situation, the repair period does not begin until the landlord has received the insurance proceeds. (These types of problems will be discussed in more detail later in this chapter.)

Written Lease Provisions

The remedies under this section of the code do not apply if, in the written lease, the tenant has waived his rights to them as provided for in Section 92.006. However, there are only certain conditions under which the repair and deduct remedy can be waived. (see Sec. 92.006 (d)-(f).) If, at the beginning of the lease term, the landlord owns only one rental dwelling, and the property is at that time free from any condition that would materially affect the physical health or safety of an ordinary tenant, and the landlord has no reason to think any condition like that will occur, then the parties can agree that the tenant will secure and pay for any repairs. This agreement must be contained in a written lease, and either be in boldface type, underlined, or contained in a separate written agreement. If the landlord chooses to use boldface or underlining, it is also a good idea to have the tenant place his or her initials by these sections so that it will be clear later on that the tenant was aware of these provisions at the time the lease was signed.

The code also says that the agreement must be made for *consideration*. That means that the tenant must receive something from the landlord above and beyond what would otherwise be received in the lease in exchange for agreeing to be responsible for the repairs.

The landlord and tenant can agree that the tenant will be responsible for certain repairs so long as the damage is not the landlord's fault. These repairs include those necessary:

✪   for damage caused by pipes in the tenant's dwelling that are blocked because of foreign objects;

✪   for damage to doors, windows, or screens; or,

✪   that resulted from a door or window being left open.

Although this section of the Property Code does not require this clause in the lease to be in boldface type or underlined, it is a good idea to do it this way. Once again, it is a good idea to have the tenant initial this provision when the lease is signed.

If the landlord and tenant have agreed in the lease that the tenant would be responsible for certain repairs, a landlord can use **LANDLORD'S NOTICE TO TENANT FOR REPAIRS** (form 11, p.177) to notify the tenant of any needed repairs.

Property Sold before Repairs are Made

If the property is sold before the repairs have been made, then the tenant still has the option of terminating the lease. However, unless the needed repairs are for sewage backup or overflow inside the dwelling or a cutoff of potable water, then the tenant cannot exercise the repair and deduct remedies until he or she has given the new landlord notice of the problem. Basically, this means that the repair process starts over from the beginning with the new landlord. The repair and deduct remedy remains available to the tenant without any notices to the new landlord for the sewage and lack of potable water conditions. If the new landlord violates the affidavit for delay, they can be fined up to $2,000 plus one month's rent, actual damages, and attorney's fees.

Court Proceedings

As previously mentioned, the tenant can also take the landlord to court. Section 92.0563 lists the remedies available through a court proceeding. A tenant can ask the judge to sign an order instructing the landlord to take action to repair the problem. The judge can also order that the tenant's rent be reduced as of the date of the first repair notice. In this situation, the rent reduction is the amount by which the uncorrected problem reduces the rental value of the property. The judge can fine the landlord up to the amount of one month's rent, plus $500, or can enter a judgment against the landlord for the tenant's actual damages. With any of these rulings by the judge, the landlord can also be ordered to pay the tenant's court costs and attorney's fees.

Landlord Remedies

In a situation where repairs need to be made, and the tenant improperly withholds rent, or has repairs made when not legally authorized to do so, the landlord can sue the tenant to recover the actual damages caused to the landlord by the tenant. If a tenant makes repairs or continues to withhold rent after being notified by the landlord that the action the tenant is taking is illegal, then the tenant can be fined by a judge. The fine amount is one month's rent, plus $500. The notice the landlord gives the tenant must also include notification about this penalty to which the tenant is subject under this section of the code. A sample **LANDLORD'S NOTICE TO TENANT FOR WRONGFULLY WITHHOLDING RENT** (form 12, p.178) in Appendix D can be used. Before a landlord can have this fine assessed against the tenant, the landlord must prove:

✪ the tenant was given notice of the illegality of his or her actions and the penalties for the violation of the law and

✪ acting in bad faith, the tenant still continued to violate the law.

Insured Losses

In instances where the problems with the property are caused by *insured casualty losses,* the tenant has the right to terminate the lease if the dwelling is totally unusable for residential purposes, so long as the casualty loss was not caused by either the tenant, a member of the tenant's family, or a guest of the tenant. The landlord also has the right to terminate the lease if an insured casualty loss caused the property to be uninhabitable. The only requirement is that the party desiring to terminate the lease, give the other party written notice any time before repairs to the property are completed. The tenant is entitled to a *pro rata refund* of rent from the date the tenant moves out and to a refund of the security deposit.

If the dwelling is only partially unusable as a residence, then the tenant is entitled to a reduction in rent. The amount of the reduction depends on the extent to which the dwelling is unusable. Additionally, the tenant can only get this reduction if the tenant files a suit against the landlord in either a county court, or district court, unless in the written lease, the landlord and tenant have agreed to a reduction under these circumstances.

Code Violations

If the condition of the property is such that it is in violation of any building codes or municipal ordinances, a landlord faces additional liability to the government for the code violations. These fines can be very expensive. Landlords should respond immediately to any code violation notices and get the property in compliance as soon as possible. When the violation has been corrected, you may want to obtain written confirmation from the code compliance officials that the property is now up to code.

8 SECURITY DEVICES

Most types of residential leased property are subject to laws regarding security devices. As with most laws, there are some exceptions. Motel and hotel rooms,and housing operated by accredited colleges and universities and prep schools, are exempt from these rules, as are rentals that are part of a contract for sale where the buyer occupies the property prior to the completion of the sale. Otherwise, these rules apply to residential leases, including rooms, mobile homes, single-family dwellings, apartments, condominiums, and townhomes. The rules are found in Sections 92.151 through 92.170.

Required Equipment

In Texas, the general rule is that every rental dwelling to which these laws apply must be *equipped with*:

- ✪ a window latch on each exterior window;

- ✪ a doorknob lock or keyed deadbolt lock on each exterior door;

- ✪ a sliding door pin lock on each exterior sliding glass door;

✪ a sliding door handle latch or sliding door security bar on each exterior sliding glass door; and,

✪ a keyless bolting device and a door viewer on each exterior door.

Dwellings that have French doors have an additional requirement. One of the doors must meet the general requirements above and the other door must have bolts that go into the top and bottom of the doorjamb. These *security devices* are to be installed at the landlord's expense and do not require a specific request from the tenant.

Senior Housing

The code does allow for exceptions in certain instances related to housing for senior citizens and the disabled. If the dwelling is part of a multi-unit complex in which the majority of tenants are over age 55 or have a mental or physical disability, and as part of a written lease or some other written agreement, the landlord is expressly required or permitted to periodically check on the health and welfare of the tenant, then the unit does not have to have a keyless bolting device. In other dwellings that do not meet that criteria, if the property is rented to a tenant who is either over 55, has a mental or physical disability, and requests in writing that the landlord not install the keyless bolting device, then one is not required. It is important to note that this request from the tenant cannot be contained in the lease agreement, but must be in a separate document.

For example, if an elderly woman in poor health decides to move to an assisted living center, part of the rules and regulations of the center (not to mention part of the benefit to the resident) is that the staff checks on the welfare of the resident. Therefore, the landlord for the facility is not required to install a keyless bolting device. On the other hand, if a disabled person moves into a regular apartment complex and does not want a keyless bolting device because home health workers must have access to the apartment, then that tenant will have to ask the landlord in writing not to install the device.

Specifications

Section 92.154 contains the technical specifications for many of the devices. A keyed dead bolt or keyless bolting device must be installed at least 36 inches from the floor, and cannot be higher than 48 inches from the floor. (Any of these devices that were installed prior to September 1, 1993, can be 54 inches from the floor.) They must have a strike plate screwed into the doorjamb or be installed into a door with a metal doorjamb. The bolt must have a throw of at least one inch. (The one inch requirement does not apply to bolts installed prior to September 1, 1993.) The sliding glass door pin lock or security bar must be no more than 48 inches from the floor, (or 54 inches if installed prior to the September 1, 1993 date). So long as all the requirements are met, the landlord has the discretion to select the type and brand of device.

Rekeying

The Property Code also contains provisions that require a landlord to rekey exterior locks operated by keys or cards no later than seven days after each change of tenant. The code, in Section 92.156, requires that this expense be borne by the landlord. Any additional rekeying or a change of the security device, if requested by the tenant, must be paid for by the tenant.

If a tenant requests the landlord to rekey, or if a device needs repair or replacement, the landlord must act within a reasonable time. Section 92.161 states that a reasonable time is presumed to be *seven days*. There is an exception to this time limit if the tenant notifies the landlord that there has been an unauthorized entry into the dwelling, or another unit, in a multi-unit complex, or if a crime of personal violence has occurred in the multi-unit complex within the two months prior to the request. If one of those conditions is present, then the reasonable time period is lowered to seventy two hours. The amount of time that is considered reasonable can be increased if the landlord, through no fault of his or her own, does not know of the tenant's request, if the materials or labor or utilities are unavailable, or if the delay is caused by things beyond the control of the landlord.

When a tenant signs a lease to move into a rented house for the first time, the landlord has seven days from the day the new tenant moves in to change the locks. This expense is the landlord's, for obvious reasons. Every previous tenant of that property should not have a key to get access to the new tenant's home. However, once the landlord has performed this initial change of locks, if the tenant loses a key or for some other reason wants the locks changed, then the tenant has to pay for the change.

Repairs and Replacement of Security Devices

The general rule under Section 92.162 is that repairs and replacements of security devices caused by normal wear and tear are the landlord's responsibility. There is an exception to this rule if the repair or replacement is due to damage or misuse of the device by the tenant. However, before the tenant can be required to pay this cost, there must be a provision in the lease authorizing the landlord to charge the tenant. The Property Code requires that this provision be *underlined* in the lease.

A landlord can require the tenant to pay these charges in advance of the repair or replacement if:

- ✪ the written lease authorizes advance payment;

- ✪ the landlord notifies the tenant within a reasonable time after the tenant makes the request that advance payment will be required; and,

- ✪ the tenant is more than thirty (30) days delinquent in reimbursing the landlord for damages to a security device caused by the tenant. The tenant can also be required to pay in advance if the tenant has requested a repair or change to the same security device, including a request to rekey, within the previous thirty days.

Unless the written lease says something to the contrary, it is sufficient if the tenant gives the landlord oral notice. However, the lease can require written notice from the tenant.

Remedies

If the landlord does not comply with the laws regarding security devices, then Section 92.164 lists the remedies available to the tenant. The tenant's first option is to install or rekey the security device him or herself and deduct the costs of material, labor, taxes, and extra keys from the next rent payment. The tenant is limited to reasonable costs.

The second option is for the tenant to send a written request for compliance with the security device laws to the landlord. A **TENANT'S REQUEST FOR COMPLIANCE WITH SECURITY DEVICE REQUIREMENTS** (form 13, p.179) is included in Appendix D. If the landlord does not comply by the third day after receipt of the notice, then the tenant can terminate the lease. This provision is subject to some limitations found in Section 92.164, if the lease has a clause that is either underlined or in bold type that restricts this right and authorizes the tenant to install the device and withhold the cost from the rent.

The third option available to the tenant is to take the landlord to court for violating the laws on security devices. If the tenant does not give the landlord a written request for compliance, then the tenant can ask the court to award actual damages, court costs, and attorney's fees. There are some limits in this section on recovery of attorney's fees. If the tenant's actual damages are for property damage, personal injury, or wrongful death, then the court cannot award the attorney's fees.

If the tenant has given the landlord the written request for compliance, the court can order the landlord to bring the dwelling into compliance with the law, and the tenant can also recover actual damages, punitive damages, a civil penalty of one month's rent, plus $500, court costs, and attorney's fees (subject to the limitation on attorney's fees discussed above.)

Limitations   It is permissible for the written lease to contain provisions that specifically authorize the tenant to install or rekey a security device that is required by law and deduct the costs from the rent so long as these provisions are found in the lease in boldface type or are underlined. If this language is present in the lease, then the tenant cannot terminate the lease based on the lack of mandatory security devices, nor can the tenant take the landlord to court for failing to provide the security devices. In order for these remedies to be available to the tenant, the tenant must be current on the rent at the time the request is made to the landlord.

Management Companies

There are some additional rules in Section 92.167 that provide protection for management companies or agents, if they do not have funds of the property owner in their possession or control to make the repairs or install the device. In that event, the manager is obligated to give written notice to the owner to comply and also to give the tenant written notice within three days of the fact that they do not have the owner's funds and that they have requested compliance from the owner. If the management company tells the tenant that the owner will not comply or has not provided the necessary funds, then the tenant can either terminate the lease or take the owner to court.

9 | SMOKE DETECTORS

Subchapter F of Chapter 92 of the Property Code contains the provisions of the law related to smoke detectors in residential properties. In addition to these laws, many cities have local ordinances that address this issue. A landlord leasing residential property must comply with both the state laws and any applicable municipal ones. This book will address only the state laws, so you will need to check to see what the laws of your city are.

General Requirements

State law requires that a smoke detector be designed to detect both visible and invisible products of combustion, have an alarm that is audible to the bedroom it serves, be powered either by battery, alternating current, or other power source (this will be determined by local ordinance), be approved by Underwriters Laboratories, Inc., Factory Mutual Research Corporation, or United States Testing Company, Inc., and be in good working order.

Each bedroom must have its own smoke detector, unless the bedrooms are served by a single corridor. The detectors must be outside the bedroom, but near to it. If a bedroom is located above the living and cooking areas, then the detector must be installed in the center of the ceiling directly above the top of the stairway. If the dwelling uses only one room for dining, living, and sleeping, then the smoke detector should be installed inside that room.

State law requires that the smoke detector be installed either on the ceiling or the wall. If it is on the ceiling, it cannot be within six inches of the wall. If it is placed on the wall, it must be within six and twelve inches of the ceiling.

Duty to Inspect   At the beginning of each tenant's possession, the landlord has the duty to check the smoke detector to ensure that it is in working order. On the **PROPERTY REPORT** (form 8, p.173), smoke detectors are included and should be checked. During the term of the lease or during an extension or renewal, the landlord does not have a duty to inspect the detector unless the tenant gives the landlord notice that there is a malfunction or requests that the landlord inspect or repair the detector. The **TENANT'S REPAIR NOTICE TO LANDLORD** (form 10, p.176) can be used by a tenant to notify the landlord of a problem with a smoke detector. When the tenant makes this request, the law requires the landlord to comply with the request within a reasonable time. The law sets *seven days* as the amount of time that is presumed to be reasonable. The exception to this duty is when the damage to the smoke detector is caused by the tenant, or a guest of the tenant. In that event, the landlord does not have to act unless the tenant pays in advance for the reasonable repair or replacement costs.

The duty to inspect is complied with as long as the landlord has either used the testing button or followed other test procedures recommended by the manufacturer.

Remedies   If the landlord violates the laws related to smoke detectors, the tenant has several remedies available, but the tenant must be sure to give the landlord written notice of the smoke detector problem, and request action by the landlord (see form 10, p.176). These remedies are listed in Section 92.260 and include going to court to get an order directing the landlord to comply with the tenant's request. The tenant can also get a judgment against the landlord for damages suffered by the tenant because of the landlord's violation, as well as a civil penalty of one month's rent, plus $100 dollars, court costs, and attorney's fees. If the landlord fails to act after written notice, the tenant can also terminate the lease.

The landlord is not liable to the tenant if the tenant is not current on the rent when the written notice is given or has not paid the costs in advance.

Tenant's Obligations The tenant is liable to the landlord if the tenant damages or disables a smoke detector. In order for the landlord to hold the tenant liable, the lease must contain language either underlined or in boldface type, which states that the tenant must not disconnect or intentionally damage a smoke detector and may be liable for damages, civil penalties, and attorney's fees if they do so. (see Sec. 92.260 (d) (1).) The landlord must give the tenant written notice in a separate document furnished to the tenant that the landlord intends to exercise his or her remedies if the tenant does not reconnect, repair, or replace the smoke detector within seven days after being notified.

A **LANDLORD'S NOTICE TO TENANT REGARDING SMOKE DETECTOR** (form 14, p.180) is included in Appendix D. Then, if the tenant does not comply, the landlord can go to court and get an order requiring the tenant to comply. The landlord can also get a judgment for a civil penalty of one month's rent plus $100, court costs, and attorney's fees.

Tenant's Guest

If a guest of the tenant suffers damage as the result of an absent or broken smoke detector, the guest can sue to recover the damages. If the landlord failed to inspect, repair, or replace the detector, when required to by law, then the landlord is the one who is liable to the tenant's guest. However, if the tenant disconnected or disabled the detector, then it is the tenant, not the landlord, who is liable for the guest's damages.

10 | UTILITY CUTOFFS

If the landlord either expressly implies or agrees in a lease to provide and pay for water, gas, or electric service, the landlord is liable to the tenant if the utility company either cuts off service to the tenant's dwelling or gives the tenant notice that the utilities are about to be cut off for nonpayment of the bill by the landlord.

Tenant's Remedies

Section 92.301 lists the remedies available to the tenant. The tenant can pay the utility company whatever amount of money is required to reconnect the utilities to avoid the cutoff, and then deduct the amounts paid to the utility company from the rent. The tenant can also terminate the lease, so long as written notice of the lease termination is given to the landlord and the move-out date is within thirty days of the date the tenant has notice of a future, or actual cutoff, whichever is sooner. **A TENANT'S NOTICE OF TERMINATION—UTILITY CUTOFF** (form 15, p.181) is included in Appendix D.

If the tenant terminates the lease, the tenant can deduct any rent due from the security deposit without having to file suit. The tenant is also entitled to a refund of the security deposit. If the tenant terminates, and the tenant has paid any rents in advance, then the tenant is entitled to a pro rata refund from the date of the termination or the date the tenant moves out, whichever is later. The tenant can also sue to recover actual damages, including moving costs, utility connection fees, storage fees, and lost wages in addition to court costs and attorney's fees.

The tenant loses the right to these remedies if the landlord provides written evidence from the utility company that all delinquent sums have been paid in full. This evidence must be provided prior to termination of the lease by the tenant, and prior to the filing of a lawsuit under this section by the tenant.

II | RETALIATION

In many of the preceding chapters, the rights and remedies of tenants have been discussed. Unfortunately, in the past, many landlords have tried to punish tenants for exercising their legal rights. Therefore, the Texas state legislature passed laws protecting tenants from retaliation by landlords. These laws are found in Sections 92.231 through 92.335.

Against Tenant

The general rule is that a landlord cannot take certain actions against a tenant if the tenant, in good faith, exercises, or attempts to exercise a right granted by the lease, municipal ordinance, federal law, or state law. This would include such actions as the tenant giving the landlord a repair notice or complaining to a governmental entity responsible for enforcing building and housing codes. The law states that the landlord cannot, within six months after the date of the tenant's action:

- ✪ deprive the tenant of the use of the property (except for reasons authorized by law such as failure to pay rent);

✪ decrease services to the tenant or increase the rent (unless the written lease already contains automatic escalation provisions or the change is part of a change to all units in a multi-unit complex); or,

✪ terminate the tenant's lease.

The landlord cannot act in bad faith to materially interfere with the tenant's rights under the lease.

Filing an eviction proceeding against the tenant, within six months, is also considered retaliation unless the tenant:

✪ is delinquent on the rent;

✪ has damaged the property;

✪ threatens the personal safety of the landlord, the landlord's employees, or another tenant;

✪ has materially breached the lease in some way; or,

✪ has held over in violation of the law.

If the landlord retaliates against a tenant, the tenant can sue the landlord for a civil penalty of one month's rent, plus $500, actual damages, court costs, and attorney's fees.

Against Landlord

If a tenant files a retaliation complaint against a landlord in *bad faith*, the landlord can sue the tenant. The court can evict the tenant from the premises, as well as penalizing the tenant one month's rent, plus $500, court costs, and attorney's fees. There is a provision in this section that creates a presumption of bad faith if the tenant files a complaint with a governmental entity, they investigate and find that the building or housing code violation or utility problem did not exist.

12 COLLECTING UNPAID RENT

A landlord has two basic options to collect unpaid rent. They are: 1) using a *landlord's lien* and following the procedures for seizing and selling a tenant's property, and 2) taking the tenant to court.

Statutory Lien

Section 54.041 gives a residential landlord a *statutory lien* for unpaid rent that is due. The lien attaches to *nonexempt property* that is in the residence or that the tenant has stored in a storage room.

Exempt Property Section 54.042 lists the property belonging to the tenant that is exempt from the lien. Items that are exempt from the lien are:

✪ wearing apparel;

✪ tools;

✪ apparatus;

✪ books of a trade or profession;

✪ schoolbooks;

✪ a family library;

✪ family portraits and pictures;

✪ one couch;

✪ two living room chairs;

✪ a dining room table and chairs;

✪ beds and bedding;

✪ kitchen furniture and utensils;

✪ food and foodstuffs;

✪ medicine and medical supplies;

✪ one automobile and one truck;

✪ agricultural implements;

✪ children's toys not commonly used by adults;

✪ goods that the landlord or the landlord's agent knows are owned by a person other than the tenant or an occupant of the residence; and,

✪ goods that the landlord or the landlord's agent knows are subject to a recorded mortgage or financing agreement.

The property on this list cannot be taken by the landlord. In order to enforce this lien, the landlord must file formal foreclosure proceedings against the tenant.

Contracted Liens

The written lease can also provide for a landlord's lien. This is a *contractual lien*, not a *statutory lien*. There are several advantages to including this language in your written lease. The primary ones being that you can, if the proper language is included, satisfy this lien without the necessity for formal foreclosure proceedings. Section 54.043 states that the contractual lien must be either underlined in the lease or in boldface type in the lease. Otherwise, it is not enforceable.

Seizing Property

If the landlord wants to have the right to *seize* nonexempt property (which is anything not on the list of exempt property) and sell it, these rights must be contained in the written lease. Otherwise, even though the property code creates a statutory lien, the landlord cannot take and then sell the tenant's property.

Section 54.044 covers the seizure of property. In addition to the requirement of the written lease authorizing seizure, the landlord must also be able to take the property without a *breach of the peace*. That means that the landlord may use his or her master key and take the property while the tenant is not present, but cannot use force to take the property while the tenant is present.

If seizure is authorized by the lease, then the landlord can take the tenant's nonexempt property found in the residence or in a storage building on the property. Immediately upon taking the property, the law requires the landlord, or the landlord's agent, to leave a written *notice of entry* for the tenant. This notice must state:

✪   the amount of delinquent rent;

✪   the name, address, and telephone number of the person the tenant may contact regarding the amount owed;

✪   an itemized list of the items taken; and,

✪ statement that the property will be promptly returned on full payment of the delinquent rent.

The notice must be left in a *conspicuous* place within the dwelling. Unless it is authorized in the written lease, the landlord cannot collect charges for packing, removing, or storing the property seized. A **LANDLORD'S NOTICE TO TENANT OF ENTRY OF PREMISES AND SEIZURE OF PROPERTY** (form 16, p.182) is provided in Appendix D.

Sale of Seized Property

The rules regarding sale of the seized property are found in Section 54.045. This section requires the landlord to give the tenant notice of the sale not later than thirty days prior to the date of the sale. This notice must be sent both regular first class mail and by certified mail, return receipt requested, to the tenant's last known address. The notice must contain:

✪ the date, time, and place of the sale;

✪ an itemized account of the amount owed by the tenant to the landlord; and,

✪ the name, address, and telephone number of the person the tenant may contact regarding the sale.

A **NOTICE OF SALE OF SEIZED PROPERTY** (form 17, p.184) is included in Appendix D.

Tenant's Right to Redeem

The tenant must also be told he or she has a right to *redeem* his or her property by paying to the landlord, or the landlord's agent, prior to the sale, all delinquent rents, and the charges for packing, moving, and storing the property (if these charges are authorized by the written lease). If any of the property to be sold has another lien on it, such as a mortgage or purchase money lien, then that lien must be satisfied first before the landlord can keep any of the money from the sale of that piece of property.

All of the property must be sold on a cash basis to the highest bidder. Proceeds from the sale are applied first to the delinquent rent, and then to the packing, moving, and storage costs. If there is any money left after the payment of these amounts, then that money must be mailed to the tenant within thirty days of the sale, at the tenant's last known address. An accounting of the sale proceeds, and how they were applied must also be given to the tenant at that time.

Replevy

In addition to the tenant's *right to redeem* the property by paying the amounts owed, there is another method by which the tenant can keep the property from being sold. This is called a *replevy* and this procedure is found in Section 54.048. This requires a tenant to post a *bond* in an amount approved by the court, payable to the landlord. The bond is conditioned on the outcome of a court proceeding. If the landlord wins, then the bond proceeds are used to pay the judgment awarded to the landlord. This replevy bond must be posted prior to the entry of a judgment against the tenant in a suit for unpaid rent and prior to the sale of the property.

Additional Tenant Remedies

If the landlord violates the rules regarding the seizure and sale of a tenant's property, the tenant has the right to take the landlord to court and sue for:

- actual damages;

- the return of any property that has been seized, but not sold;

- the return of the proceeds of any sale of seized property;

- one month's rent or $500 (whichever is greater); and,

- reasonable attorney's fees.

Any amounts for which the tenant is liable are deducted from the amount of the judgement granted to the tenant.

Suing for Unpaid Rent

If the tenant has already moved out of the residence, but still owes rent, then the landlord can file a suit to collect the unpaid rent. While most landlord-tenant suits must be filed in justice court, a suit just for the unpaid rent is different. Because it is simply a *breach of contract* suit, the court in which you should file your suit depends on the amount of unpaid rent.

All courts have what are called *jurisdictional limits.* This means that, in some courts, there is a maximum amount of damages you can claim in your suit and, in other courts, a minimum amount. Since these amounts vary from county to county, you should call the clerk of the courts and ask what the amount is. If the amount owed is small enough, you should file your case in *justice court.* For regular civil cases like this, you will often hear the court referred to as *small claims court,* but for all practical purposes, justice court and small claims court are the same.

Cases with dollar amounts that are too high for small claims or justice court must be filed in county court. You should consider hiring an attorney to help you with these kinds of lawsuits. The rules in *county court* are more complex and strict than they are in small claims court. A **LANDLORD'S DEMAND FOR UNPAID RENT** (form 18, p.185), as well as an **ORIGINAL PETITION TO COLLECT UNPAID RENT** (form 19, p.186) are included in Appendix D.

13 MANUFACTURED HOUSING

Subchapter A of Chapter 94 of the Property Code covers landlords renting lots on which manufactured homes, sometimes known as mobile homes, or recreational vehicles, are located as part of a manufactured home community. A *community* is defined by the statutes as a parcel of land in which four or more lots are offered for lease for installing and occupying manufactured homes. These laws do not apply to the relationship between an owner of a mobile home who is renting the home and the tenant of that property. That relationship is governed by the regular rules for residential tenancies.

This subchapter has a provision that says that any attempt in a lease to waive a right or to exempt a landlord or tenant from a duty established by these laws is void.

Landlord's Entry

The landlord of a manufactured home community cannot enter the tenant's home unless the tenant is present and has given consent, or unless the tenant has previously given written consent to the landlord. This written consent must specify the date and time the entry is permitted, and is valid only for that date and time.

Common Areas

The law requires all the common areas of the community to be open or available to all of the tenants.

Community Rules

The landlord is allowed to establish rules applicable to the community, so long as the rules are not arbitrary or capricious. This means that the rules should be reasonable and apply equally to all tenants. The tenants get thirty days notice of any changes to the rules and ninety days if the rule change is going to require them to expend money to comply with the rule. The rules become part of the lease agreement and can be enforced by the landlord just like any other term of the lease.

The landlord of a manufactured home community is required to disclose to each tenant the name and address of the owner of record of the property, as well as the name and address of any off-site entity responsible for the management of the community.

Lease Term

Section 94.052 requires the landlord to offer the tenant a six month lease. The landlord and the tenant may agree to either a shorter or longer lease term than the six month term required to be offered. The law also requires the landlord to give the tenant at least sixty days notice prior to the end of the lease term if the landlord does not intend to renew the lease.

While the law entitles a tenant to a minimum six month lease, there may be reasons the landlord and tenant would agree to a shorter period. For example, if the tenant were waiting for his purchase of a piece of property on which he planned to permanently install the home to be complete, and the landlord had an unused space, the parties might just do a three month lease. On the other hand, if both the landlord and tenant want their business relationship to continue for some time (for example, if the tenant had already rented from the landlord for a couple of years and the landlord had no plans to sell the property), the parties might agree on a longer term lease of several years.

Lease Requirements

Section 94.053 sets out the legal requirements for a lease in a manufactured home community. In addition to being in writing, either typed or written legibly, and signed by both the landlord and the tenant, the lease must contain:

✪   the address or number of the lot on which the home will be located;

✪   the number and location of any accompanying parking spaces;

✪   the lease term;

✪   the rental amount;

✪   the interval at which the rent must be paid (monthly, for example);

✪   the date on which the periodic payments are due (the first day of the month, for example);

✪   any late charge, or fee, or charge for any service or facility;

✪   the amount of any security deposit;

✪   a description of the landlord's maintenance responsibilities;

✪   the phone number of the person who may be contacted for emergency maintenance;

✪   the name and address of the person designated to accept official notices for the landlord;

✪   the penalty the landlord may impose for the tenant's early termination of the lease;

✪   the grounds for eviction;

✪   a disclosure of the landlord's right to terminate the lease agreement if there is a change in the land use of the community;

✪ a prominent disclosure informing the tenant that Chapter 94 governs the rights granted to tenants, and obligations imposed on the landlord by law;

✪ a disclosure of any incorporation by reference of any addendum related to submetering of utilities;

✪ any other conditions of occupancy not expressly included in the community rules; and,

✪ the expiration date of any temporary zoning permits covering the land.

Any lease provision requiring an increase in rent or in fees charged during the lease term must be initialed by the tenant or it is void. The tenant is required by law to disclose to the landlord the name and address of any lienholder on the manufactured home.

Security Deposits

Chapter 94 also includes provisions for the handling of security deposits. Landlords of manufactured home communities *do* have the right to require security deposits from their tenants. The landlord is required to refund the security deposit no later than thirty days after the date the tenant surrenders the lot back to the landlord. If the landlord wants to impose a condition that the tenant give *advance notice of surrender* in order for the security deposit to be refunded, that clause in the lease must either be underlined or printed in bold type. In situations where the tenant signs the lease and pays a security deposit, but then does not take possession of the lot, the landlord must refund the tenant's security deposit. In addition, the landlord must refund any rent prepayment, if either the tenant or the landlord secures a replacement tenant by the commencement date of the lease signed by the original tenant.

There are some conditions under which the landlord can retain some, or all, of the security deposit. However, as with other types of leases, the landlord cannot withhold any portion of the security deposit for normal *wear and tear*. If the landlord withholds part of the deposit to cover damage to the property for which the tenant is liable or for damages caused by the tenant's breach of the lease, then the landlord must give the tenant a written description and an itemized list of all deductions at the time the balance of the security deposit is returned to the tenant. The landlord is exempt from the accounting requirement if the tenant owes rent when the tenant surrenders possession of the lot and there is no controversy about the amount of rent owed by the tenant. The landlord's duty to refund the security deposit and give the accounting does not become effective until the tenant gives the landlord a forwarding address. However, the landlord's duty does not just go away. The landlord must continue to hold the tenant's security deposit until such time as the tenant does provide the address.

If the landlord wrongfully withholds the tenant's security deposit, the tenant can sue the landlord for an amount equal to the sum of $100, three times the portion of the security deposit wrongfully withheld, and the tenant's attorney's fees. If the landlord fails to give the tenant the required accounting, then the landlord loses the right to retain any part of the deposit, and also loses the right to file suit against the tenant for damages to the property. The landlord can also be ordered to pay the tenant's attorney's fees if the tenant sues the landlord to get back the remainder of the security deposit.

Maintenance Requirements

In manufactured home communities, the landlord has certain maintenance requirements. The landlord has to comply with any laws, such as local codes and ordinances, that establish rules applicable to the mobile home park. In addition, the landlord must:

✪ maintain all of the common areas in a clean and useable condition;

✪ maintain all of the utility lines installed in the community by the landlord (unless the utility company is responsible for this task);

✪ maintain individual mailboxes for the tenants in compliance with Postal Service regulations;

✪ maintain roads in the community to the extent necessary to allow each tenant access to his or her lot;

✪ provide services for collection of garbage and solid waste from the community; and,

✪ repair or remedy conditions on the property that materially affect the physical health or safety of ordinary tenants in the community.

The landlord's duty to repair does not extend to conditions present in or on the tenant's manufactured home or to damages to the landlord's property caused by the tenant or a guest of the tenant.

Tenant's Responsibilities

The tenant must give the landlord notice of the problem that the landlord needs to repair or remedy. If the landlord fails to act, the tenant's remedies include the right to terminate the lease, have the condition repaired himself and deduct the cost of repairs from the rent, or file suit against the landlord.

Time Limits for Repairs

The rules regarding time limits for repairs and procedures are generally the same as those for regular residential leases. The rules also include provisions for the landlord to sign an affidavit for delay, justifying the delay in making the repairs to avoid liability to the tenant for failing to make the repairs soon enough.

This part of the Property Code also contains provisions setting out the respective liabilities of the tenant and the landlord. These provisions are basically the same as those for other residential leases. If you are dealing with these issues in a manufactured home community setting, refer to the information contained in the residential lease section.

NOTE: *If you have to give any written notices or file any suits in court, you should reference the statute numbers in this part of the code and not the ones in the general residential section.*

14 COMMERCIAL LEASES

Chapter 93 of the Property Code contains the provisions specifically addressing commercial tenancies. You will note that there are many similarities between the residential rules and the commercial ones, but generally the laws regarding residential leases are more extensive, and offer more detailed rights for the tenants.

Commercial Property

Commercial property is defined as all property not covered by the definition of residential property contained in the residential leases chapter of the Property Code (Chapter 92). As a reminder, residential property covers dwellings, and dwellings are defined as one or more rooms rented for use as a permanent residence. That means that everything else is legally defined as a commercial lease.

Utility Cutoffs

Section 93.002 contains the rules about utility cutoffs in commercial leases, and it says that a landlord may not interrupt or cause the interruption of utility services that are paid directly by the tenant to the utility company unless the interruption is necessary because of *bona fide* repairs, construction, or an emergency.

Removal of Tenant's Property

Section 93.002 also contains the rules the cover removal of the tenant's property by the landlord. A landlord cannot remove a door, window, attic hatchway, cover, lock, latch, hinge, hinge pin, doorknob, or other mechanism connected to a door, window, or attic hatchway cover, or remove furniture, fixtures, or appliances furnished by the landlord for any reason other than legitimate repairs or replacement. If an item is removed for repair or replacement, the repair or replacement must be completed promptly.

Abandoned Property A landlord is allowed to remove a tenant's property from the leased premises if the tenant has abandoned the premises. Section 93.002 (d) states that a tenant is presumed to have *abandoned* the premises, if goods, equipment, or other property in an amount substantial enough to indicate a probable intent to abandon the premises is being or has been removed from the premises, as long as the removal is not within the normal course of the tenant's business. If the landlord removes property based on abandonment, the landlord must store the tenant's property, and give the tenant an opportunity to reclaim the property. The tenant must be notified by certified mail sent to the tenant's last known mailing address that the landlord is storing the property. The notice must tell the tenant that the landlord may dispose of the property if the tenant does not claim it within sixty days after the date the property is stored. A **LANDLORD'S NOTICE TO TENANT REGARDING DISPOSAL OF ABANDONED PROPERTY** (form 20, p.189) is included in Appendix D.

Banning Tenant's Entry

The law also prohibits landlords from intentionally excluding tenants from the leased premises without a court order. There are exceptions allowing a landlord to exclude a tenant if the exclusion is necessary because of repairs to, or construction of the premises, or as the result of an emergency.

Lockouts The landlord can, however, change the locks of a tenant who is delinquent in paying at least part of the rent. If the landlord does change the locks, the law requires the landlord or the landlord's agent, to place a written notice on the tenant's front door stating the name and the address or telephone number of the individual or company from which the new key may be obtained. A **NOTICE OF CHANGING OF LOCK TO COMMERCIAL TENANT** (form 21, p.190) is included in Appendix D. The new key is only required to be supplied during the tenant's regular business hours and only upon payment of the delinquent rent.

Tenant Remedies

If the landlord improperly interrupts the utilities, removes a tenant's property, or excludes the tenant from the leased premises, the tenant may either regain possession of the leased premises or terminate the lease. In addition, the tenant can sue the landlord for one month's rent or $500, whichever is greater, plus the tenant's actual damages, attorney's fees, and court costs. Any delinquent rents, or other amounts owed will be deducted from the amount of money awarded to the tenant in the court order.

However, it is important for both tenants and landlords to take note that, if the lease contains provisions that conflict with these laws (Section 93.002), the terms of the lease supersede the statutory provisions. Therefore, both tenants and landlords should know the terms of the lease that apply to these situations before filing suit or taking any of these actions just discussed.

Writ of Re-Entry

Section 93.003 sets out the procedure that must be followed by the tenant if the tenant plans to take the landlord to court to regain possession of the premises after the landlord has violated the unlawful lockout provisions of section 93.002. The tenant must file the lawsuit in justice court in the precinct in which the rental premises are located. The tenant files a *sworn complaint* (which means that the written document containing the tenant's allegations against the landlord must be notarized). This complaint must also specify the facts of the alleged unlawful lockout. In addition, the tenant must orally state to the justice the facts of the alleged lockout.

Once the tenant has taken both of these steps, then the judge determines whether an unlawful lockout has occurred. If the judge believes it has, the judge can issue an *ex parte order* (meaning an order that is issued without notice to the other party and without any further hearings), called a *writ of re-entry* that entitles the tenant to immediate possession of the premises pending a final hearing in court on the issues. The writ of re-entry must be formally served on either the landlord, or the landlord's management company, the on-site manager, or rent collector by the sheriff or constable.

This writ of re-entry will tell the landlord that he or she has the right to have a hearing on the tenant's allegations. It is the landlord's job to request the hearing from the justice court. The hearing must be held not earlier than the first day and not later than the seventh day, after the date the landlord requests the hearing. Further, the landlord must request this hearing within seven days from the date the landlord is served with the writ of re-entry. If the landlord fails to request this hearing, the justice court can enter a judgment against the landlord for court costs.

A landlord must follow all of the conditions in the writ of re-entry or face being held in *contempt of court*. That means that, if the landlord is served with the writ of re-entry and either fails to immediately comply with the writ, or later disobeys the writ, then the tenant can file an affidavit with the justice court setting out how the landlord has disobeyed the writ. The justice court will schedule a hearing, and give the landlord an opportunity to defend the allegations. If, after that hearing, the justice court judge decides that the landlord has in fact disobeyed the writ of re-entry, the landlord can be put in jail and held there without bail until the landlord has complied with the writ of re-entry.

Landlord's Remedies

If the tenant acts in bad faith when he or she goes to court and swears out the unlawful lockout complaint, then the landlord has the right to take the tenant to court and sue for the greater of one month's rent, or $500, plus actual damages, attorney's fees, and court costs.

Security Deposits

The issues related to the handling of security deposits in commercial tenancies are similar to those in residential leases. Sections 93.004 through 93.006 cover security deposits in commercial situations. The commercial landlord is allowed to deduct damages and other charges for which the tenant is legally liable from the security deposit, as well as damages and charges that result from a breach of the lease. However, the landlord cannot hold any part of the deposit to cover normal wear and tear. The statute defines normal *wear and tear* as deterioration that results from the intended use of the commercial premises, including breakage or malfunction due to age or deteriorated condition. Damage that results from negligence, carelessness, accident, or abuse of the premises, equipment, or other property by the tenant or any guest of the tenant can be withheld from the security deposit.

Deductions Generally, the landlord must give the tenant a written description and itemized list of all deductions if any part of the security deposit will be retained. The written accounting should be given to the tenant at the time the balance of the security deposit is returned. The deadline for the return of the security deposit is no later than the 30th day after the tenant surrenders possession of the premises and provides notice of the tenant's forwarding address. If the tenant owes rent when possession of the premises is surrendered and there is no controversy between the landlord and tenant as to the amount of rent owed, then the landlord does not have to give the tenant this written documentation on the amounts withheld from the deposit.

If the tenant fails to give the landlord a forwarding address, then the landlord is not obligated to return the deposit until that address is provided by the tenant. But the fact that the tenant does not give the required notice does not mean that the landlord just gets to keep the security deposit forever because the law says that a tenant's failure to give the address is not a *forfeiture* of the deposit. That means that the landlord must be prepared to refund the deposit at any time in the future that the tenant complies with the forwarding address notice requirement.

Security Deposit It is illegal for a tenant to fail to pay rents due on the grounds that the security
as Rent deposit can be taken to satisfy the unpaid rent. This provision is found in Section 93.010. A tenant who fails to pay all rent due, in violation of this section, can be sued by the landlord and be ordered to pay the landlord an amount equal to three times the rent wrongfully withheld, plus the landlord's attorney's fees.

Retaining If the landlord retains a security deposit in bad faith, then the landlord can be
Security required to pay the tenant an amount equal to the sum of $100, plus three times
Deposits the amount of the deposit wrongfully withheld, plus the tenant's attorney's fees. If the landlord, in bad faith, does not provide the tenant with the required writ-

ten accounting of the amounts withheld from the deposit, then section 93.011 states that the landlord forfeits the right to withhold any of the security deposit, and also loses the right to sue the tenant for damages to the premises. In addition, the landlord can be ordered to pay the tenant's attorney's fees.

Bad Faith

You will notice that all of these penalty provisions apply when the landlord acts in *bad faith*. Fortunately, the law gives a definition of what is meant by *bad faith* in this instance. If a landlord fails to return the security deposit or to provide a written description and itemization of the deductions on or before the 30th day after the date the tenant surrenders possession of the premises, he or she is presumed to be acting in bad faith. (see Section 93.011 (d).)

New Ownership

If ownership of the property changes during the term of the lease, then the new owner is liable for the return of the security deposit. This liability is assumed by the new owner as of the date that new owner acquires legal title to the property. The prior owner also remains liable for the return of the deposit until such time as the new owner gives the tenant a signed statement acknowledging that the new owner has received, and is responsible for, the security deposit. This written notice to the tenant should also contain the exact dollar amount of the security deposit. The one exception to these rules is that they do not apply to a new owner who was the real estate mortgage holder for the prior owner and who has acquired title to the property as a result of foreclosure.

You should note that the Property Code does not contain all of the requirements for maintenance responsibilities, security devices, and smoke detectors that are found in the residential rules. Since there is no specific set of rules determining responsibility for these items, the rules should be agreed upon by the parties and the respective duties of each should be set out in the written lease agreement.

I5 COMMERCIAL LANDLORD'S LIENS

The *commercial landlord's lien* is called a *building landlord's lien*, and the laws governing this type of lien are found in sections 54.021 through 54.025 of the Property Code. The law gives a person, who leases all or part of a building for nonresidential purposes, a *preference lien* on the property of the tenant or subtenant in the building, This lien is for rent that is due and for rent that is to become due during the current twelve-month period. The twelve-month period is the date of the beginning of the rental agreement, or an anniversary of that date. Basically, what this means is that the lien only covers rent due for the current lease year. If you signed the lease on August 1, then your lease year runs from August 1 to July 31. If the tenant becomes delinquent in June, then the landlord's lien on that rent expires two months later, on August 1.

Lien Statement

The lien also does not cover rent that is more than six months past due unless the landlord files a lien statement with the county clerk of the county in which the building is located. This lien statement must be signed and notarized, and contain:

✪   an account, itemized month by month, of the rent for which the lien is claimed;

✪   the name and address of the tenant or subtenant;

✪   a description of the leased premises; and,

✪   the beginning and termination dates of the lease.

When the lien statement is recorded, it lasts while the tenant occupies the building up until one month after the day that the tenant surrenders or abandons the building.

Distress Warrants

Because of the time restrictions, a commercial landlord should not let unpaid rent accrue for any significant period without taking action. As you can see, a failure to act can mean that the commercial landlord loses the protection afforded by the lien laws. You should also note that the law does not give a commercial landlord *self-help protections*, such as the right to seize and sell property without going to court. The only way for a commercial landlord to enforce the lien, is by filing a suit to foreclose on the lien or by applying to the justice court for a *distress warrant.*

The distress warrant provisions are found in Section 54.025 of the Property Code, and Rules 610 through 620 of the Rules of Civil Procedure. They permit the landlord to ask for a distress warrant if the tenant owes rent and is either about to abandon the building or remove the tenant's property from the building. The application must be accompanied by an affidavit stating that the amounts claimed are for rent, that the request is not for the purpose of harassing or vexing the tenant, and must state the grounds supporting the request.

The application is presented to the justice of the peace, who must make a finding to support the grounds for the warrant, and set a maximum value for the property to be seized. The landlord will have to post a bond, and the justice will set the amount of this bond at the time the distress warrant is approved.

The distress warrant must be served formally on the tenant by either the sheriff or constable. The sheriff or constable will take the property and hold it until the court makes additional orders after a trial on the merits of the landlord's claim. There is, however, an exception that allows the justice court to order the property sold prior to trial if it will be seriously damaged or destroyed by the delay, or the storage costs will be so high that it will not have any value by the time of the trial.

Replevy At any time prior to the entry of a final judgment (assuming the property has not already been sold), the tenant has the right to replevy the property (in other words, get his property back) by posting a bond. The amount of the bond will be determined by the justice court at the time the distress warrant is issued.

Landlord's Other Remedies

Since both the procedures to obtain a distress warrant and to prosecute a foreclosure suit are fairly detailed and complex, the commercial landlord should seriously consider hiring an attorney for representation on both of these issues. As a reminder, if you prevail in court, you have a good chance of having the court order the tenant to reimburse you for some or all of your attorney's fees.

Sometimes, the tenant will have already moved out of the building and there will not be any property left to use to satisfy a lien. If that is the case, the landlord still has the right to sue the former tenant in court for the unpaid rent. The procedure for this is the same as for a residential landlord's suit for unpaid rent described in Chapter 12.

16 | TERMINATING LEASES

The relationship between a landlord and tenant commonly ends as a result of the lease term expiring and the tenant vacating the premises. However, there will be times that one of the parties will want to end the relationship sooner. There are a variety of ways this can happen with both residential and commercial leases.

Month-to-Month Tenancies

A month-to-month tenancy may be terminated by either the landlord or the tenant. The procedure for termination is that the party desiring to end the tenancy gives a termination notice to the other party. If the rent is paid on at least a monthly basis, as most rents are, then the tenancy terminates on the later of the date stated in the termination notice or one month after the day on which the termination notice is given. This provision, found in Section 91.001, means that the terminating party must give the other party at least thirty days notice of the termination of the lease. The **LANDLORD'S NOTICE TO TERMINATE LEASE** (form 4, p.167) found in Appendix D may be used for this purpose. If you are a tenant, you can adapt this form to simply state that you will not be renewing the lease and give the landlord your move out date.

If the rent paying period is less than one month, such as week-to-week, then the non-terminating party gets a notice period that is at least equal to the rent-paying period. If the tenancy terminates in the middle of a rent paying period, then the tenant's last rent payment must only cover the portion of the rental period that falls within the tenancy. For example, if the tenant pays rent on a monthly basis, and the tenancy terminates in the middle of the month, the tenant's final rent would only be for half of the month.

The landlord and tenant can agree to handle the termination in a different manner. However, Section 91.001 requires this agreement to be in writing and signed by both the landlord and the tenant. These notice requirements also do not apply to situations in which there has been a breach of the lease by one of the parties. In that event, the non-breaching party is not required to comply with these notice provisions.

Tenant Convicted of a Crime

Section 91.003 establishes another legal ground that authorizes the landlord to terminate the lease. If the tenant or another occupant uses the property for an activity that results in a conviction under Chapter 43 of the Penal Code, then the landlord can, within six months after the conviction becomes final, terminate the lease. Chapter 43 of the Penal Code contains the criminal laws related to public indecency. Offenses include prostitution, promotion of prostitution, obscenity, and child pornography. Convictions of the tenant for any of these crimes will authorize the landlord to terminate the lease if the tenant used the leased premises in the commission of the crime. A conviction becomes final when the accused person has been found guilty and exhausted all of their appeals.

Other Terminating Issues

Other than these factors that the Property Code sets up to terminate the tenancy, the tenancy will either end on its own terms when the lease expires, because of one of the situations discussed or because one of the parties breaches the lease in some way. If the landlord breaches the lease, the tenant generally has the right to sue the landlord in court for damages. Section 91.004 gives the tenant a *statutory lien* on the landlord's nonexempt property in the tenant's possession, and on the rent due the landlord to satisfy a judgment for damages assessed against the landlord.

Death of Tenant

If the tenant dies, it might seem that this event brings an end to the tenancy and ends the tenant's obligation to pay rent. However, the tenant's estate remains liable to the landlord for payment of all the rent that remains due through the end of the leased premises. A landlord can request, in writing, that the tenant give the landlord the name and address and phone number of the person to contact in case of the tenant's death and authorize the landlord to permit this person to take the tenant's property from the premises if the tenant dies. If the landlord has obtained this authorization, he or she must give the designated person written notice, by certified mail, return receipt requested, that they must retrieve the tenant's property within thirty days. If the designated person does not have the property removed by the deadline, then the landlord is authorized to discard it. If the landlord does not have this written authorization, he or she will have to go to court to deal with terminating the tenancy and obtaining authorization to remove the tenant's property. These rules are found in Section 92.014 of the Property Code.

Example: Assume that Jane's sister, Jean, has rented a house from Bill. The lease is for six months and Jean has been in the house for four of those months. When Jean dies unexpectedly, Bill must decide what to do with Jean's property that is in the house. If, at the time Jean rented the house, she signed a document designating Jane as the person to contact in case of her death and authorizing the landlord to permit Jane to take her property, then Bill must send Jane a letter by certified mail, return receipt requested, giving her thirty days to remove Jean's belongings from the house. If Jane misses the deadline, then Bill can dispose of Jean's property.

Agreement to Terminate before Lease Signed

Another example of the end of a tenancy is the landlord-tenant relationship that ends before the tenant actually signs the lease. If the prospective tenant agrees to lease and then does not sign the actual lease, the landlord has a claim against the tenant for breach of contract. In this instance, the breached contract is not the lease agreement, but rather the agreement to lease. While this is a valid claim, it will almost never be worth the time and effort it would take to actually sue the tenant on this basis. In this situation, it is best for all parties to just walk away from the situation. If the tenant has paid a deposit, the refundability of this deposit depends on the facts of each case, and any agreements between the parties.

> ***Example:*** Assume Jean had looked over a house belonging to Bill and told him she planned to rent the house from him and would be in on Tuesday to sign the lease. On Monday, she called him back and told him she would not be coming to sign after all because she had changed her mind about renting the house. Jean has completed the application but not paid a deposit. In this instance, Bill cannot force Jean to rent the house because the lease was never signed.

Agreement to Terminate after Lease Signed

The situation is different, however, if the tenant changes his or her mind about renting after already signing the lease. Once the lease is signed, it is binding on both parties, and the tenant is obligated to make all the rent payments unless the landlord is able to relet the premises. The only exceptions to this rule are situations in which the tenant has a legal defense to the enforcement of the lease. Examples of legal defenses would be some sort of fraud in the negotiating of the lease, such as a *material factual misrepresentation* (for example, if the landlord lied about some significant feature of the premises just to get the tenant to sign the lease), the *impossibility of performance* (for example, if the premises were leased for use as a residence but something happens to the house after the lease is signed that make the house uninhabitable), or *illegality of the lease* (any lease that is entered into for an illegal purpose is void).

> ***Example:*** Using the set of facts from the previous section, assume that Jean has already been to Bill's office and she and Bill have both signed the lease. After she has signed but before she moves in, Jean changes her mind and decides that she does not want to live in the house after all. Assuming that none of the defenses we mentioned apply, then Jean has a problem. While Bill cannot force her to move in and actually live in the house, he can take her to court and sue her if she does not pay the rent as agreed. Once Bill knows that Jean is not moving in, he must begin looking for a replacement tenant. Once he finds one and a new lease on the property is signed, then Jean will not have to make any more rent payments.

Self-Condemned Property

If the landlord wants to close the rental premises, he or she can terminate the lease by giving written notice, by certified mail, return receipt requested. This should be sent to the tenant, the local health officer, and the local building inspector, stating that the landlord is terminating the tenancy as soon as it is legally possible. The landlord must state in the notice that the landlord will either demolish the premises, or not longer use it for residential purposes. In this event, the landlord must pay the tenant's moving expenses, refund the security deposit, and give the tenant a pro rata refund on the rent. The tenant also has the right to sue the landlord for actual damages, a civil penalty of one month's rent, plus $500, attorney's fees, and court costs.

Sale of Premises

If the landlord sells the property, this does not terminate the tenancy. The new owner must honor all the terms and conditions of all existing leases. If you are a landlord selling a property that is leased, you should specify in the sales contract that the sale is subject to the outstanding leases and the leases should be assigned to the new owner as a part of the closing of the sale. If the selling landlord fails to take these steps, he or she can be sued for damages by the new owner.

Foreclosure

A *foreclosure* will occur when the landlord owes money to a mortgage holder on the leased premises and fails to make the payments. After several months with no payments have gone by, the lender will foreclose on the property, meaning they will post the property for sale on the courthouse steps and use the sale proceeds to satisfy the unpaid balance on the mortgage. The effect of the foreclosure is that the person or company who buys the property at the foreclosure sale is the owner and the landlord no longer owns or has any legal right to the leased premises. If the property is sold in foreclosure, then the leases are terminated by the foreclosure unless the mortgage holder specifically agrees to continue the leases.

Eviction

If the tenant is the one who breaches the lease, the landlord may want to force the tenant to vacate the premises by *evicting* the tenant. This is the procedure the landlord will want to use if the tenant *holdsover* after the expiration of the lease, and the landlord chooses not to continue the tenancy under the same terms as the original lease. If the landlord does not consent to the tenant remaining in possession of the premises, then the tenant becomes legally defined as a *trespasser*. The landlord can sue for possession of the premises, and damages in the amount of the rent value, plus double the rent.

17 | EVICTIONS

If the tenant fails to pay his or her rent or refuses to vacate the premises after the end of the lease period, then the landlord will most likely want to evict the tenant from the premises. In order to do so, the landlord will need to go to court and file an eviction proceeding. In Texas, proceedings to evict tenants are called *forcible detainer suits*. Suits by tenants relating to unlawful entries onto the leased property without their consent are *forcible entries*. You may hear both types of cases referred to as forcible entry and detainer suits or FEDs. The laws regarding forcible entry and detainer suits are found in Chapter 24 of the Property Code. You will also need to familiarize yourself with Rules 738 through 755 of the Texas Rules of Civil Procedure. These rules specifically apply to FED suits.

Procedure

It is very important that all of the steps in the eviction process be precisely followed. One reason for being careful is that a failure to follow the law can keep you from accomplishing your desired goal in court. A second reason is that the law provides that the loser in these proceedings has to pay the winner's attorney's fees.

Notice   The first step in the eviction process is to give the tenant the written notice required by Section 24.005. This section requires the landlord to give the tenant, who is either in default under the lease or is holding over after the end of the lease term, at least three days notice to vacate the premises prior to filing a forcible detainer suit. If the written lease provides for a different notice period, then what is written in the lease controls. This provision can allow for either a shorter or longer notice period. An **EVICTION NOTICE** (form 22, p.191) is included for use in situations where the tenant has failed to pay rent.

There is a different requirement if the building is purchased at a foreclosure sale, the tenant pays rent timely, and is not in default of any of the other terms of the lease. In that event, if the new owner does not want to continue the tenancy, then the tenant is entitled to thirty days notice to vacate.

The landlord must also comply with the end of the tenancy provisions in Chapter 91 of the Property Code. As a reminder, these provisions generally give the tenant a notice period that the tenancy will be ending that is equal to the rent period (monthly rental payments means that the tenant gets a month's notice).

Mail Delivery. The notice to vacate can be given to the tenant either by mail or in person. Although notice by regular mail is permitted by the statute, a landlord who elects to give the notice by mail should use certified mail, return receipt requested, so that there is proof available that the notice was given and received by the tenant. If using mail as the notice method, most courts will require you to wait at least two extra days to allow for the mail to be delivered to the tenant.

Personal Delivery. If the landlord elects to give the notice in person, the law allows the landlord to leave the notice with either the tenant, or any other person who lives at the premises who is at least 16 years old, or to affix the notice to the main entry door. Generally, the notice should be attached to the inside of the main entry door. However, if the property has no mailbox and has a keyless bolting device, alarm system, or dangerous animal that keeps the landlord from using the inside of the entry door, it is permissible to attach the vacate notice to the outside of the entry door. The time period runs from the date the notice is delivered to the tenant.

This notice to vacate should include the date by which the tenant must vacate the premises, and tell the tenant that a suit for eviction will be filed if the tenant does not vacate by the deadline date. It should also include a demand for possession of the premises. It is also advisable to include in the notice to vacate a demand for the tenant to pay the unpaid rent.

Filing Suit   If the deadline in the notice to vacate passes and the tenant remains on the property, the next step is to file the eviction proceeding. This suit has to be filed in justice court in the precinct in which the property is located. If you are not sure which precinct is the correct one, you should call one of the justice courts. The clerks should be able to tell you in which precinct your property is located.

Court Forms. There is a sample eviction petition in the appendix to this book. Your local justice court may also have forms available for your use. Once you determine which precinct you are in, you should ask the clerk of that court if they have forms available. If your county has a website, you can also check that website for forms you can download. If your court has established a form, you should use that form instead of the one in the appendix. This ensures that you will have complied with all of the requirements of your court and that your paperwork is in a form that will be met with approval by the judge.

Petition. This eviction must be *notarized*, so you should be sure to sign before a notary public. Some courts will also let you swear to the truth of the allegations in front of the court's clerk when you file your petition. At the time you file your petition, you will need to be prepared to pay the filing fees. These fees will vary from county to county, so you will need to get this information from the clerk of your court.

The eviction petition should contain the following information:

- ✪ the landlord's name;

- ✪ the tenant's name and home and work addresses;

- ✪ the address of the leased premises;

- ✪ the date the tenant breached the lease agreement; and,

- ✪ the way in which the agreement was breached (for example, the date the tenant failed to pay rent).

The petition should state that the written demand for possession, and notice to vacate was given to the tenant, and that the landlord is suing for immediate possession of the property. If there is unpaid rent, the petition should also state that the landlord is suing for unpaid rent and state the amount of the past due rent. The petition should also ask for recovery of court costs. If the landlord is represented by an attorney, then the petition will also contain a request that the tenant pay the attorney's fees. If you are drafting your own petition, be sure to sign the petition. Underneath your signature, include your name, address, and phone number. The petition should list all persons who signed the lease as defendants. An **Eviction Petition** (form 23, p.192) is included in Appendix D.

When you file the petition in court, be sure to bring the original and two copies. However, if there is more than one person on the lease, you will need more copies. You will have to serve this petition on each tenant, and you will want to have a *file-marked copy* of the petition for your records. When you file the petition, you need to tell the clerk that you want to have the petition served.

The court clerk will then issue a *citation*, which will set a date and time for the the tenant to appear in court. Rule 739 of the *Rules of Civil Procedure* states that the hearing must be not more than ten days, and not less than six days, from the date of service of the citation. This appearance is not the final trial of the case, but is simply the deadline for the tenant to file an *answer* with the court. The *answer* is the written document that the tenant files denying the allegations in the complaint. If the answer is filed, then the case will be set for trial. If the tenant does not file an answer, then the allegations in the eviction petition will be deemed to be true, and a *default judgment* will be entered against the tenant.

Court Hearing   If there is a trial, the landlord will have to prove in court that the tenant is in breach of the lease, and should be evicted. If, for instance, the tenant has breached the lease by failing to pay rent, the landlord should come to court with a copy of the lease agreement and have the tenant's rent payment records so that he or she can tell the judge when the last payment was made and what payments are due as of the time of the trial.

At a minimum, the landlord should always bring a copy of the written lease agreement. The landlord should also bring a copy of the notice to vacate and, if available, the proof of delivery to the tenant. If the lease is oral, the landlord will need to be prepared to testify in court as to what the terms of the lease agreement are. This is because the landlord must prove in court that he or she has a right to possession of the property as a result of the tenant's breach of the lease agreement. If the tenant has failed to pay the rent, the right to possession by the landlord is clear. For other types of breaches of the lease agreement, the right to possession must be established by the terms of the lease. If, after carefully reading your lease, you have any doubt about whether the facts entitle you, as a landlord, to regain possession, you should consult an attorney to assist with this evaluation. This consultation should be done prior to filing your eviction suit in court.

Possession Bonds

If a landlord wants to obtain possession of the premises prior to the final trial, the landlord can file a *possession bond*. This bond can be done at any time after the complaint is filed, and prior to the final trial. The amount of the bond is determined by the judge of the justice court. It will be based on the probable amount of the costs of the suit, plus any damages that might result to the tenant, if the eviction suit has been improperly filed. If a possession bond is filed, the justice court is required to notify the tenant of the filing of the bond. Most courts will have this form available for you.

Tenants Counterbond

In order for the tenant to remain in possession of the premises while the suit is pending, the tenant must file a *counterbond* with the court. As with the possession bond itself, the judge of the justice court determines the amount of the counterbond. Likewise, it will set the amount based on the probable amount of the costs of the suit, plus any damages that would result to the landlord if the tenant is improperly withholding possession of the premises. Most courts will have this form available for you.

This counterbond must be filed within six days from the date the tenant is served with the notice of the filing of the landlord's bond. Alternatively, the tenant can demand that a trial on the eviction suit take place within the six day period from the date the tenant is served with the notice of the possession bond. If the tenant elects to have the trial within the six day period, and the justice court decides that the landlord is entitled to possession of the premises, the tenant must be out of the premises within five days or the sheriff or constable will remove the tenant from the property.

If the tenant neither files a counterbond nor demands that the trial occur within the six day period, then the tenant must be out of the property within six days of the date the tenant is served with the notice of the filing of the possession bond. If the tenant does not leave voluntarily, then the sheriff or constable will force them out and remove their property from the premises.

Final Trial   The final trial on the eviction suit will be conducted by the judge of the justice court unless one of the parties requests a jury trial and pays the jury fee. Rule 744 of the *Rules of Civil Procedure* says that the demand for a jury trial must be made within five days of the date the tenant is served with the citation.

Attorney Representation   In forcible entry and detainer suits for nonpayment of rent or for holding over beyond the rental term, the landlord can represent himself or be represented by an authorized agent. In the justice court, the authorized agent does not have to be an attorney. However, the losing party in justice court has the right to appeal the decision of the justice court to county court. If the case is appealed to county court, the landlord cannot appear in court via an agent. Also, if the property is owned by a corporation, partnership, or any other form of ownership other than sole proprietorship, then the landlord must be represented by an attorney in county court. While an individual person has the right to represent themselves in court, a corporation, partnership or other legal entity does not have this right. The landlord cannot simply send a representative from a management company, either.

Appeals   Any appeal from a decision by the justice court is done by filing an *appeal bond* that is approved by the judge of the justice court. This bond must be filed within five days of the date the judgment is rendered by the justice court. When the bond has been approved, the appealing party has to give notice of the filing of the bond to the other party. The form for the appeal bond is found in Rule 750 of the Rules of Civil Procedure. It should also be available from the justice court.

Writ of Possession

A landlord who wins an eviction suit gets a *judgment for possession* and a *writ of possession*. The writ of possession is the name for the legal document that authorizes the sheriff or constable to forcibly remove the tenant from the premises if they do not leave voluntarily. The writ orders the sheriff or constable to post a written warning on a page that is at least 8 1/2 by 11 inches in size on the exterior door. This warning tells the tenant that a writ of possession has been issued and that the writ will be executed on or after a specific date or time. This date and time must be stated in the warning, and must be at least 24 hours after the time that the warning is posted on the door. The warning instructs the tenant to leave immediately, or he or she will be physically removed. The warning also tells the tenant that the landlord is authorized to remove the tenant's property from the rented premises and placed outside. The landlord is not required to store the property, but is prohibited from leaving it outside if it is raining, sleeting, or snowing. Most courts will have this form available for you.

Storing Tenants Property

If the landlord elects to store the tenant's property, the tenant is responsible for all costs associated with the storage. If the landlord has the tenant's property stored in a bonded or insured public warehouse, the warehouseman has a *statutory lien* on the property for the amount of the storage costs and moving costs. If the property is stored, a written notice containing the complete name and address and telephone number of the location at which the tenant's property can be redeemed, must be given to the tenant seventy two hours after the execution of the writ of possession. The tenant must also be notified, in boldface type, or by underlined section, that he or she can redeem the property without payment of moving and storage costs if done while the warehouseman is in the process of removing the property, and prior to the time the warehouseman leaves the tenant's premises for the last time. If the property has not been redeemed within thirty days from the date of storage, the warehouseman can sell the property. A blank **LANDLORD'S NOTICE TO TENANT REGARDING STORAGE OF PROPERTY AFTER WRIT OF POSSESSION** (form 24, p.194) is included in Appendix D.

Release of Judgment

If you get a judgment, either as a landlord or a tenant, and the losing party pays you all the money owed under the judgment, you need to file a **RELEASE OF JUDGMENT** (form 25, p.195) with the court, stating that the judgment has been paid in full.

Public Hearing

If you have tenants in Section 8 housing, you must serve the housing authority with a notice of your eviction proceedings in writing *prior* to having the tenant served with the eviction. The tenant is also entitled to an extra notice period of fourteen days if the eviction is based on nonpayment of rent, not just the three days required in other instances. To be safe, a landlord should give the tenant in public housing both a fourteen day notice and a three day notice. The notice can be done in such a manner that the tenant has just one deadline to pay rent, before facing an eviction. The fourteen day notice must also inform the tenant that they have the right to use the grievance procedure. In Section 236 housing, the tenant must be told that, if legal proceedings are instituted, the tenant has a right to present any valid defenses in court.

For lease breaches other than nonpayment of rent, the landlord of a Section 236 rental must give the tenant a thirty day notice (except in cases of emergencies) that gives the tenant specific reasons for the termination. The landlord must give the tenant notice of the fact that he or she has an opportunity to reply to the landlord's allegations, and also the right to request a grievance hearing. If a *grievance hearing* is requested, the tenant gets another thirty day notice after the hearing, even if the tenant loses the grievance hearing.

Possible Tenant Defenses

The only issue in an eviction proceeding is whether the tenant has breached the lease and whether the landlord is therefore entitled to possession of the premises. Some tenants may try to use tactics, such as claiming the eviction laws are unconstitutional or claiming that the landlord has not proved that they own the property. As a general rule, neither of these approaches is helpful for the tenant.

Constitutionality   If, prior to the final trial, the issue of constitutionality comes up, you should either consult an attorney or check the annotated statutes as there may be case law that specifically addresses the tenant's claim. If this issue comes up for the first time at the final trial, you will not have an opportunity to do these things.

Landlord's Ownership Interest   If the tenant tries to litigate the landlord's ownership interest in the property, you should object to this tactic. The landlord statutes state that the landlord's ownership of the property is not a proper issue for the court to rule on in these types of cases. This means that the judge should not allow the tenant to talk in court about whether the landlord actually owns the property, but should limit the proceedings to whether the tenant has paid the rent due or not.

Amount of Rent Due   If the tenant disputes the amount of rent due, this is not a defense to eviction. The standard that allows the landlord to evict is if there is any rent due and owing. However, it is important for the landlord to calculate the correct amount of rent due in the three day notice to the tenant. It is possible that the case could be dismissed by the judge if the amount stated in that notice is found to be incorrect.

I8 | HIRING AN ATTORNEY

Most of the time, the judges of the justice courts follow the rules and requirements of the law exactly as they are written. On occasion, however, you may run into a situation where the judge does something that is not specifically authorized in the statutes, or does not exactly follow some of the time requirements. If that happens and your case becomes complicated or you are confused about the effect of a decision made by the judge, you should consult an attorney with experience in the landlord-tenant area.

When looking for an attorney, you will need to find someone who is experienced in landlord-tenant matters. There are several ways to find an attorney. Ask a friend or another landlord for a referral, contact your local bar association if you live in a city that is large enough to have one, or check with the State Bar of Texas. The state bar has a website that will direct you to referral services. The address is **www.texasbar.com**. Some employers offer legal benefits to their employees, so check with your benefits department to see if this is an option. There may also be local apartment associations who can direct you to an attorney. If you are a tenant, some cities will have tenant's associations that can help you find a lawyer.

You should feel free to meet with more than one attorney. Many will offer either free or low cost consultations, which will make it easier for you to find an attorney with whom you feel comfortable. Be sure to find out what the attorney's fees will be. Some attorneys will handle landlord-tenant cases on a flat fee, while others will charge an hourly rate. If you decide to use an attorney that works on a flat fee, keep in mind that the flat fee will only cover cases that proceed with just the filing of the petition and a short hearing. If a case becomes contested or more complicated, most attorneys will require you to make additional fee arrangements to cover the extra work that will be needed in that situation.

If you are working with an attorney on an hourly basis, you need to keep in mind that you will be paying for everything that attorney does on your case. While you should make sure that all your questions are answered, and you are prepared for any hearings, remember that you will be charged for every phone call to the attorney, and every office visit. Therefore, you should be organized so that you are not wasting the attorney's time (and your money).

Landlords   As a landlord, you should always evaluate whether or not to hire an attorney when you contemplate filing to evict a tenant. The laws allow the winning party to recover their attorney's fees from the loser. While you will have to pay your attorney's fees up front, this does mean that the court might make the tenant reimburse you for some or all of the fees that you paid. Certainly, if the tenant contests the case and hires an attorney, the careful landlord will at least invest in a consultation with a lawyer, and should probably hire one. It is very difficult for an individual with little or no experience in the court systems to represent themselves against an experienced attorney. In most instances, when there is a lawyer representing the tenant, the case will move more quickly if both parties have representation. Often times, paying the money to have an attorney represent you will save money in the long run.

Tenants   From the tenant's point of view, the same is true if he or she is considering challenging an eviction on legal grounds, or filing a suit against the landlord for violations of the law. An attorney can help you evaluate the strengths and weaknesses of your claim, and perhaps save you time and money overall. Additionally, tenants can sometimes get their attorney's fees paid by the landlord if the tenant wins in court.

19 RECOVERING POSSESSION

A landlord recovers possession to a premise in a number of ways. One way the landlord can recover possession of the premises is to go to court and have the tenant evicted from the property. Another way is for the tenant to voluntarily move at the end of the lease period. There is a third way that landlords sometimes regain possession, that occurs when the tenant abandons the leased premises prior to the expiration of the lease term.

Abandonment

Under the law, a tenant surrenders possession when he or she tells the landlord he or she is leaving or leaves the keys. Sometimes, however, the tenant does not make his or her intention clear. Under those circumstances, the landlord may need to determine whether or not the tenant has abandoned the premises.

If the tenant is not making rent payments and has not notified the landlord to the contrary, and has been absent for at least half of the rental term, the landlord may presume that the tenant has abandoned the property and re-take possession. If the tenant has removed all of the property from the premises, and ceases paying rent, the landlord can also likely treat this as abandonment by the tenant. There may be other fact situations in which the landlord can also assume the tenant has abandoned. Each case, if later contested by the tenant, will be reviewed individually by the court, and the court will decide whether or not the landlord made the correct decision.

Agreeing to End the Tenancy

There may be some instances in which the landlord wants the tenant to leave because the tenant is in breach of the agreement or there are other problems in the landlord-tenant relationship, but wants to avoid going to court for formal eviction proceedings. One alternative for the parties to consider is an agreement between them to end the tenancy. As a landlord, if you want to avoid court, but are having trouble getting the tenant to leave, you can consider making a cash offer to the tenant, essentially buying them out of the rest of the lease.

The advantages are that the tenant may leave the premises in better condition than if a formal eviction process occurs, and the landlord is able to avoid the additional costs, and sometimes significant delays, in taking the tenant to court. This may ultimately make it cheaper in the long run to settle with the tenant. There is no certain amount of money that a landlord should offer to a tenant. The amount depends on the facts of each situation. While it will not work in every situation, it is something that the landlord should consider in deciding how to best approach a problem situation.

Acceptance of Past Due Rent

In most instances, you can accept past due rent even if you have already given the notice to vacate or filed the eviction suit and still proceed with the eviction. However, if your lease contains a clause to the contrary and says you lose your right to evict if you accept the rent, then you should not do so unless you are willing to stop the eviction proceedings and start over from the beginning if the tenant becomes delinquent in the future. Also, there are some courts that rule that acceptance of past due rent waives your right to evict. While this is not the law, you should check with your local justice of the peace to see what his or her policies are on this issue. In order to protect your rights to accept past due rent as much as possible, your written lease should include a clause that says that you have the right to accept payments of past due rent after notice to vacate is given, without waiving your rights to continue with the eviction. The **RESIDENTIAL LEASE** (form 2, p.159) includes this language.

You should never accept any payments for future rent due unless you have decided not to go forward with the eviction.

Tenant's Bankruptcy

As soon as the landlord is notified of the tenant's bankruptcy filing, he or she must immediately stop all legal proceedings against the tenant. This is true even if the only notice the landlord has of the bankruptcy filing is a verbal notice from the tenant. You should, however, call the clerk of the bankruptcy court in your area to verify the filing.

It is very important for landlords to stop any actions, including such obvious things as filing an action in court and taking the security deposit to cover unpaid rent. This is because the instant a person files a bankruptcy petition, they are protected by what is called an *automatic stay*. This stay immediately stops all actions against the person filing for bankruptcy, and anyone who violates the stay can be held in contempt of court by the bankruptcy judge. If you are a landlord dealing with a tenant problem and the tenant files for bankruptcy, you should consult an attorney at once. This is true especially if you have already filed your eviction suit and it is pending in court.

There is a method by which the landlord can eventually go forward with the eviction, but it requires getting permission from the bankruptcy court. This is done by way of a *motion to lift stay*. There are several procedural requirements that must be met. You should not attempt this process on your own. Instead, you should hire an attorney to help you through the process. The automatic stay does not cover rent that becomes due after the filing of the bankruptcy petition, so the landlord can sue for eviction and unpaid rents on post bankruptcy filing rents without obtaining the permission of the bankruptcy court first.

The automatic stay remains in effect until it is either lifted by the bankruptcy court, the property is abandoned or surrendered, the debts are discharged by the bankruptcy court, or the case is dismissed.

These same rules apply to tenants if they have filed a suit against the landlord and the landlord is the one who files for bankruptcy. If you are a tenant and involved in litigation with a landlord and you learn that the landlord has filed for bankruptcy, you should consult an attorney since you can be held in contempt of court by the bankruptcy court if you violate the rules.

20 | OTHER LIABILITIES

The majority of this book discusses issues and liabilities between landlords and their tenants arising out of the rental relationship. But there are other ways in which liability can be created between them and between either the landlord or tenant and third parties.

Personal Injuries

One of the most common of these situations involves injuries sustained on the leased premises. Who is legally responsible if someone is hurt? The answer depends on the situations of each case, and where on the property the injury occurs. If the third person is injured inside a rented dwelling, the tenant may be liable. But if the injury is caused by some defect or maintenance issue, the landlord may also be liable. If the injuries are sustained outside, in a single-family dwelling rental, legal liability will ultimately fall on the one with control of whatever caused the injury. In an apartment setting, the landlord is responsible for the care and maintenance of the common areas, so the landlord has potential liability and the tenant does not.

The general rule is that the landlords are not liable for injuries on the portions of the leased premises that are not within the landlord's control. However, if there is a dangerous condition on the property and the landlord is aware of the condition, then the landlord can be liable for injuries that are caused by that condition, regardless of whether or not the condition is located in an area of the premises that is within the landlord's control.

If the condition of the leased premises is in violation of the law, and the landlord caused the condition, the landlord may also be held liable for injuries to third parties. Additionally, if there is a problem on the premises and the landlord is either responsible for the repairs or makes the repairs (regardless of which party is responsible under the lease for them), and the third party's injuries are caused in some way by the repairs, then the landlord can be liable to the third party for their injuries.

As between the tenant and the landlord, the provisions of the written lease may help determine which one of them is responsible for injuries to third parties, particularly in the case of a single family dwelling rental. In an apartment situation, the landlord will primarily be the liable party because no matter what the lease says, the landlord is still responsible for the common areas of the complex. As a general rule, landlords have greater maintenance responsibility for the inside of the dwellings and, therefore, are generally the ones responsible for injuries.

Insurance   This is why all landlords should carry appropriate amounts of *liability insurance*. In deciding what kind of insurance to buy, you will need to consider insurance to cover losses and damages to the property itself and liability insurance to protect you if someone is injured on the property. If you fail to purchase regular property insurance and your property is damaged by a storm, you will have to pay the repair costs yourself. If you do not carry liability insurance, and someone is hurt on the property, you may be responsible for paying all of the damages suffered by that person out of your own pocket. If you have employees who work for you, you might also consider worker's compensation insurance in case one of them was injured while working for you.

As a tenant renting a single-family dwelling, you may also want to consider purchasing liability insurance as well. This type of insurance will protect your personal assets if a guest of yours gets hurt while they are in your home. You should also consider renter's insurance to cover losses to your personal property, for example in a theft or storm loss. The landlord's insurance does not generally provide coverage for you in these types of cases.

Criminal Acts of Third Parties

Another area that has created litigation in recent years is the issue of liability for injuries caused by the actions of third parties. Most often, the litigation will be triggered because either the tenant or a guest of the tenant, suffers damage as the result of a crime. Traditionally, the landlord was not liable for injuries and damages caused by the criminal acts of another. The trend has begun to change though, and there are now instances in which landlords have been held liable. This holds true more for landlords of multi-unit complexes, and not usually for landlords of single family dwellings.

The courts will approach the liability issue by examining the degree to which the injuries suffered were *foreseeable* to the landlord. If the complex is located in an area of town noted for its high crime rate, the landlord may need to do more to protect the tenants and their guests from criminal activity. The amount and location of lighting, the existence of gates to control access to the property, the availability of security guards or patrols, and other crime-reduction activities will be factors that go into this analysis.

If the landlord is aware of a condition that makes it easier for a tenant to become a crime victim, and does not act to correct the problem, the likelihood that the landlord will be held liable by a court increases. For example, if there have been several rapes and break-ins in a complex, and the tenant has notified the landlord that the door lock is not working, then the landlord could be liable to the tenant for damages because the landlord has a legal duty to provide adequate door locks.

The same could be true if the landlord hires an employee with a criminal record for violence or theft, and gives that employee access to the units. If that employee harms a tenant, the landlord could be liable.

Tenant's Criminal Activity

If a landlord is aware of criminal activity by a tenant, the landlord could face liability to third parties harmed by the tenant. This is particularly true where the tenant is using the leased premises for the criminal activity.

Landlords also need to be aware of *forfeiture laws* for property used in drug sales. If a landlord knowingly allows a tenant to sell drugs from the leased premises, without taking action to evict the tenant, particularly a single-family dwelling, the landlord faces the possibility that the government will try to seize and sell the leased premises under the drug forfeiture laws.

21 | CONCLUSION

Being a landlord can be a positive business experience, but it is important for the landlord to know his or her rights and responsibilities. As we have seen, there are penalties for not following the rules and it can be expensive to get caught up in the system. For tenants, it is easier to negotiate and have a good working relationship with the landlord, if the tenant knows what rights he or she has.

As a reminder, check the laws yourself if you are involved in a conflict in Texas, to be sure that you have the most current information. This book can be a helpful guide for you as you navigate the landlord-tenant relationship, but it should not be used as the only resource since laws change and each case is different.

GLOSSARY

A

abandonment. Occurs legally when a tenant, without notifying the landlord, stops paying rent and has been absent for half of the rental term or stops paying rent and removes all personal property from the premises.

Americans with Disabilities Act (ADA). Requires that reasonable accommodations be made to commercial buildings to allow access for persons with disabilities. Modification should be made without undue burden or undue hardship.

application deposit. Sum of money given to the landlord with a rental application; money is returned if the applicant is rejected or applied towards rental costs, if the applicant is accepted.

application fee. Sum of money that a landlord charges applicants to offset the cost of tenant screening.

assumed name. Any name used for business that is not the owner's legal name. This name must be registered with the county in which business is transacted and, in some cases, with the state.

B

bad faith. Occurs when a landlord does not fulfill contractual terms, as when the landlord fails to return a security deposit to the tenant after the tenant has vacated the premises.

breach of contract. Occurs when either the landlord or the tenant does not fulfill the terms of the written lease. This often occurs when a tenant does not pay rent and can be litigated in court.

breach of the peace. Occurs when a landlord uses force to seize property under statutory lien. (This is not allowed under Texas code.)

burden of proof. The standard that must be met in court by a party filing a claim for relief in order to win the case.

C

citation. The legal document issued by the court that notifies a person that a lawsuit has been filed against them.

Civil Rights Act of 1968. Federal law that bars any policy with a discriminatory effect. Civil court can award up to $1000 in actual and punitive damages to violators of this law. Owners of three or fewer single-family dwellings are not subject if certain conditions are met.

code. A collection of laws passed by the legislature.

commercial. Any property leased for use as other than a residence.

community. Defined under Texas law as a parcel of land in which four or more lots are offered for lease for installing and occupying manufactured homes.

consideration. Something of value, including a promise to do some act or refrain from doing an act a party is legally entitled to do, given in exchange for something of value from the other party to the transaction.

contractual lien. A landlord's lien provided by the written lease. Not enforceable unless underlined or in boldface type in the lease.

D

distress warrant. A legal document issued by a court allowing a landlord to take possession of a commercial tenant's property.

dwelling. One or more rooms rented for use as a residence.

E

eviction. A proceeding filed with the court to remove a tenant from property when the tenant refuses to pay rent or after the lease has expired.

ex parte. An order signed by a judge after hearing evidence from one party outside the presence of other parties to the lawsuit.

F

familial status. Refers to whether an applicant has minor children. Under Texas law, landlords cannot use this category to discriminate when selecting a tenant.

Federal Reporter. Set of books that contain decisions from the Texas Fifth Court of Appeals. Useful for legal research.

forcible entry and detainer. See *eviction.*

foreclosure. Legal proceeding that allows a lender to take title of or force sale of a borrower's property in order to satisfy the borrower's unpaid debts. Foreclosure results in the termination of a renter's lease unless an agreement is reached with the new property owner.

forfeiture laws. Apply when property is used in the commission of a crime and a landlord takes no action to evict a tenant from leased premises used in the crime. In these cases, the government may seize and sell the landlord's property.

H

holdover tenant. A tenant who remains on the property after the end of a lease term. If the written lease does not address the holdover and the landlord continues to accept rental payments, the law considers the parties to have agreed to a new lease under the same conditions of the existing written lease.

I

implied lease. A judge may rule that this exists if the landlord allows a tenant possession of the premises without a written lease. This situation can lead to many problems for the landlord and should always be voided.

J

judgment for possession. Document awarded by a court, along with a *writ of possession*, to a landlord who wins an eviction suit. Allows the landlord to regain possession of the premises in question.

jurisdictional limits. Refers to the limits set on damages that litigating parties can claim in certain types of court. Some courts set *minimum jurisdictional limits*; others set *maximum jurisdictional limits*.

L

landlord. The owner of a property.

lease. The agreement between the landlord and tenant that authorized the tenant to take possession on a temporary basis of property owned by another.

lessee. Another word for tenant.

lessor. Another word for landlord.

liability insurance. Landlords should always carry appropriate amounts of this in case they are held responsible for injury sustained on their property.

lien. A lender's legal right to a debtor's property. This sometimes, but not usually, results in the lender taking possession of the debtor's property.

M

mitigation of damages. Refers to the legal requirement that a landlord minimize any losses he or she may suffer when a tenant breaches a lease.

N

nonexempt property. Refers to the property that a landlord can legally seize under statutory lien from a tenant who refuses to pay rent. The landlord cannot legally seize certain, exempt, categories of property from a tenant.

O

oral lease. Agreement to rent that is not based in a written document. The *statute of frauds* requires that any lease with a term of more than one year must be in writing.

ordinance. A local law.

P

periodic tenancy. Lease agreement that allows the tenant possession of the property for a certain period of time. This type of tenancy renews automatically if rent is paid and no notice of termination is given.

practice manual. A book that contains summaries of the law and applicable forms. These books can be found in most law libraries.

R

redeem. Recover property by paying debt it was taken to satisfy.

rekey. Changing locks so they are operated by a different set of keys or cards. Texas Property Code requires a landlord to change exterior locks operated by keys or cards within seven days after each change of tenant.

replevy. Reclaiming property formally seized under a court order.

reported decision. The verdict, or *opinion*, on a federal district court case. These are collected in a set of books called *The Federal Supplement*.

residential. Property leased for person to live in.

S

security deposit. Any advance of money, other than a rental application deposit or advance payment of rent, that is intended primarily to secure performance under a lease.

statute. A law passed by the legislature, as opposed to a rule of law established in a case by a judge.

statute of frauds. A legal doctrine that requires some contracts to be in writing to be enforceable.

statutory lien. Refers to a landlord's legal right to seize certain categories of (nonexempt) property from the rented residence or storage area of a tenant who refuses to pay rent.

sublet. Occurs when a tenant agrees to rent property to a third party in order to fulfill the terms of a lease. (This is not legal in Texas unless the landlord agrees in writing.)

sworn complaint. A petition filed in court that must be notarized.

T

tenant. A person authorized by a lease to occupy premises to the exclusion of another.

tenancy. Lease agreement that specifies how long a tenant may occupy the premises and how the occupancy will be terminated.

Texas Fair Housing Act. Texas Property Code that bans discrimination based on race, religion, sex, national origin, handicap, or familial status.

tenancy at sufferance. Occurs when a tenant holdsover after the term of the lease but the landlord does not accept rent payments. A landlord can terminate this tenancy at any time.

tenancy at will. Lease agreement that allows the tenant to occupy the premises so long as the rent is paid. This type of tenancy can be terminated by any party at any time.

U

unconscionable. A lease provision that is so burdensome on one party that the courts will not enforce it against that party.

W

wear and tear. Damage that results from the normal use of property. Landlords may not withhold any money from security deposits for this type of property damage.

writ of possession. Legal document that authorizes a sheriff or constable to forcibly remove an evicted tenant from the rental property. A landlord who wins an eviction suit is awarded this along with a *judgement for possession*.

Y

year-to-year tenancy. *Periodic tenancy* created when parties agree to an annual amount of rent and do not set a specific lease ending date.

APPENDIX A:
TEXAS LANDLORD AND
TENANT STATUTES

TITLE 8. LANDLORD AND TENANT

CHAPTER 91. PROVISIONS GENERALLY APPLICABLE TO LANDLORDS AND TENANTS
§ 91.001. Notice for Terminating Certain Tenancies
(a) A monthly tenancy or a tenancy from month to month may be terminated by the tenant or the landlord giving notice of termination to the other.
(b) If a notice of termination is given under Subsection (a) and if the rent-paying period is at least one month, the tenancy terminates on whichever of the following days is the later:
(1) the day given in the notice for termination; or
(2) one month after the day on which the notice is given.
(c) If a notice of termination is given under Subsection (a) and if the rent-paying period is less than a month, the tenancy terminates on whichever of the following days is the later:
(1) the day given in the notice for termination; or
(2) the day following the expiration of the period beginning on the day on which notice is given and extending for a number of days equal to the number of days in the rent-paying period.
(d) If a tenancy terminates on a day that does not correspond to the beginning or end of a rent-paying period, the tenant is liable for rent only up to the date of termination.
(e) Subsections (a), (b), (c), and (d) do not apply if:
(1) a landlord and a tenant have agreed in an instrument signed by both parties on a different period of notice to terminate the tenancy or that no notice is required; or
(2) there is a breach of contract recognized by law.
§ 91.003. Termination of Lease Because of Public Indecency Conviction
(a) A landlord may terminate a lease executed or renewed after June 15, 1981, if:
(1) the tenant or occupant of the leasehold uses the property for an activity for which the tenant or occupant or for which an agent or employee of the tenant or occupant is convicted under Chapter 43, Penal Code, as amended; and
(2) the convicted person has exhausted or abandoned all avenues of direct appeal from the conviction.
(b) The fee owner or an intermediate lessor terminates the lease by giving written notice of termination to the tenant or occupant within six months after the right to terminate arises under this section. The right to possess the property reverts to the landlord on the 10th day after the date the notice is given.
(c) This section applies regardless of a term of the lease to the contrary.

§ 91.004. Landlord's Breach of Lease; Lien

(a) If the landlord of a tenant who is not in default under a lease fails to comply in any respect with the lease agreement, the landlord is liable to the tenant for damages resulting from the failure.

(b) To secure payment of the damages, the tenant has a lien on the landlord's nonexempt property in the tenant's possession and on the rent due to the landlord under the lease.

§ 91.005. Subletting Prohibited

During the term of a lease, the tenant may not rent the leasehold to any other person without the prior consent of the landlord.

§ 91.006. Landlord's Duty to Mitigate Damages

(a) A landlord has a duty to mitigate damages if a tenant abandons the leased premises in violation of the lease.

(b) A provision of a lease that purports to waive a right or to exempt a landlord from a liability or duty under this section is void.

CHAPTER 92. RESIDENTIAL TENANCIES
SUBCHAPTER A. GENERAL PROVISIONS

§ 92.001. Definitions

Except as otherwise provided by this chapter, in this chapter:

(1) "Dwelling" means one or more rooms rented for use as a permanent residence under a single lease to one or more tenants.

(2) "Landlord" means the owner, lessor, or sublessor of a dwelling, but does not include a manager or agent of the landlord unless the manager or agent purports to be the owner, lessor, or sublessor in an oral or written lease.

(3) "Lease" means any written or oral agreement between a landlord and tenant that establishes or modifies the terms, conditions, rules, or other provisions regarding the use and occupancy of a dwelling.

(4) "Normal wear and tear" means deterioration that results from the intended use of a dwelling, including, for the purposes of Subchapters B and D, breakage or malfunction due to age or deteriorated condition, but the term does not include deterioration that results from negligence, carelessness, accident, or abuse of the premises, equipment, or chattels by the tenant, by a member of the tenant's household, or by a guest or invitee of the tenant.

(5) "Premises" means a tenant's rental unit, any area or facility the lease authorizes the tenant to use, and the appurtenances, grounds, and facilities held out for the use of tenants generally.

(6) "Tenant" means a person who is authorized by a lease to occupy a dwelling to the exclusion of others and, for the purposes of Subchapters D, E, and F, who is obligated under the lease to pay rent.

§ 92.002. Application

This chapter applies only to the relationship between landlords and tenants of residential rental property.

§ 92.003. Landlord's Agent for Service of Process

(a) In a lawsuit by a tenant under either a written or oral lease for a dwelling or in a suit to enforce a legal obligation of the owner as landlord of the dwelling, the owner's agent for service of process is determined according to this section.

(b) If written notice of the name and business street address of the company that manages the dwelling has been given to the tenant, the management company is the owner's sole agent for service of process.

(c) If Subsection (b) does not apply, the owner's management company, on-premise manager, or rent collector serving the dwelling is the owner's authorized agent for service of process unless the owner's name and business street address have been furnished in writing to the tenant.

§ 92.004. Harassment

A party who files or prosecutes a suit under Subchapter B, D, E, or F in bad faith or for purposes of harassment is liable to the defendant for one month's rent plus $100 and for attorney's fees.

§ 92.005. Attorney's Fees

(a) A party who prevails in a suit brought under this subchapter or Subchapter B, E, or F may recover the party's costs of court and reasonable attorney's fees in relation to work reasonably expended.

(b) This section does not authorize a recovery of attorney's fees in an action brought under Subchapter E or F for damages that relate to or arise from property damage, personal injury, or a criminal act.

§ 92.006. Waiver or Expansion of Duties and Remedies

(a) A landlord's duty or a tenant's remedy concerning security deposits, security devices, the landlord's disclosure of ownership and management, or utility cutoffs, as provided by Subchapter C, D, E, or G, respectively, may not be waived. A landlord's duty to install a smoke detector under Subchapter F may not be waived, nor may a tenant waive a remedy for the landlord's noninstallation or waive the tenant's limited right of installation and removal. The landlord's duty of inspection and repair of smoke detectors under Subchapter F may be waived only by written agreement.

(b) A landlord's duties and the tenant's remedies concerning security devices, the landlord's disclosure of ownership and management, or smoke detectors, as provided by Subchapter D, E, or F, respectively, may be enlarged only by specific written agreement.

(c) A landlord's duties and the tenant's remedies under Subchapter B, which covers conditions materially affecting the physical health or safety of the ordinary tenant, may not be waived except as provided in Subsections (d), (e), and (f) of this section.

(d) A landlord and a tenant may agree for the tenant to repair or remedy, at the landlord's expense, any condition covered by Subchapter B.

(e) A landlord and a tenant may agree for the tenant to repair or remedy, at the tenant's expense, any condition covered by Subchapter B if all of the following conditions are met:

(1) at the beginning of the lease term the landlord owns only one rental dwelling;

(2) at the beginning of the lease term the dwelling is free from any condition which would materially affect the physical health or safety of an ordinary tenant;

(3) at the beginning of the lease term the landlord has no reason to believe that any condition described in Subdivision (2) of this subsection is likely to occur or recur during the tenant's lease term or during a renewal or extension; and

(4)(A) the lease is in writing;

(B) the agreement for repairs by the tenant is either underlined or printed in boldface in the lease or in a separate written addendum;

(C) the agreement is specific and clear; and

(D) the agreement is made knowingly, voluntarily, and for consideration.

(f) A landlord and tenant may agree that, except for those conditions caused by the negligence of the landlord, the tenant has the duty to pay for repair of the following conditions that may occur during the lease term or a renewal or extension:

(1) damage from wastewater stoppages caused by foreign or improper objects in lines that exclusively serve the tenant's dwelling;

(2) damage to doors, windows, or screens; and

(3) damage from windows or doors left open.

This subsection shall not affect the landlord's duty under Subchapter B to repair or remedy, at the landlord's expense, wastewater stoppages or backups caused by deterioration, breakage, roots, ground conditions, faulty construction, or malfunctioning equipment. A landlord and tenant may agree to the provisions of this subsection only if the agreement meets the requirements of Subdivision (4) of Subsection (e) of this section.

§ 92.007. Venue

Venue for an action under this chapter is governed by Section 15.0115, Civil Practice and Remedies Code.

§ 92.008. Interruption of Utilities

(a) A landlord or a landlord's agent may not interrupt or cause the interruption of utility service paid for directly to the utility company by a tenant unless the interruption results from bona fide repairs, construction, or an emergency.

(b) Except as provided by Subsections (c) and (d), a landlord may not interrupt or cause the interruption of water, wastewater, gas, or electric service furnished to a tenant by the landlord as an incident of the tenancy or by other agreement unless the interruption results from bona fide repairs, construction, or an emergency.

(c) A landlord may interrupt or cause the interruption of electrical service furnished to a tenant by the landlord as an incident of the tenancy or by other agreement if:

(1) the electrical service furnished to the tenant is individually metered or submetered for the dwelling unit;

(2) the electrical service connection with the utility company is in the name of the landlord or the landlord's agent; and

(3) the landlord complies with the rules adopted by the Public Utility Commission of Texas for discontinuance of submetered electrical service.

(d) A landlord may interrupt or cause the interruption of electrical service furnished to a tenant by the landlord as an incident of the tenancy or by other agreement if:

(1) the electrical service furnished to the tenant is not individually metered or submetered for the dwelling unit;

(2) the electrical service connection with the utility company is in the name of the landlord or the landlord's agent;

(3) the tenant is at least seven days late in paying the rent;

(4) the landlord has mailed or hand-delivered to the tenant at least five days before the date the electrical service is interrupted a written notice that states:

(A) the earliest date of the proposed interruption of electrical service;

(B) the amount of rent the tenant must pay to avert the interruption; and

(C) the name and location of the individual to whom or the location of the on-site management office where the delinquent rent may be paid during the landlord's normal business hours;

(5) the interruption does not begin before or after the landlord's normal business hours; and

(6) the interruption does not begin on a day, or on a day immediately preceding a day, when the landlord or other designated individual is not available or the on-site management office is not open to accept rent and restore electrical service.

(e) A landlord who interrupts electrical service under Subsection (c) or (d) shall restore the service not later than two hours after the time the tenant tenders, during the landlord's normal business hours, payment of the delinquent electric bill or rent owed to the landlord.

(f) If a landlord or a landlord's agent violates this section, the tenant may:

(1) either recover possession of the premises or terminate the lease; and

(2) recover from the landlord an amount equal to the sum of the tenant's actual damages, one month's rent or $500, whichever is greater, reasonable attorney's fees, and court costs, less any delinquent rents or other sums for which the tenant is liable to the landlord.

(g) A provision of a lease that purports to waive a right or to exempt a party from a liability or duty under this section is void.

§ 92.0081. Removal of Property and Exclusion of Residential Tenant

(a) A landlord may not remove a door, window, or attic hatchway cover or a lock, latch, hinge, hinge pin, doorknob, or other mechanism connected to a door, window, or attic hatchway cover from premises leased to a tenant or remove furniture, fixtures, or appliances furnished by the landlord from premises leased to a tenant unless the landlord removes the item for a bona fide repair or replacement. If a landlord removes any of the items listed in this subsection for a bona fide repair or replacement, the repair or replacement must be promptly performed.

(b) A landlord may not intentionally prevent a tenant from entering the leased premises except by judicial process unless the exclusion results from:

(1) bona fide repairs, construction, or an emergency;

(2) removing the contents of premises abandoned by a tenant; or

(3) changing the door locks of a tenant who is delinquent in paying at least part of the rent.

(c) If a landlord or a landlord's agent changes the door lock of a tenant who is delinquent in paying rent, the landlord or the landlord's agent must place a written notice on the tenant's front door stating:

(1) an on-site location where the tenant may go 24 hours a day to obtain the new key or a telephone number that is

answered 24 hours a day that the tenant may call to have a key delivered within two hours after calling the number;

(2) the fact that the landlord must provide the new key to the tenant at any hour, regardless of whether or not the tenant pays any of the delinquent rent; and

(3) the amount of rent and other charges for which the tenant is delinquent.

(d) A landlord may not intentionally prevent a tenant from entering the leased premises under Subsection (b)(3) unless:

(1) the tenant is delinquent in paying all or part of the rent; and

(2) the landlord has locally mailed not later than the fifth calendar day before the date on which the door locks are changed or hand-delivered to the tenant or posted on the inside of the main entry door of the tenant's dwelling not later than the third calendar day before the date on which the door locks are changed a written notice stating:

(A) the earliest date that the landlord proposes to change the door locks;

(B) the amount of rent the tenant must pay to prevent changing of the door locks; and

(C) the name and street address of the individual to whom, or the location of the on-site management office at which, the delinquent rent may be paid during the landlord's normal business hours.

(e) A landlord may not change the locks on the door of a tenant's dwelling under Subsection (b)(3) on a day, or on a day immediately before a day, on which the landlord or other designated individual is not available, or on which any on-site management office is not open, for the tenant to tender the delinquent rent.

(f) A landlord who intentionally prevents a tenant from entering the tenant's dwelling under Subsection (b)(3) must provide the tenant with a key to the changed lock on the dwelling without regard to whether the tenant pays the delinquent rent.

(g) If a landlord arrives at the dwelling in a timely manner in response to a tenant's telephone call to the number contained in the notice as described by Subsection (c)(1) and the tenant is not present to receive the key to the changed lock, the landlord shall leave a notice on the front door of the dwelling stating the time the landlord arrived with the key and the street address to which the tenant may go to obtain the key during the landlord's normal office hours.

(h) If a landlord violates this section, the tenant may:

(1) either recover possession of the premises or terminate the lease; and

(2) recover from the landlord a civil penalty of one month's rent plus $500, actual damages, court costs, and reasonable attorney's fees in an action to recover property damages, actual expenses, or civil penalties , less any delinquent rent or other sums for which the tenant is liable to the landlord.

(i) If a landlord violates Subsection (f), the tenant may recover, in addition to the remedies provided by Subsection (h), an additional civil penalty of one month's rent.

(j) A provision of a lease that purports to waive a right or to exempt a party from a liability or duty under this section is void.

§ 92.009. Residential Tenant's Right of Reentry After Unlawful Lockout

(a) If a landlord has locked a tenant out of leased premises in violation of Section 92.008, the tenant may recover possession of the premises as provided by this section.

(b) The tenant must file with the justice court in the precinct in which the rental premises are located a sworn complaint for reentry, specifying the facts of the alleged unlawful lockout by the landlord or the landlord's agent. The tenant must also state orally under oath to the justice the facts of the alleged unlawful lockout.

(c) If the tenant has complied with Subsection (b) and if the justice reasonably believes an unlawful lockout has likely occurred, the justice may issue, ex parte, a writ of reentry that entitles the tenant to immediate and temporary possession of the premises, pending a final hearing on the tenant's sworn complaint for reentry.

(d) The writ of reentry must be served on either the landlord or the landlord's management company, on-premises manager, or rent collector in the same manner as a writ of possession in a forcible detainer action. A sheriff or constable may use reasonable force in executing a writ of reentry under this section.

(e) The landlord is entitled to a hearing on the tenant's sworn complaint for reentry. The writ of reentry must notify the landlord of the right to a hearing. The hearing shall be held not earlier than the first day and not later than the seventh day after the date the landlord requests a hearing.

(f) If the landlord fails to request a hearing on the tenant's sworn complaint for reentry before the eighth day after the date of service of the writ of reentry on the landlord under Subsection (d), a judgment for court costs may be rendered against the landlord.

(g) A party may appeal from the court's judgment at the hearing on the sworn complaint for reentry in the same manner as a party may appeal a judgment in a forcible detainer suit.

(h) If a writ of possession is issued, it supersedes a writ of reentry.

(i) If the landlord or the person on whom a writ of reentry is served fails to immediately comply with the writ or later disobeys the writ, the failure is grounds for contempt of court against the landlord or the person on whom the writ was served, under Section 21.002, Government Code. If the writ is disobeyed, the tenant or the tenant's attorney may file in the court in which the reentry action is pending an affidavit stating the name of the person who has disobeyed the writ and describing the acts or omissions constituting the disobedience. On receipt of an affidavit, the justice shall issue a show cause order, directing the person to appear on a designated date and show cause why he should not be adjudged in contempt of court. If the justice finds, after considering the evidence at the hearing, that the person has directly or indirectly disobeyed the writ, the justice may commit the person to jail without bail until the person purges himself of the contempt in a manner and form as the justice may direct. If the person disobeyed the writ before receiving the show cause order but has complied with the writ after receiving the order, the justice may find the person in contempt and assess punishment under Section 21.002(c), Government Code.

(j) This section does not affect a tenant's right to pursue a separate cause of action under Section 92.008.

(k) If a tenant in bad faith files a sworn complaint for reentry resulting in a writ of reentry being served on the landlord or landlord's agent, the landlord may in a separate cause of action recover from the tenant an amount equal to actual damages, one month's rent or $500, whichever is greater, reasonable attorney's fees, and costs of court, less any sums for which the landlord is liable to the tenant.

(l) The fee for filing a sworn complaint for reentry is the same as that for filing a civil action in justice court. The fee for service of a writ of reentry is the same as that for service of a writ of possession. The fee for service of a show cause order is the same as that for service of a civil citation. The justice may defer payment of the tenant's filing fees and service costs for the sworn complaint for reentry and writ of reentry. Court costs may be waived only if the tenant executes a pauper's affidavit.

(m) This section does not affect the rights of a landlord or tenant in a forcible detainer or forcible entry and detainer action.

§ 92.010. Occupancy Limits

(a) Except as provided by Subsection (b), the maximum number of adults that a landlord may allow to occupy a dwelling is three times the number of bedrooms in the dwelling.

(b) A landlord may allow an occupancy rate of more than three adult tenants per bedroom:

(1) to the extent that the landlord is required by a state or federal fair housing law to allow a higher occupancy rate; or

(2) if an adult whose occupancy causes a violation of Subsection (a) is seeking temporary sanctuary from family violence, as defined by Section 71.01, Family Code, for a period that does not exceed one month.

(c) An individual who owns or leases a dwelling within 3,000 feet of a dwelling as to which a landlord has violated this section, or a governmental entity or civic association acting on behalf of the individual, may file suit against a landlord to enjoin the violation. A party who prevails in a suit under this subsection may recover court costs and reasonable attorney's fees from the other party. In addition to court costs and reasonable attorney's fees, a plaintiff who prevails under this subsection may recover from the landlord $500 for each violation of this section.

(d) In this section:

(1) "Adult" means an individual 18 years of age or older.

(2) "Bedroom" means an area of a dwelling intended as sleeping quarters. The term does not include a kitchen, dining room, bathroom, living room, utility room, or closet or storage area of a dwelling.

§ 92.011. Cash Rental Payments

(a) A landlord shall accept a tenant's timely cash rental payment unless a written lease between the landlord and tenant requires the tenant to make rental payments by check, money order, or other traceable or negotiable instrument.

(b) A landlord who receives a cash rental payment shall:

(1) provide the tenant with a written receipt; and

(2) enter the payment date and amount in a record book maintained by the landlord.

(c) A tenant or a governmental entity or civic association acting on the tenant's behalf may file suit against a landlord to enjoin a violation of this section. A party who prevails in a suit brought under this subsection may recover court costs and reasonable attorney's fees from the other party. In addition to court costs and reasonable attorney's fees, a tenant who prevails under this subsection may recover from the landlord the greater of one month's rent or $500 for each violation of this section.

§ 92.012. Notice to Tenant at Primary Residence

(a) If, at the time of signing a lease or lease renewal, a tenant gives written notice to the tenant's landlord that the tenant does not occupy the leased premises as a primary residence and requests in writing that the landlord send notices to the tenant at the tenant's primary residence and provides to the landlord the address of the tenant's primary residence, the landlord shall mail to the tenant's primary residence:

(1) all notices of lease violations;

(2) all notices of lease termination;

(3) all notices of rental increases at the end of the lease term; and

(4) all notices to vacate.

(b) The tenant shall notify the landlord in writing of any change in the tenant's primary residence address. Oral notices of change are insufficient.

(c) A notice to a tenant's primary residence under Subsection (a) may be sent by regular United States mail and shall be considered as having been given on the date of postmark of the notice.

(d) If there is more than one tenant on a lease, the landlord is not required under this section to send notices to the primary residence of more than one tenant.

(e) This section does not apply if notice is actually hand delivered to and received by a person occupying the leased premises.

§ 92.013. Notice of Rule or Policy Change Affecting Tenant's Personal Property

(a) A landlord shall give prior written notice to a tenant regarding a landlord rule or policy change that is not included in the lease agreement and that will affect any personal property owned by the tenant that is located outside the tenant's dwelling, including any change in vehicle towing rules or policies.

(b) The notice must be given in person or by mail to the affected tenant. Notice in person may be by personal delivery to the tenant or any person residing at the tenant's dwelling who is 16 years of age or older or by personal delivery to the tenant's dwelling and affixing the notice to the inside of the main entry door. Notice by mail may be by regular mail, by registered mail, or by certified mail, return receipt requested. If the dwelling has no mailbox and has a keyless bolting device, alarm system, or dangerous animal that prevents the landlord from entering the premises to leave the notice on the inside of the main entry door, the landlord may securely affix the notice on the outside of the main entry door.

(c) A landlord who fails to give notice as required by this section is liable to the tenant for any expense incurred by the tenant as a result of the landlord's failure to give the notice.

§ 92.014. Personal Property and Security Deposit of Deceased Tenant

(a) Upon written request of a landlord, the landlord's tenant shall:

(1) provide the landlord with the name, address, and telephone number of a person to contact in the event of the tenant's death; and

(2) sign a statement authorizing the landlord in the event of the tenant's death to:

(A) grant to the person designated under Subdivision (1) access to the premises at a reasonable time and in the presence of the landlord or the landlord's agent;

(B) allow the person designated under Subdivision (1) to remove any of the tenant's property found at the leased premises; and

(C) refund the tenant's security deposit, less lawful deductions, to the person designated under Subdivision (1).

(b) A tenant may, without request from the landlord, provide the landlord with the information in Subsection (a).

(c) Except as provided in Subsection (d), in the event of the death of a tenant who is the sole occupant of a rental dwelling:

(1) the landlord may remove and store all property found in the tenant's leased premises;

(2) the landlord shall turn over possession of the property to the person who was designated by the tenant under Subsection (a) or (b) or to any other person lawfully entitled to the property if the request is made prior to the property being discarded under Subdivision (5);

(3) the landlord shall refund the tenant's security deposit, less lawful deductions, including the cost of removing and storing the property, to the person designated under Subsection (a) or (b) or to any other person lawfully entitled to the refund;

(4) the landlord may require any person who removes the property from the tenant's leased premises to sign an inventory of the property being removed; and

(5) the landlord may discard the property removed by the landlord from the tenant's leased premises if:

(A) the landlord has mailed a written request by certified mail, return receipt requested, to the person designated under Subsection (a) or (b), requesting that the property be removed;

(B) the person failed to remove the property by the 30th day after the postmark date of the notice; and

(C) the landlord, prior to the date of discarding the property, has not been contacted by anyone claiming the property.

(d) In a written lease or other agreement, a landlord and a tenant may agree to a procedure different than the procedure in this section for removing, storing, or disposing of property in the leased premises of a deceased tenant.

(e) If a tenant, after being furnished with a copy of this subchapter, knowingly violates Subsection (a), the landlord shall have no responsibility after the tenant's death for removal, storage, disappearance, damage, or disposition of property in the tenant's leased premises.

(f) If a landlord, after being furnished with a copy of this subchapter, knowingly violates Subsection (c), the landlord shall

be liable to the estate of the deceased tenant for actual damages.

SUBCHAPTER B. REPAIR OR CLOSING OF LEASEHOLD

§ 92.051. Application

This subchapter applies to a lease executed, entered into, renewed, or extended on or after September 1, 1979.

§ 92.052. Landlord's Duty to Repair or Remedy

(a) A landlord shall make a diligent effort to repair or remedy a condition if:

(1) the tenant specifies the condition in a notice to the person to whom or to the place where rent is normally paid;

(2) the tenant is not delinquent in the payment of rent at the time notice is given; and

(3) the condition materially affects the physical health or safety of an ordinary tenant.

(b) Unless the condition was caused by normal wear and tear, the landlord does not have a duty during the lease term or a renewal or extension to repair or remedy a condition caused by:

(1) the tenant;

(2) a lawful occupant in the tenant's dwelling;

(3) a member of the tenant's family; or

(4) a guest or invitee of the tenant.

(c) This subchapter does not require the landlord:

(1) to furnish utilities from a utility company if as a practical matter the utility lines of the company are not reasonably available; or

(2) to furnish security guards.

(d) The tenant's notice under Subsection (a) must be in writing only if the tenant's lease is in writing and requires written notice.

§ 92.053. Burden of Proof

(a) Except as provided by this section, the tenant has the burden of proof in a judicial action to enforce a right resulting from the landlord's failure to repair or remedy a condition under Section 92.052.

(b) If the landlord does not provide a written explanation for delay in performing a duty to repair or remedy on or before the fifth day after receiving from the tenant a written demand for an explanation, the landlord has the burden of proving that he made a diligent effort to repair and that a reasonable time for repair did not elapse.

§ 92.054. Casualty Loss

(a) If a condition results from an insured casualty loss, such as fire, smoke, hail, explosion, or a similar cause, the period for repair does not begin until the landlord receives the insurance proceeds.

(b) If after a casualty loss the rental premises are as a practical matter totally unusable for residential purposes and if the casualty loss is not caused by the negligence or fault of the tenant, a member of the tenant's family, or a guest or invitee of the tenant, either the landlord or the tenant may terminate the lease by giving written notice to the other any time before repairs are completed. If the lease is terminated, the tenant is entitled only to a pro rata refund of rent from the date the tenant moves out and to a refund of any security deposit otherwise required by law.

(c) If after a casualty loss the rental premises are partially unusable for residential purposes and if the casualty loss is not caused by the negligence or fault of the tenant, a member of the tenant's family, or a guest or invitee of the tenant, the tenant is entitled to reduction in the rent in an amount proportionate to the extent the premises are unusable because of the casualty, but only on judgment of a county or district court. A landlord and tenant may agree otherwise in a written lease.

§ 92.055. Closing the Rental Premises

(a) A landlord may close a rental unit at any time by giving written notice by certified mail, return receipt requested, to the tenant and to the local health officer and local building inspector, if any, stating that:

(1) the landlord is terminating the tenancy as soon as legally possible; and

(2) after the tenant moves out the landlord will either immediately demolish the rental unit or no longer use the unit for residential purposes.

(b) After a tenant receives the notice and moves out:

(1) the local health officer or building inspector may not allow occupancy of or utility service by separate meter to the rental unit until the officer certifies that he knows of no condition that materially affects the physical health or safety of an ordinary tenant; and

(2) the landlord may not allow reoccupancy or reconnection of utilities by separate meter within six months after the date the tenant moves out.

(c) If the landlord gives the tenant the notice closing the rental unit:

(1) before the tenant gives a repair notice to the landlord, the remedies of this subchapter do not apply;

(2) after the tenant gives a repair notice to the landlord but before the landlord has had a reasonable time to make repairs, the tenant is entitled only to the remedies under Subsection (d) of this section and Subdivisions (3), (4), and (5) of Subsection (a) of Section 92.0563; or

(3) after the tenant gives a repair notice to the landlord and after the landlord has had a reasonable time to make repairs, the tenant is entitled only to the remedies under Subsection (d) of this section and Subdivisions (3), (4), and (5) of Subsection (a) of Section 92.0563.

(d) If the landlord closes the rental unit after the tenant gives the landlord a notice to repair and the tenant moves out on or before the end of the rental term, the landlord must pay the tenant's actual and reasonable moving expenses, refund a pro rata portion of the tenant's rent from the date the tenant moves out, and, if otherwise required by law, return the tenant's security deposit.

(e) A landlord who violates Subsection (b) or (d) is liable to the tenant for an amount equal to the total of one month's rent plus $100 and attorney's fees.

(f) The closing of a rental unit does not prohibit the occupancy of other apartments, nor does this subchapter prohibit occupancy of or utility service by master or individual meter to other rental units in an apartment complex that have not been closed under this section. If another provision of this subchapter conflicts with this section, this section controls.

§ 92.056. Landlord Liability and Tenant Remedies; Notice and Time for Repair

(a) A landlord's liability under this section is subject to Section 92.052(b) regarding conditions that are caused by a tenant and Section 92.054 regarding conditions that are insured casualties.

(b) A landlord is liable to a tenant as provided by this subchapter if:

(1) the tenant has given the landlord notice to repair or remedy a condition by giving that notice to the person to whom or to the place where the tenant's rent is normally paid;

(2) the condition materially affects the physical health or safety of an ordinary tenant;

(3) the tenant has given the landlord a subsequent written notice to repair or remedy the condition after a reasonable time to repair or remedy the condition following the notice given under Subdivision (1) or the tenant has given the notice under Subdivision (1) by sending that notice by certified mail, return receipt requested, or by registered mail;

(4) the landlord has had a reasonable time to repair or remedy the condition after the landlord received the tenant's notice under Subdivision (1) and, if applicable, the tenant's subsequent notice under Subdivision (3);

(5) the landlord has not made a diligent effort to repair or remedy the condition after the landlord received the tenant's notice under Subdivision (1) and, if applicable, the tenant's subsequent notice under Subdivision (3); and

(6) the tenant was not delinquent in the payment of rent at the time any notice required by this subsection was given.

(c) For purposes of Subsection (b)(4) or (5), a landlord is considered to have received the tenant's notice when the landlord or the landlord's agent or employee has actually received the notice or when the United States Postal Service has attempted to deliver the notice to the landlord.

(d) For purposes of Subsection (b)(3) or (4), in determining whether a period of time is a reasonable time to repair or remedy a condition, there is a rebuttable presumption that seven days is a reasonable time. To rebut that presumption, the date on which the landlord received the tenant's notice, the severity and nature of the condition, and the reasonable availability of materials and labor and of utilities from a utility company must be considered.

(e) Except as provided in Subsection (f), a tenant to whom a landlord is liable under Subsection (b) of this section may:

(1) terminate the lease;

(2) have the condition repaired or remedied according to Section 92.0561;

(3) deduct from the tenant's rent, without necessity of judicial action, the cost of the repair or remedy according to Section 92.0561; and

(4) obtain judicial remedies according to Section 92.0563.

(f) A tenant who elects to terminate the lease under Subsection (e) is:

(1) entitled to a pro rata refund of rent from the date of termination or the date the tenant moves out, whichever is later;

(2) entitled to deduct the tenant's security deposit from the tenant's rent without necessity of lawsuit or obtain a refund of the tenant's security deposit according to law; and

(3) not entitled to the other repair and deduct remedies under Section 92.0561 or the judicial remedies under Subdivisions (1) and (2) of Subsection (a) of Section 92.0563.

§ 92.0561. Tenant's Repair and Deduct Remedies

(a) If the landlord is liable to the tenant under Section 92.056(b), the tenant may have the condition repaired or remedied and may deduct the cost from a subsequent rent payment as provided in this section.

(b) The tenant's deduction for the cost of the repair or remedy may not exceed the amount of one month's rent under the lease or $500, whichever is greater. However, if the tenant's rent is subsidized in whole or in part by a governmental agency, the deduction limitation of one month's rent shall mean the fair market rent for the dwelling and not the rent that the tenant pays. The fair market rent shall be determined by the governmental agency subsidizing the rent, or in the absence of such a determination, it shall be a reasonable amount of rent under the circumstances.

(c) Repairs and deductions under this section may be made as often as necessary so long as the total repairs and deductions in any one month do not exceed one month's rent or $500, whichever is greater.

(d) Repairs under this section may be made only if all of the following requirements are met:

(1) The landlord has a duty to repair or remedy the condition under Section 92.052, and the duty has not been waived in a written lease by the tenant under Subsection (e) or (f) of Section 92.006.

(2) The tenant has given notice to the landlord as required by Section 92.056(b)(1), and, if required, a subsequent notice under Section 92.056(b)(3), and at least one of those notices states that the tenant intends to repair or remedy the condition. The notice shall also contain a reasonable description of the intended repair or remedy.

(3) Any one of the following events has occurred:

(A) The landlord has failed to remedy the backup or overflow of raw sewage inside the tenant's dwelling or the flooding from broken pipes or natural drainage inside the dwelling.

(B) The landlord has expressly or impliedly agreed in the lease to furnish potable water to the tenant's dwelling and the water service to the dwelling has totally ceased.

(C) The landlord has expressly or impliedly agreed in the lease to furnish heating or cooling equipment; the equipment is producing inadequate heat or cooled air; and the landlord has been notified in writing by the appropriate local housing, building, or health official or other official having jurisdiction that the lack of heat or cooling materially affects the health or safety of an ordinary tenant.

(D) The landlord has been notified in writing by the appropriate local housing, building, or health official or other official having jurisdiction that the condition materially affects the health or safety of an ordinary tenant.

(e) If the requirements of Subsection (d) of this section are met, a tenant may:

(1) have the condition repaired or remedied immediately following the tenant's notice of intent to repair if the condition involves sewage or flooding as referred to in Paragraph (A) of Subdivision (3) of Subsection (d) of this section;

(2) have the condition repaired or remedied if the condition involves a cessation of potable water as referred to in Paragraph (A) of Subdivision (3) of Subsection (d) of this section and if the landlord has failed to repair or remedy the condition within three days following the tenant's delivery of notice of intent to repair;

(3) have the condition repaired or remedied if the condition involves inadequate heat or cooled air as referred to in Paragraph (C) of Subdivision (3) of Subsection (d) of this section and if the landlord has failed to repair the condition within three days after delivery of the tenant's notice of intent to repair; or

(4) have the condition repaired or remedied if the condition is not covered by Paragraph (A), (B), or (C) of Subdivision (3) of Subsection (d) of this section and involves a condition affecting the physical health or safety of the ordinary tenant as referred to in Paragraph (D) of Subdivision (3) of Subsection (d) of this section and if the landlord has failed to repair or remedy the condition within seven days after delivery of the tenant's notice of intent to repair.

(f) Repairs made pursuant to the tenant's notice must be made by a company, contractor, or repairman listed in the yellow or business pages of the telephone directory or in the classified advertising section of a newspaper of the local city, county, or adjacent county at the time of the tenant's notice of intent to repair. Unless the landlord and tenant agree otherwise under Subsection (g) of this section, repairs may not be made by the tenant, the tenant's immediate family, the tenant's employer or employees, or a company in which the tenant has an ownership interest. Repairs may not be made to the foundation or load-bearing structural elements of the building if it contains two or more dwelling units.

(g) A landlord and a tenant may mutually agree for the tenant to repair or remedy, at the landlord's expense, any condition of the dwelling regardless of whether it materially affects the health or safety of an ordinary tenant. However, the landlord's duty to repair or remedy conditions covered by this subchapter may not be waived except as provided by Subsection (e) or (f) of Section 92.006.

(h) Repairs made pursuant to the tenant's notice must be made in compliance with applicable building codes, including a building permit when required.

(i) The tenant shall not have authority to contract for labor or materials in excess of what the tenant may deduct under this section. The landlord is not liable to repairmen, contractors, or material suppliers who furnish labor or materials to repair or remedy the condition. A repairman or supplier shall not have a lien for materials or services arising out of repairs contracted for by the tenant under this section.

(j) When deducting the cost of repairs from the rent payment, the tenant shall furnish the landlord, along with payment of the balance of the rent, a copy of the repair bill and the receipt for its payment. A repair bill and receipt may be the same document.

(k) If the landlord repairs or remedies the condition or delivers an affidavit for delay under Section 92.0562 to the tenant after the tenant has contacted a repairman but before the repairman commences work, the landlord shall be liable for the cost incurred by the tenant for the repairman's trip charge, and the tenant may deduct the charge from the tenant's rent as if it were a repair cost.

§ 92.0562. Landlord Affidavit for Delay

(a) The tenant must delay contracting for repairs under Section 92.0561 if, before the tenant contracts for the repairs, the landlord delivers to the tenant an affidavit, signed and sworn to under oath by the landlord or his authorized agent and complying with this section.

(b) The affidavit must summarize the reasons for the delay and the diligent efforts made by the landlord up to the date of the affidavit to get the repairs done. The affidavit must state facts showing that the landlord has made and is making diligent efforts to repair the condition, and it must contain dates, names, addresses, and telephone numbers of contractors, suppliers, and repairmen contacted by the owner.

(c) Affidavits under this section may delay repair by the tenant for:

(1) 15 days if the landlord's failure to repair is caused by a delay in obtaining necessary parts for which the landlord is not at fault; or

(2) 30 days if the landlord's failure to repair is caused by a general shortage of labor or materials for repair following a natural disaster such as a hurricane, tornado, flood, extended freeze, or widespread windstorm.

(d) Affidavits for delay based on grounds other than those listed in Subsection (c) of this section are unlawful, and if used, they are of no effect. The landlord may file subsequent affidavits, provided that the total delay of the repair or remedy extends no longer than six months from the date the landlord delivers the first affidavit to the tenant.

(e) The affidavit must be delivered to the tenant by any of the following methods:

(1) personal delivery to the tenant;

(2) certified mail, return receipt requested, to the tenant; or

(3) leaving the notice inside the dwelling in a conspicuous place if notice in that manner is authorized in a written lease.

(f) Affidavits for delay by a landlord under this section must be submitted in good faith. Following delivery of the affidavit, the landlord must continue diligent efforts to repair or remedy the condition. There shall be a rebuttable presumption that the landlord acted in good faith and with continued diligence for the first affidavit for delay the landlord delivers to the tenant. The landlord shall have the burden of pleading and proving good faith and continued diligence for subsequent affidavits for delay. A landlord who violates this section shall be liable to the tenant for all judicial remedies under Section 92.0563 except that the civil penalty under Subdivision (3) of Subsection (a) of Section 92.0563 shall be one month's rent plus $1,000.

(g) If the landlord is liable to the tenant under Section 92.056 and if a new landlord, in good faith and without knowledge of the tenant's notice of intent to repair, has acquired title to the tenant's dwelling by foreclosure, deed in lieu of foreclosure, or general warranty deed in a bona fide purchase, then the following shall apply:

(1) The tenant's right to terminate the lease under this subchapter shall not be affected, and the tenant shall have no duty to give additional notice to the new landlord.

(2) The tenant's right to repair and deduct for conditions involving sewage backup or overflow, flooding inside the dwelling, or a cutoff of potable water under Subsection (e) of

Section 92.0561 shall not be affected, and the tenant shall have no duty to give additional notice to the new landlord.

(3) For conditions other than those specified in Subdivision (2) of this subsection, if the new landlord acquires title as described in this subsection and has notified the tenant of the name and address of the new landlord or the new landlord's authorized agent and if the tenant has not already contracted for the repair or remedy at the time the tenant is so notified, the tenant must deliver to the new landlord a written notice of intent to repair or remedy the condition, and the new landlord shall have a reasonable time to complete the repair before the tenant may repair or remedy the condition. No further notice from the tenant is necessary in order for the tenant to repair or remedy the condition after a reasonable time has elapsed.

(4) The tenant's judicial remedies under Section 92.0563 shall be limited to recovery against the landlord to whom the tenant gave the required notices until the tenant has given the new landlord the notices required by this section and otherwise complied with Section 92.056 as to the new landlord.

(5) If the new landlord violates this subsection, the new landlord is liable to the tenant for a civil penalty of one month's rent plus $2,000, actual damages, and attorney's fees.

(6) No provision of this section shall affect any right of a foreclosing superior lienholder to terminate, according to law, any interest in the premises held by the holders of subordinate liens, encumbrances, leases, or other interests and shall not affect any right of the tenant to terminate the lease according to law.

§ 92.0563. Tenant's Judicial Remedies

(a) A tenant's judicial remedies under Section 92.056 shall include:

(1) an order directing the landlord to take reasonable action to repair or remedy the condition;

(2) an order reducing the tenant's rent, from the date of the first repair notice, in proportion to the reduced rental value resulting from the condition until the condition is repaired or remedied;

(3) a judgment against the landlord for a civil penalty of one month's rent plus $500;

(4) a judgment against the landlord for the amount of the tenant's actual damages; and

(5) court costs and attorney's fees, excluding any attorney's fees for a cause of action for damages relating to a personal injury.

(b) A landlord who knowingly violates Section 92.006 by contracting orally or in writing with a tenant to waive the landlord's duty to repair under this subchapter shall be liable to the tenant for actual damages, a civil penalty of one month's rent plus $2,000, and reasonable attorney's fees. For purposes of this subsection, there shall be a rebuttable presumption that the landlord acted without knowledge of the violation. The tenant shall have the burden of pleading and proving a knowing violation. If the lease is in writing and is not in violation of Section 92.006, the tenant's proof of a knowing violation must be clear and convincing. A mutual agreement for tenant repair under Subsection (g) of Section 92.0561 is not a violation of Section 92.006.

(c) The justice, county, and district courts have concurrent jurisdiction of an action under Subsection (a) of this section except that the justice court may not order repairs under Subdivision (1) of Subsection (a) of this section.

§ 92.058. Landlord Remedy for Tenant Violation

(a) If the tenant withholds rents, causes repairs to be performed, or makes rent deductions for repairs in violation of this subchapter, the landlord may recover actual damages from the tenant. If, after a landlord has notified a tenant in writing of (1) the illegality of the tenant's rent withholding or the tenant's proposed repair and (2) the penalties of this subchapter, the tenant withholds rent, causes repairs to be performed, or makes rent deductions for repairs in bad faith violation of this subchapter, the landlord may recover from the tenant a civil penalty of one month's rent plus $500.

(b) Notice under this section must be in writing and may be given in person, by mail, or by delivery to the premises.

(c) The landlord has the burden of pleading and proving, by clear and convincing evidence, that the landlord gave the tenant the required notice of the illegality and the penalties and that the tenant's violation was done in bad faith. In any litigation under this subsection, the prevailing party shall recover reasonable attorney's fees from the nonprevailing party.

§ 92.060. Agents for Delivery of Notice

A managing agent, leasing agent, or resident manager is the agent of the landlord for purposes of notice and other communications required or permitted by this subchapter.

§ 92.061. Effect on Other Rights

The duties of a landlord and the remedies of a tenant under this subchapter are in lieu of existing common law and other statutory law warranties and duties of landlords for maintenance, repair, security, habitability, and nonretaliation, and remedies of tenants for a violation of those warranties and duties. Otherwise, this subchapter does not affect any other right of a landlord or tenant under contract, statutory law, or common law that is consistent with the purposes of this subchapter or any right a landlord or tenant may have to bring an action for personal injury or property damage under the law of this state. This subchapter does not impose obligations on a landlord or tenant other than those expressly stated in this subchapter.

SUBCHAPTER C. SECURITY DEPOSITS

§ 92.101. Application

This subchapter applies to all residential leases.

§ 92.102. Security Deposit

A security deposit is any advance of money, other than a rental application deposit or an advance payment of rent, that is intended primarily to secure performance under a lease of a dwelling that has been entered into by a landlord and a tenant.

§ 92.103. Obligation to Refund

(a) Except as provided by Section 92.107, the landlord shall refund a security deposit to the tenant on or before the 30th day after the date the tenant surrenders the premises.

(b) A requirement that a tenant give advance notice of surrender as a condition for refunding the security deposit is effective only if the requirement is underlined or is printed in conspicuous bold print in the lease.

(c) The tenant's claim to the security deposit takes priority over the claim of any creditor of the landlord, including a trustee in bankruptcy.

§ 92.1031. Conditions for Retention of Security Deposit or Rent Prepayment

(a) Except as provided in Subsection (b), a landlord who receives a security deposit or rent prepayment for a dwelling from a tenant who fails to occupy the dwelling according to a lease between the landlord and the tenant may not retain the security deposit or rent prepayment if:

(1) the tenant secures a replacement tenant satisfactory to the landlord and the replacement tenant occupies the dwelling on or before the commencement date of the lease; or

(2) the landlord secures a replacement tenant satisfactory to the landlord and the replacement tenant occupies the dwelling on or before the commencement date of the lease.

(b) If the landlord secures the replacement tenant, the landlord may retain and deduct from the security deposit or rent prepayment either:

(1) a sum agreed to in the lease as a lease cancellation fee; or

(2) actual expenses incurred by the landlord in securing the replacement, including a reasonable amount for the time of the landlord in securing the replacement tenant.

§ 92.104. Retention of Security Deposit; Accounting

(a) Before returning a security deposit, the landlord may deduct from the deposit damages and charges for which the tenant is legally liable under the lease or as a result of breaching the lease.

(b) The landlord may not retain any portion of a security deposit to cover normal wear and tear.

(c) If the landlord retains all or part of a security deposit under this section, the landlord shall give to the tenant the balance of the security deposit, if any, together with a written description and itemized list of all deductions. The landlord is not required to give the tenant a description and itemized list of deductions if:

(1) the tenant owes rent when he surrenders possession of the premises; and

(2) there is no controversy concerning the amount of rent owed.

§ 92.1041. Presumption of Refund or Accounting

A landlord is presumed to have refunded a security deposit or made an accounting of security deposit deductions if, on or before the date required under this subchapter, the refund or accounting is placed in the United States mail and postmarked on or before the required date.

§ 92.105. Cessation of Owner's Interest

(a) If the owner's interest in the premises is terminated by sale, assignment, death, appointment of a receiver, bankruptcy, or otherwise, the new owner is liable for the return of security deposits according to this subchapter from the date title to the premises is acquired, regardless of whether notice is given to the tenant under Subsection (b) of this section.

(b) The person who no longer owns an interest in the rental premises remains liable for a security deposit received while the person was the owner until the new owner delivers to the tenant a signed statement acknowledging that the new owner has received and is responsible for the tenant's security deposit and specifying the exact dollar amount of the deposit.

(c) Subsection (a) does not apply to a real estate mortgage lienholder who acquires title by foreclosure.

§ 92.106. Records
The landlord shall keep accurate records of all security deposits.

§ 92.107. Tenant's Forwarding Address
(a) The landlord is not obligated to return a tenant's security deposit or give the tenant a written description of damages and charges until the tenant gives the landlord a written statement of the tenant's forwarding address for the purpose of refunding the security deposit.

(b) The tenant does not forfeit the right to a refund of the security deposit or the right to receive a description of damages and charges merely for failing to give a forwarding address to the landlord.

§ 92.108. Liability for Withholding Last Month's Rent
(a) The tenant may not withhold payment of any portion of the last month's rent on grounds that the security deposit is security for unpaid rent.

(b) A tenant who violates this section is presumed to have acted in bad faith. A tenant who in bad faith violates this section is liable to the landlord for an amount equal to three times the rent wrongfully withheld and the landlord's reasonable attorney's fees in a suit to recover the rent.

§ 92.109. Liability of Landlord
(a) A landlord who in bad faith retains a security deposit in violation of this subchapter is liable for an amount equal to the sum of $100, three times the portion of the deposit wrongfully withheld, and the tenant's reasonable attorney's fees in a suit to recover the deposit.

(b) A landlord who in bad faith does not provide a written description and itemized list of damages and charges in violation of this subchapter:

(1) forfeits the right to withhold any portion of the security deposit or to bring suit against the tenant for damages to the premises; and

(2) is liable for the tenant's reasonable attorney's fees in a suit to recover the deposit.

(c) In an action brought by a tenant under this subchapter, the landlord has the burden of proving that the retention of any portion of the security deposit was reasonable.

(d) A landlord who fails either to return a security deposit or to provide a written description and itemization of deductions on or before the 30th day after the date the tenant surrenders possession is presumed to have acted in bad faith.

SUBCHAPTER D. SECURITY DEVICES
§ 92.151. Definitions
In this subchapter:
(1) "Doorknob lock" means a lock in a doorknob, with the lock operated from the exterior by a key, card, or combination and from the interior without a key, card, or combination.

(2) "Door viewer" means a permanently installed device in an exterior door that allows a person inside the dwelling to view a person outside the door. The device must be:

(A) a clear glass pane or one-way mirror; or

(B) a peephole having a barrel with a one-way lens of glass or other substance providing an angle view of not less than 160 degrees.

(3) "Exterior door" means a door providing access from a dwelling interior to the exterior. The term includes a door between a living area and a garage but does not include a sliding glass door or a screen door.

(4) "French doors" means a set of two exterior doors in which each door is hinged and abuts the other door when closed. The term includes double-hinged patio doors.

(5) "Keyed dead bolt" means:
(A) a door lock not in the doorknob that:
(i) locks with a bolt into the doorjamb; and
(ii) is operated from the exterior by a key, card, or combination and from the interior by a knob or lever without a key, card, or combination; or
(B) a doorknob lock that contains a bolt with at least a one-inch throw.

(6) "Keyless bolting device" means a door lock not in the doorknob that locks:
(A) with a bolt into a strike plate screwed into the portion of the doorjamb surface that faces the edge of the door when the door is closed or into a metal doorjamb that serves as the strike plate, operable only by knob or lever from the door's interior and not in any manner from the door's exterior, and that is commonly known as a keyless dead bolt;
(B) by a drop bolt system operated by placing a central metal plate over a metal doorjamb restraint that protrudes from the doorjamb and that is affixed to the doorjamb frame by means of three case-hardened screws at least three inches in length. One-half of the central plate must overlap the interior surface of the door and the other half of the central plate must overlap the doorjamb when the plate is placed over the doorjamb restraint. The drop bolt system must prevent the door from being opened unless the central plate is lifted off of the doorjamb restraint by a person who is on the interior side of the door.

The term "keyless bolting device" does not include a chain latch, flip latch, surface-mounted slide bolt, mortise door bolt, surface-mounted barrel bolt, surface-mounted swing bar door guard, spring-loaded nightlatch, foot bolt, or other lock or latch; or

(C) by a metal bar or metal tube that is placed across the entire interior side of the door and secured in place at each end of the bar or tube by heavy-duty metal screw hooks. The screw hooks must be at least three inches in length and must be screwed into the door frame stud or wall stud on each side of the door. The bar or tube must be capable of being secured to both of the screw hooks and must be permanently attached in some way to the door frame stud or wall stud. When secured to the screw hooks, the bar or tube must prevent the door from being opened unless the bar or tube is removed by a person who is on the interior side of the door.

(7) "Landlord" means a dwelling owner, lessor, sublessor, management company, or managing agent, including an on-site manager.

(8) "Multiunit complex" means two or more dwellings in one or more buildings that are:
(A) under common ownership;

(B) managed by the same owner, agent, or management company; and

(C) located on the same lot or tract or adjacent lots or tracts of land.

(9) "Possession of a dwelling" means occupancy by a tenant under a lease, including occupancy until the time the tenant moves out or a writ of possession is issued by a court. The term does not include occupancy before the initial occupancy date authorized under a lease.

(10) "Rekey" means to change or alter a security device that is operated by a key, card, or combination so that a different key, card, or combination is necessary to operate the security device.

(11) "Security device" means a doorknob lock, door viewer, keyed dead bolt, keyless bolting device, sliding door handle latch, sliding door pin lock, sliding door security bar, or window latch in a dwelling.

(12) "Sliding door handle latch" means a latch or lock:

(A) located near the handle on a sliding glass door;

(B) operated with or without a key; and

(C) designed to prevent the door from being opened.

(13) "Sliding door pin lock" means a lock on a sliding glass door that consists of a pin or nail inserted from the interior side of the door at the side opposite the door's handle and that is designed to prevent the door from being opened or lifted.

(14) "Sliding door security bar" means a bar or rod that can be placed at the bottom of or across the interior side of the fixed panel of a sliding glass door and that is designed to prevent the door from being opened.

(15) "Tenant turnover date" means the date a tenant moves into a dwelling under a lease after all previous occupants have moved out. The term does not include dates of entry or occupation not authorized by the landlord.

(16) "Window latch" means a device on a window that prevents the window from being opened and that is operated without a key and only from the interior.

§ 92.152. Application of Subchapter

(a) This subchapter does not apply to:

(1) a room in a hotel, motel, or inn or to similar transient housing;

(2) residential housing owned or operated by a public or private college or university accredited by a recognized accrediting agency as defined under Section 61.003, Education Code;

(3) residential housing operated by preparatory schools accredited by the Texas Education Agency, a regional accrediting agency, or any accrediting agency recognized by the commissioner of education; or

(4) a temporary residential tenancy created by a contract for sale in which the buyer occupies the property before closing or the seller occupies the property after closing for a specific term not to exceed 90 days.

(b) Except as provided by Subsection (a), a dwelling to which this subchapter applies includes:

(1) a room in a dormitory or rooming house;

(2) a mobile home;

(3) a single family house, duplex, or triplex; and

(4) a living unit in an apartment, condominium, cooperative, or townhome project.

§ 92.153. Security Devices Required Without Necessity of Tenant Request

(a) Except as provided by Subsections (b), (e), (f), (g), and (h) and without necessity of request by the tenant, a dwelling must be equipped with:

(1) a window latch on each exterior window of the dwelling;

(2) a doorknob lock or keyed dead bolt on each exterior door;

(3) a sliding door pin lock on each exterior sliding glass door of the dwelling;

(4) a sliding door handle latch or a sliding door security bar on each exterior sliding glass door of the dwelling; and

(5) a keyless bolting device and a door viewer on each exterior door of the dwelling.

(b) If the dwelling has French doors, one door of each pair of French doors must meet the requirements of Subsection (a) and the other door must have:

(1) a keyed dead bolt or keyless bolting device capable of insertion into the doorjamb above the door and a keyless bolting device capable of insertion into the floor or threshold, each with a bolt having a throw of one inch or more; or

(2) a bolt installed inside the door and operated from the edge of the door, capable of insertion into the doorjamb above the door, and another bolt installed inside the door and operated from the edge of the door capable of insertion into the floor or threshold, each bolt having a throw of three-fourths inch or more.

(c) A security device required by Subsection (a) or (b) must be installed at the landlord's expense.

(d) Subsections (a) and (b) apply only when a tenant is in possession of a dwelling.

(e) A keyless bolting device is not required to be installed at the landlord's expense on an exterior door if:

(1) the dwelling is part of a multiunit complex in which the majority of dwelling units are leased to tenants who are over 55 years of age or who have a physical or mental disability;

(2) a tenant or occupant in the dwelling is over 55 years of age or has a physical or mental disability; and

(3) the landlord is expressly required or permitted to periodically check on the well-being or health of the tenant as a part of a written lease or other written agreement.

(f) A keyless bolting device is not required to be installed at the landlord's expense if a tenant or occupant in the dwelling is over 55 years of age or has a physical or mental disability, the tenant requests, in writing, that the landlord deactivate or not install the keyless bolting device, and the tenant certifies in the request that the tenant or occupant is over 55 years of age or has a physical or mental disability. The request must be a separate document and may not be included as part of a lease agreement. A landlord is not exempt as provided by this subsection if the landlord knows or has reason to know that the requirements of this subsection are not fulfilled.

(g) A keyed dead bolt or a doorknob lock is not required to be installed at the landlord's expense on an exterior door if at the time the tenant agrees to lease the dwelling:

(1) at least one exterior door usable for normal entry into the dwelling has both a keyed dead bolt and a keyless bolting

device, installed in accordance with the height, strike plate, and throw requirements of Section 92.154; and

(2) all other exterior doors have a keyless bolting device installed in accordance with the height, strike plate, and throw requirements of Section 92.154.

(h) A security device required by this section must be operable throughout the time a tenant is in possession of a dwelling. However, a landlord may deactivate or remove the locking mechanism of a doorknob lock or remove any device not qualifying as a keyless bolting device if a keyed dead bolt has been installed on the same door.

(i) A landlord is subject to the tenant remedies provided by Section 92.164(a)(4) if the landlord:

(1) deactivates or does not install a keyless bolting device, claiming an exemption under Subsection (e), (f), or (g); and

(2) knows or has reason to know that the requirements of the subsection granting the exemption are not fulfilled.

§ 92.154. Height, Strike Plate, and Throw Requirements—Keyed Dead Bolt or Keyless Bolting Device

(a) A keyed dead bolt or a keyless bolting device required by this subchapter must be installed at a height:

(1) not lower than 36 inches from the floor; and

(2) not higher than:

(A) 54 inches from the floor, if installed before September 1, 1993; or

(B) 48 inches from the floor, if installed on or after September 1, 1993.

(b) A keyed dead bolt or a keyless bolting device described in Section 92.151(6)(A) or (B) in a dwelling must:

(1) have a strike plate screwed into the portion of the door-jamb surface that faces the edge of the door when the door is closed; or

(2) be installed in a door with a metal doorjamb that serves as the strike plate.

(c) A keyed dead bolt or keyless dead bolt, as described by Section 92.151(6)(A), installed in a dwelling on or after September 1, 1993, must have a bolt with a throw of not less than one inch.

(d) The requirements of this section do not apply to a keyed dead bolt or a keyless bolting device in one door of a pair of French doors that is installed in accordance with the requirements of Section 92.153(b)(1) or (2).

§ 92.155. Height Requirements—Sliding Door Security Devices

A sliding door pin lock or sliding door security bar required by this subchapter must be installed at a height not higher than:

(1) 54 inches from the floor, if installed before September 1, 1993; or

(2) 48 inches from the floor, if installed on or after September 1, 1993.

§ 92.156. Rekeying or Change of Security Devices

(a) A security device operated by a key, card, or combination shall be rekeyed by the landlord at the landlord's expense not later than the seventh day after each tenant turnover date.

(b) A landlord shall perform additional rekeying or change a security device at the tenant's expense if requested by the tenant. A tenant may make an unlimited number of requests under this subsection.

(c) The expense of rekeying security devices for purposes of the use or change of the landlord's master key must be paid by the landlord.

(d) This section does not apply to locks on closet doors or other interior doors.

§ 92.157. Security Devices Requested by Tenant

(a) At a tenant's request made at any time, a landlord, at the tenant's expense, shall install:

(1) a keyed dead bolt on an exterior door if the door has:

(A) a doorknob lock but not a keyed dead bolt; or

(B) a keyless bolting device but not a keyed dead bolt or doorknob lock; and

(2) a sliding door pin lock or sliding door security bar if the door is an exterior sliding glass door without a sliding door pin lock or sliding door security bar.

(b) At a tenant's request made before January 1, 1995, a landlord, at the tenant's expense, shall install on an exterior door of a dwelling constructed before September 1, 1993:

(1) a keyless bolting device if the door does not have a keyless bolting device; and

(2) a door viewer if the door does not have a door viewer.

(c) If a security device required by Section 92.153 to be installed on or after January 1, 1995, without necessity of a tenant's request has not been installed by the landlord, the tenant may request the landlord to immediately install it, and the landlord shall immediately install it at the landlord's expense.

§ 92.158. Landlord's Duty to Repair or Replace Security Device

During the lease term and any renewal period, a landlord shall repair or replace a security device on request or notification by the tenant that the security device is inoperable or in need of repair or replacement.

§ 92.159. When Tenant's Request or Notice Must be in Writing

A tenant's request or notice under this subchapter may be given orally unless the tenant has a written lease that requires the request or notice to be in writing and that requirement is underlined or in boldfaced print in the lease.

§ 92.160. Type, Brand, and Manner of Installation

Except as otherwise required by this subchapter, a landlord may select the type, brand, and manner of installation, including placement, of a security device installed under this subchapter. This section does not apply to a security device installed, repaired, changed, replaced, or rekeyed by a tenant under Section 92.164(a)(1) or 92.165(1).

§ 92.161. Compliance With Tenant Request Required Within Reasonable Time

(a) Except as provided by Subsections (b) and (c), a landlord must comply with a tenant's request for rekeying, changing, installing, repairing, or replacing a security device under Section 92.156, 92.157, or 92.158 within a reasonable time. A reasonable time for purposes of this subsection is presumed to be not later than the seventh day after the date the request is received by the landlord.

(b) If within the time allowed under Section 92.162(c) a landlord requests advance payment of charges that the landlord is entitled to collect under that section, the landlord shall comply with a tenant's request under Section 92.156(b),

92.157(a), or 92.157(b) within a reasonable time. A reasonable time for purposes of this subsection is presumed to be not later than the seventh day after the date a tenant's advance payment is received by the landlord, except as provided by Subsection (c).

(c) A reasonable time for purposes of Subsections (a) and (b) is presumed to be not later than 72 hours after the time of receipt of the tenant's request and any required advance payment if at the time of making the request the tenant informed the landlord that:

(1) an unauthorized entry occurred or was attempted in the tenant's dwelling;

(2) an unauthorized entry occurred or was attempted in another unit in the multiunit complex in which the tenant's dwelling is located during the two months preceding the date of the request; or

(3) a crime of personal violence occurred in the multiunit complex in which the tenant's dwelling is located during the two months preceding the date of the request.

(d) A landlord may rebut the presumption provided by Subsection (a) or (b) if despite the diligence of the landlord:

(1) the landlord did not know of the tenant's request, without the fault of the landlord;

(2) materials, labor, or utilities were unavailable; or

(3) a delay was caused by circumstances beyond the landlord's control, including the illness or death of the landlord or a member of the landlord's immediate family.

(e) This section does not apply to a landlord's duty to install or rekey, without necessity of a tenant's request, a security device under Section 92.153 or 92.156(a).

§ 92.162. Payment of Charges; Limits on Amount Charged

(a) A landlord may not require a tenant to pay for repair or replacement of a security device due to normal wear and tear. A landlord may not require a tenant to pay for other repairs or replacements of a security device except as provided by Subsections (b), (c), and (d).

(b) A landlord may require a tenant to pay for repair or replacement of a security device if an underlined provision in a written lease authorizes the landlord to do so and the repair or replacement is necessitated by misuse or damage by the tenant, a member of the tenant's family, an occupant, or a guest, and not by normal wear and tear. Misuse of or damage to a security device that occurs during the tenant's occupancy is presumed to be caused by the tenant, a family member, an occupant, or a guest. The tenant has the burden of proving that the misuse or damage was caused by another party.

(c) A landlord may require a tenant to pay in advance charges for which the tenant is liable under this subchapter if a written lease authorizes the landlord to require advance payment, and the landlord notifies the tenant within a reasonable time after the tenant's request that advance payment is required, and:

(1) the tenant is more than 30 days delinquent in reimbursing the landlord for charges to which the landlord is entitled under Subsection (b); or

(2) the tenant requested that the landlord repair, install, change, or rekey the same security device during the 30 days

preceding the tenant's request, and the landlord complied with the request.

(d) A landlord authorized by this subchapter to charge a tenant for repairing, installing, changing, or rekeying a security device under this subchapter may not require the tenant to pay more than the total cost charged by a third-party contractor for material, labor, taxes, and extra keys. If the landlord's employees perform the work, the charge may include a reasonable amount for overhead but may not include a profit to the landlord. If management company employees perform the work, the charge may include reasonable overhead and profit but may not exceed the cost charged to the owner by the management company for comparable security devices installed by management company employees at the owner's request and expense.

(e) The owner of a dwelling shall reimburse a management company, managing agent, or on-site manager for costs expended by that person in complying with this subchapter. A management company, managing agent, or on-site manager may reimburse itself for the costs from the owner's funds in its possession or control.

§ 92.163. Removal or Alteration of Security Device by Tenant

A security device that is installed, changed, or rekeyed under this subchapter becomes a fixture of the dwelling. Except as provided by Section 92.164(a)(1) or 92.165(1) regarding the remedy of repair-and-deduct, a tenant may not remove, change, rekey, replace, or alter a security device or have it removed, changed, rekeyed, replaced, or altered without permission of the landlord.

§ 92.164. Tenant Remedies for Landlord's Failure to Install or Rekey Certain Security Devices

(a) If a landlord does not comply with Section 92.153 or 92.156(a) regarding installation or rekeying of a security device, the tenant may:

(1) install or rekey the security device as required by this subchapter and deduct the reasonable cost of material, labor, taxes, and extra keys from the tenant's next rent payment, in accordance with Section 92.166;

(2) serve a written request for compliance on the landlord, and, except as provided by Subsections (b) and (c), if the landlord does not comply on or before the third day after the date the notice is received, unilaterally terminate the lease without court proceedings;

(3) file suit against the landlord without serving a request for compliance and obtain a judgment for:

(A) a court order directing the landlord to comply, if the tenant is in possession of the dwelling;

(B) the tenant's actual damages;

(C) court costs; and

(D) attorney's fees except in suits for recovery of property damages, personal injuries, or wrongful death; and

(4) serve a written request for compliance on the landlord, and, except as provided by Subsections (b) and (c), if the landlord does not comply on or before the third day after the date the notice is received, file suit against the landlord and obtain a judgment for:

(A) a court order directing the landlord to comply and bring all dwellings owned by the landlord into compliance, if the tenant serving the written request is in possession of the dwelling;

(B) the tenant's actual damages;

(C) punitive damages if the tenant suffers actual damages;

(D) a civil penalty of one month's rent plus $500;

(E) court costs; and

(F) attorney's fees except in suits for recovery of property damages, personal injuries, or wrongful death.

(b) A tenant may not unilaterally terminate the lease under Subsection (a)(2) or file suit against the landlord to obtain a judgment under Subsection (a)(4) unless the landlord does not comply on or before the seventh day after the date the written request for compliance is received if the lease includes language underlined or in boldface print that in substance provides the tenant with notice that:

(1) the landlord at the landlord's expense is required to equip the dwelling, when the tenant takes possession, with the security devices described by Sections 92.153(a)(1)-(4) and (6);

(2) the landlord is not required to install a doorknob lock or keyed dead bolt at the landlord's expense if the exterior doors meet the requirements of Section 92.153(f);

(3) the landlord is not required to install a keyless bolting device at the landlord's expense on an exterior door if the landlord is expressly required or permitted to periodically check on the well-being or health of the tenant as provided by Section 92.153(e)(3); and

(4) the tenant has the right to install or rekey a security device required by this subchapter and deduct the reasonable cost from the tenant's next rent payment, as provided by Subsection (a)(1).

(c) Regardless of whether the lease contains language complying with the requirements of Subsection (b), the additional time for landlord compliance provided by Subsection (b) does not apply if at the time the tenant served the written request for compliance on the landlord the tenant informed the landlord that an unauthorized entry occurred or was attempted in the tenant's dwelling, an unauthorized entry occurred or was attempted in another unit in the multiunit complex in which the tenant's dwelling is located during the two months preceding the date of the request, or a crime of personal violence occurred in the multiunit complex in which the tenant's dwelling is located during the two months preceding the date of the request, unless despite the diligence of the landlord:

(1) the landlord did not know of the tenant's request, without the fault of the landlord;

(2) materials, labor, or utilities were unavailable; or

(3) a delay was caused by circumstances beyond the landlord's control, including the illness or death of the landlord or a member of the landlord's immediate family.

§ 92.1641. Landlord's Defenses Relating to Installing or Rekeying Certain Security Devices

The landlord has a defense to liability under Section 92.164 if:

(1) the tenant has not fully paid all rent then due from the tenant on the date the tenant gives a request under Subsection (a) of Section 92.157 or the notice required by Section 92.164 ; or

(2) on the date the tenant terminates the lease or files suit the tenant has not fully paid costs requested by the landlord and authorized by Section 92.162.

§ 92.165. Tenant Remedies for Other Landlord Violations

If a landlord does not comply with a tenant's request regarding rekeying, changing, adding, repairing, or replacing a security device under Section 92.156(b), 92.157, or 92.158 in accordance with the time limits and other requirements of this subchapter, the tenant may:

(1) install, repair, change, replace, or rekey the security devices as required by this subchapter and deduct the reasonable cost of material, labor, taxes, and extra keys from the tenant's next rent payment in accordance with Section 92.166;

(2) unilaterally terminate the lease without court proceedings; and

(3) file suit against the landlord and obtain a judgment for:

(A) a court order directing the landlord to comply, if the tenant is in possession of the dwelling;

(B) the tenant's actual damages;

(C) punitive damages if the tenant suffers actual damages and the landlord's failure to comply is intentional, malicious, or grossly negligent;

(D) a civil penalty of one month's rent plus $500;

(E) court costs; and

(F) attorney's fees except in suits for recovery of property damages, personal injuries, or wrongful death.

§ 92.166. Notice of Tenant's Deduction of Repair Costs From Rent

(a) A tenant shall notify the landlord of a rent deduction attributable to the tenant's installing, repairing, changing, replacing, or rekeying of a security device under Section 92.164(a)(1) or 92.165(1) after the landlord's failure to comply with this subchapter. The notice must be given at the time of the reduced rent payment.

(b) Unless otherwise provided in a written lease, a tenant shall provide one duplicate of the key to any key-operated security device installed or rekeyed by the tenant under Section 92.164(a)(1) or 92.165(1) within a reasonable time after the landlord's written request for the key.

§ 92.167. Landlord's Defenses Relating to Compliance With Tenant's Request

(a) A landlord has a defense to liability under Section 92.165 if on the date the tenant terminates the lease or files suit the tenant has not fully paid costs requested by the landlord and authorized by this subchapter.

(b) A management company or managing agent who is not the owner of a dwelling and who has not purported to be the owner in the lease has a defense to liability under Sections 92.164 and 92.165 if before the date the tenant is in possession of the dwelling or the date of the tenant's request for installation, repair, replacement, change, or rekeying and before any property damage or personal injury to the tenant, the management company or managing agent:

(1) did not have funds of the dwelling owner in its possession or control with which to comply with this subchapter;

(2) made written request to the dwelling owner that the owner fund and allow installation, repair, change, replacement, or rekeying of security devices as required under this

subchapter and mailed the request, certified mail return receipt requested, to the dwelling owner; and

(3) not later than the third day after the date of receipt of the tenant's request, provided the tenant with a written notice:

(A) stating that the management company or managing agent has taken the actions in Subdivisions (1) and (2);

(B) stating that the owner has not provided or will not provide the necessary funds; and

(C) explaining the remedies available to the tenant for the landlord's failure to comply.

§ 92.168. Tenant's Remedy on Notice From Management Company

The tenant may unilaterally terminate the lease or exercise other remedies under Sections 92.164 and 92.165 after receiving written notice from a management company that the owner of the dwelling has not provided or will not provide funds to repair, install, change, replace, or rekey a security device as required by this subchapter.

§ 92.169. Agent for Delivery of Notice

A managing agent or an agent to whom rent is regularly paid, whether residing or maintaining an office on-site or off-site, is the agent of the landlord for purposes of notice and other communications required or permitted by this subchapter.

§ 92.170. Effect on Other Landlord Duties and Tenant Remedies

The duties of a landlord and the remedies of a tenant under this subchapter are in lieu of common law, other statutory law, and local ordinances relating to a residential landlord's duty to install, change, rekey, repair, or replace security devices and a tenant's remedies for the landlord's failure to install, change, rekey, repair, or replace security devices, except that a municipal ordinance adopted before January 1, 1993, may require installation of security devices at the landlord's expense by an earlier date than a date required by this subchapter. This subchapter does not affect a duty of a landlord or a remedy of a tenant under Subchapter B regarding habitability.

SUBCHAPTER E. DISCLOSURE OF OWNERSHIP AND MANAGEMENT

§ 92.201. Disclosure of Ownership and Management

(a) A landlord shall disclose to a tenant, or to any government official or employee acting in an official capacity, according to this subchapter:

(1) the name and either a street or post office box address of the holder of record title, according to the deed records in the county clerk's office, of the dwelling rented by the tenant or inquired about by the government official or employee acting in an official capacity; and

(2) if an entity located off-site from the dwelling is primarily responsible for managing the dwelling, the name and street address of the management company.

(b) Disclosure to a tenant under Subsection (a) must be made by:

(1) giving the information in writing to the tenant on or before the seventh day after the day the landlord receives the tenant's request for the information;

(2) continuously posting the information in a conspicuous place in the dwelling or the office of the on-site manager or on the outside of the entry door to the office of the on-site

manager on or before the seventh day after the date the landlord receives the tenant's request for the information; or

(3) including the information in a copy of the tenant's lease or in written rules given to the tenant before the tenant requests the information.

(c) Disclosure of information to a tenant may be made under Subdivision (1) or (2) of Subsection (b) before the tenant requests the information.

(d) Disclosure of information to a government official or employee must be made by giving the information in writing to the official or employee on or before the seventh day after the date the landlord receives the request from the official or employee for the information.

(e) A correction to the information may be made by any of the methods authorized for providing the information.

(f) For the purposes of this section, an owner or property manager may disclose either an actual name or names or an assumed name if an assumed name certificate has been recorded with the county clerk.

§ 92.202. Landlord's Failure to Disclose Information

(a) A landlord is liable to a tenant or a governmental body according to this subchapter if:

(1) after the tenant or government official or employee makes a request for information under Section 92.201, the landlord does not provide the information; and

(2) the landlord does not give the information to the tenant or government official or employee before the eighth day after the date the tenant, official, or employee gives the landlord written notice that the tenant, official, or employee may exercise remedies under this subchapter if the landlord does not comply with the request by the tenant, official, or employee for the information within seven days.

(b) If the tenant's lease is in writing, the lease may require the tenant's initial request for information to be written. A request by a government official or employee for information must be in writing.

§ 92.203. Landlord's Failure to Correct Information

A landlord who has provided information under Subdivision (2) or (3) of Subsection (b) of Section 92.201 is liable to a tenant according to this subchapter if:

(1) the information becomes incorrect because a name or address changes; and

(2) the landlord fails to correct the information on or before the seventh day after the date the tenant gives the landlord written notice that the tenant may exercise the remedies under this subchapter if the corrected information is not provided within seven days.

§ 92.204. Bad Faith Violation

A landlord acts in bad faith and is liable according to this subchapter if the landlord gives an incorrect name or address under Subsection (a) of Section 92.201 by wilfully:

(1) disclosing incorrect information under Section 92.201(b)(1) or (2) or Section 92.201(d); or

(2) failing to correct information given under Section 92.201(b)(1) or (2) or Section 92.201(d) that the landlord knows is incorrect.

§ 92.205. Remedies

(a) A tenant of a landlord who is liable under Section 92.202, 92.203, or 92.204 may obtain or exercise one or more of the following remedies:

(1) a court order directing the landlord to make a disclosure required by this subchapter;

(2) a judgment against the landlord for an amount equal to the tenant's actual costs in discovering the information required to be disclosed by this subchapter;

(3) a judgment against the landlord for one month's rent plus $100;

(4) a judgment against the landlord for court costs and attorney's fees; and

(5) unilateral termination of the lease without a court proceeding.

(b) A governmental body whose official or employee has requested information from a landlord who is liable under Section 92.202 or 92.204 may obtain or exercise one or more of the following remedies:

(1) a court order directing the landlord to make a disclosure required by this subchapter;

(2) a judgment against the landlord for an amount equal to the governmental body's actual costs in discovering the information required to be disclosed by this subchapter;

(3) a judgment against the landlord for $500; and

(4) a judgment against the landlord for court costs and attorney's fees.

§ 92.206. Landlord's Defense

A landlord has a defense to liability under Section 92.202 or 92.203 if the tenant owes rent on the date the tenant gives a notice required by either of those sections. Rent delinquency is not a defense for a violation of Section 92.204.

§ 92.207. Agents for Delivery of Notice

(a) A managing or leasing agent, whether residing or maintaining an office on-site or off-site, is the agent of the landlord for purposes of:

(1) notice and other communications required or permitted by this subchapter;

(2) notice and other communications from a governmental body relating to a violation of health, sanitation, safety, or nuisance laws on the landlord's property where the dwelling is located, including notices of:

(A) demands for abatement of nuisances;

(B) repair of a substandard dwelling;

(C) remedy of dangerous conditions;

(D) reimbursement of costs incurred by the governmental body in curing the violation;

(E) fines; and

(F) service of process.

(b) If the landlord's name and business street address in this state have not been furnished in writing to the tenant or government official or employee, the person who collects the rent from a tenant is the landlord's authorized agent for purposes of Subsection (a).

§ 92.208. Additional Enforcement by Local Ordinance

The duties of a landlord and the remedies of a tenant under this subchapter are in lieu of the common law, other statutory law, and local ordinances relating to the disclosure of ownership and management of a dwelling by a landlord to a tenant. However, this subchapter does not prohibit the adoption of a local ordinance that conforms to this subchapter but which contains additional enforcement provisions.

SUBCHAPTER F. SMOKE DETECTORS

§ 92.251. Definition

In this subchapter, "dwelling unit" means a home, mobile home, duplex unit, apartment unit, condominium unit, or any dwelling unit in a multiunit residential structure. It also means a "dwelling" as defined by Section 92.001.

§ 92.252. Application of Other Law; Municipal Regulation

(a) The duties of a landlord and the remedies of a tenant under this subchapter are in lieu of common law, other statutory law, and local ordinances regarding a residential landlord's duty to install, inspect, or repair a smoke detector in a dwelling unit. However, this subchapter does not:

(1) affect a local ordinance adopted before September 1, 1981, that requires landlords to install smoke detectors in new or remodeled dwelling units before September 1, 1981, if the ordinance conforms with or is amended to conform with this subchapter;

(2) limit or prevent adoption or enforcement of a local ordinance relating to fire safety as a part of a building, fire, or housing code, including any requirements relating to the installation of smoke detectors or the type of smoke detectors;

(3) otherwise limit or prevent the adoption of a local ordinance that conforms to this subchapter but which contains additional enforcement provisions, except as provided by Subsection (b); or

(4) affect a local ordinance that requires regular inspections by local officials of smoke detectors in dwelling units and that requires smoke detectors to be operational at the time of inspection.

(b) If a smoke detector powered by battery has been installed in a dwelling unit built before September 1, 1987, in compliance with this subchapter and local ordinances, a local ordinance may not require that a smoke detector powered by alternating current be installed in the unit unless:

(1) the interior of the unit is repaired, remodeled, or rebuilt at a projected cost of more than $2,500 and the repair, remodeling, or rebuilding requires a municipal building permit;

(2) an addition occurs to the unit at a projected cost of more than $2,500;

(3) a smoke detector powered by alternating current was actually installed in the unit at any time prior to September 1, 1987; or

(4) a smoke detector powered by alternating current was required by lawful city ordinance at the time of initial construction of the unit.

§ 92.253. Exemptions

(a) This subchapter does not apply to:

(1) a dwelling unit that is occupied by its owner, no part of which is leased to a tenant;

(2) a dwelling unit in a building five or more stories in height in which smoke detectors are required or regulated by local ordinance; or

(3) a nursing or convalescent home licensed by the Texas Department of Health and certified to meet the Life Safety Code under federal law and regulations.

(b) Notwithstanding this subchapter, a person licensed by the State Board of Insurance to install fire alarms or fire detection devices under Article 5.43-2, Insurance Code, shall comply with that article when installing smoke detectors.

§ 92.254. Smoke Detector

(a) A smoke detector must be:

(1) designed to detect both the visible and invisible products of combustion;

(2) designed with an alarm audible to the bedrooms it serves;

(3) powered by battery, alternating current, or other power source as required by local ordinance;

(4) tested and listed for use as a smoke detector by Underwriters Laboratories, Inc., Factory Mutual Research Corporation, or United States Testing Company, Inc.; and

(5) in good working order.

(b) The power system and installation procedure of a security device that is electrically operated rather than battery operated must comply with applicable local ordinances.

§ 92.255. Installation and Location in New Construction

(a) Before the first tenant takes possession of a dwelling unit, the landlord shall install at least one smoke detector outside, but in the vicinity of, each separate bedroom in the dwelling unit, except:

(1) if the dwelling unit is designed to use a single room for dining, living, and sleeping, the smoke detector must be located inside the room;

(2) if the bedrooms are served by the same corridor, at least one smoke detector must be installed in the corridor in the immediate vicinity of the bedrooms; and

(3) if at least one bedroom is located on a level above the living and cooking area, the smoke detector for the bedrooms must be placed in the center of the ceiling directly above the top of the stairway.

(b) In this section, "bedroom" means a room designed with the intent that it be used for sleeping purposes.

§ 92.256. Installation in Units Constructed or Occupied on or Before September 1, 1981

(a) If the dwelling unit was occupied as a residence on or before September 1, 1981, or the building permit for the unit was issued on or before that date, the landlord shall install at least one smoke detector in accordance with Sections 92.255 and 92.257 on or before September 1, 1984.

(b) Before September 1, 1984, a tenant may install a battery-operated smoke detector in the tenant's dwelling unit without the landlord's prior consent if the installation is made according to Sections 92.255 and 92.257. When the tenant's lease terminates, including after a renewal or extension, the tenant may remove the smoke detector, but the tenant is liable to the landlord for any unnecessary damages to the dwelling unit caused by the removal.

§ 92.257. Installation Procedure

(a) Subject to Subsections (b) and (c), a smoke detector must be installed according to the manufacturer's recommended procedures.

(b) A smoke detector must be installed on a ceiling or wall. If on a ceiling, it must be no closer than six inches to a wall. If on a wall, it must be no closer than six inches and no farther than 12 inches from the ceiling.

(c) A smoke detector may be located other than as required by Subsection (b) if a local ordinance or a local or state fire marshal approves.

§ 92.258. Inspection and Repair

(a) The landlord shall inspect and repair a smoke detector according to this section.

(b) The landlord shall determine that the smoke detector is in good working order at the beginning of the tenant's possession by testing the smoke detector with smoke, by operating the testing button on the smoke detector, or by following other recommended test procedures of the manufacturer for the particular model.

(c) During the term of a lease or during a renewal or extension, the landlord has a duty to inspect and repair a smoke detector, but only if the tenant gives the landlord notice of a malfunction or requests to the landlord that the smoke detector be inspected or repaired. This duty does not exist with respect to damage or a malfunction caused by the tenant, the tenant's family, or the tenant's guests or invitees during the term of the lease or a renewal or extension, except that the landlord has a duty to repair or replace the smoke detector if the tenant pays in advance the reasonable repair or replacement cost, including labor, materials, taxes, and overhead.

(d) The landlord must comply with the tenant's request for inspection or repair within a reasonable time, considering the availability of material, labor, and utilities.

(e) The landlord has met the duty to inspect and repair if the smoke detector is in good working order after the landlord tests the smoke detector with smoke, operates the testing button on the smoke detector, or follows other recommended test procedures of the manufacturer for the particular model.

(f) The landlord is not obligated to provide batteries for a battery-operated smoke detector after a tenant takes possession if the smoke detector was in good working order at the time the tenant took possession.

(g) A smoke detector that is in good working order at the beginning of a tenant's possession is presumed to be in good working order until the tenant requests repair of the smoke detector as provided by this subchapter.

§ 92.259. Landlord's Failure to Install, Inspect, or Repair

(a) A landlord is liable according to this subchapter if:

(1) the landlord did not install a smoke detector at the time of initial occupancy by the tenant as required by this subchapter or a municipal ordinance permitted by this subchapter; or

(2) the landlord does not install, inspect, or repair the smoke detector on or before the seventh day after the date the tenant gives the landlord written notice that the tenant may exercise his remedies under this subchapter if the landlord does not comply with the request within seven days.

(b) If the tenant gives notice under Subsection (a)(2) and the tenant's lease is in writing, the lease may require the tenant to make the initial request for installation, inspection, or repair in writing.

§ 92.260. Tenant Remedies

A tenant of a landlord who is liable under Section 92.259 may obtain or exercise one or more of the following remedies:

(1) a court order directing the landlord to comply with the tenant's request if the tenant is in possession of the dwelling unit;

(2) a judgment against the landlord for damages suffered by the tenant because of the landlord's violation;

(3) a judgment against the landlord for a civil penalty of one month's rent plus $100 if the landlord violates Section 92.259(a)(2);

(4) a judgment against the landlord for court costs;

(5) a judgment against the landlord for attorney's fees in an action under Subdivision (1) or (3); and

(6) unilateral termination of the lease without a court proceeding if the landlord violates Section 92.259(a)(2).

§ 92.261. Landlord's Defenses

The landlord has a defense to liability under Section 92.259 if:

(1) on the date the tenant gives the notice required by Section 92.259 the tenant has not paid all rent due from the tenant; or

(2) on the date the tenant terminates the lease or files suit the tenant has not fully paid costs requested by the landlord and authorized by Section 92.258.

§ 92.2611. Tenant's Disabling of a Smoke Detector

(a) A tenant is liable according to this subchapter if the tenant removes a battery from a smoke detector without immediately replacing it with a working battery or knowingly disconnects or intentionally damages a smoke detector, causing it to malfunction.

(b) Except as provided in Subsection (c), a landlord of a tenant who is liable under Subsection (a) may obtain a judgment against the tenant for damages suffered by the landlord because the tenant removed a battery from a smoke detector without immediately replacing it with a working battery or knowingly disconnected or intentionally damaged the smoke detector, causing it to malfunction.

(c) A tenant is not liable for damages suffered by the landlord if the damage is caused by the landlord's failure to repair the smoke detector within a reasonable time after the tenant requests it to be repaired, considering the availability of material, labor, and utilities.

(d) A landlord of a tenant who is liable under Subsection (a) may obtain or exercise one or more of the remedies in Subsection (e) if:

(1) a lease between the landlord and tenant contains a notice, in underlined or boldfaced print, which states in substance that the tenant must not disconnect or intentionally damage a smoke detector or remove the battery without immediately replacing it with a working battery and that the tenant may be subject to damages, civil penalties, and attorney's fees under Section 92.2611 of the Property Code for not complying with the notice; and

(2) the landlord has given notice to the tenant that the landlord intends to exercise the landlord's remedies under this subchapter if the tenant does not reconnect, repair, or replace the smoke detector or replace the removed battery within seven days after being notified by the landlord to do so.

The notice in Subdivision (2) must be in a separate document furnished to the tenant after the landlord has discovered that the tenant has disconnected or damaged the smoke detector or removed a battery from it.

(e) If a tenant is liable under Subsection (a) and the tenant does not comply with the landlord's notice under Subsection (d), the landlord shall have the following remedies against the tenant:

(1) a court order directing the tenant to comply with the landlord's notice;

(2) a judgment against the tenant for a civil penalty of one month's rent plus $100;

(3) a judgment against the tenant for court costs; and

(4) a judgment against the tenant for reasonable attorney's fees.

(f) A tenant's guest or invitee who suffers damage because of a landlord's failure to install, inspect, or repair a smoke detector as required by this subchapter may recover a judgment against the landlord for the damage. A tenant's guest or invitee who suffers damage because the tenant removed a battery without immediately replacing it with a working battery or because the tenant knowingly disconnected or intentionally damaged the smoke detector, causing it to malfunction, may recover a judgment against the tenant for the damage.

§ 92.262. Agents for Delivery of Notice

A managing or leasing agent, whether residing or maintaining an office on-site or off-site, is the agent of the landlord for purposes of notice and other communications required or permitted by this subchapter.

SUBCHAPTER G. UTILITY CUTOFF

§ 92.301. Landlord Liability to Tenant for Utility Cutoff

(a) A landlord who has expressly or impliedly agreed in the lease to furnish and pay for water, gas, or electric service to the tenant's dwelling is liable to the tenant if the utility company has cut off utility service to the tenant's dwelling or has given written notice to the tenant that such utility service is about to be cut off because of the landlord's nonpayment of the utility bill.

(b) If a landlord is liable to the tenant under Subsection (a) of this section, the tenant may:

(1) pay the utility company money to reconnect or avert the cutoff of utilities according to this section;

(2) terminate the lease if the termination notice is in writing and move-out is to be within 30 days from the date the tenant has notice from the utility company of a future cutoff or notice of an actual cutoff, whichever is sooner;

(3) deduct from the tenant's rent, without necessity of judicial action, the amounts paid to the utility company to reconnect or avert a cutoff;

(4) if the lease is terminated by the tenant, deduct the tenant's security deposit from the tenant's rent without necessity of lawsuit or obtain a refund of the tenant's security deposit pursuant to law;

(5) if the lease is terminated by the tenant, recover a pro rata refund of any advance rentals paid from the date of termination or the date the tenant moves out, whichever is later;

(6) recover actual damages, including but not limited to moving costs, utility connection fees, storage fees, and lost wages from work; and

(7) recover court costs and attorney's fees, excluding any attorney's fees for a cause of action for damages relating to a personal injury.

(c) When deducting for the tenant's payment of the landlord's utility bill under this section, the tenant shall submit to the landlord a copy of a receipt from the utility company which evidences the amount of payment made by the tenant to reconnect or avert cutoff of utilities.

(d) The tenant remedies under this section are effective on the date the tenant has notice from the utility company of a future cutoff or notice of an actual cutoff, whichever is sooner. However, the tenant's remedies under this section shall cease if:

(1) the landlord provides the tenant with written evidence from the utility that all delinquent sums due the utility have been paid in full; and

(2) at the time the tenant receives such evidence, the tenant has not yet terminated the lease or filed suit under this section.

SUBCHAPTER H. RETALIATION
§ 92.331. Retaliation by Landlord
(a) A landlord may not retaliate against a tenant by taking an action described by Subsection (b) because the tenant:

(1) in good faith exercises or attempts to exercise against a landlord a right or remedy granted to the tenant by lease, municipal ordinance, or federal or state statute;

(2) gives a landlord a notice to repair or exercise a remedy under this chapter; or

(3) complains to a governmental entity responsible for enforcing building or housing codes, a public utility, or a civic or nonprofit agency, and the tenant:

(A) claims a building or housing code violation or utility problem; and

(B) believes in good faith that the complaint is valid and that the violation or problem occurred.

(b) A landlord may not, within six months after the date of the tenant's action under Subsection (a), retaliate against the tenant by:

(1) filing an eviction proceeding, except for the grounds stated by Section 92.332;

(2) depriving the tenant of the use of the premises, except for reasons authorized by law;

(3) decreasing services to the tenant;

(4) increasing the tenant's rent or terminating the tenant's lease; or

(5) engaging, in bad faith, in a course of conduct that materially interferes with the tenant's rights under the tenant's lease.

§ 92.332. Nonretaliation
(a) The landlord is not liable for retaliation under this subchapter if the landlord proves that the action was not made for purposes of retaliation, nor is the landlord liable, unless the action violates a prior court order under Section 92.0563, for:

(1) increasing rent under an escalation clause in a written lease for utilities, taxes, or insurance; or

(2) increasing rent or reducing services as part of a pattern of rent increases or service reductions for an entire multidwelling project.

(b) An eviction or lease termination based on the following circumstances, which are valid grounds for eviction or lease termination in any event, does not constitute retaliation:

(1) the tenant is delinquent in rent when the landlord gives notice to vacate or files an eviction action;

(2) the tenant, a member of the tenant's family, or a guest or invitee of the tenant intentionally damages property on the premises or by word or conduct threatens the personal safety of the landlord, the landlord's employees, or another tenant;

(3) the tenant has materially breached the lease, other than by holding over, by an action such as violating written lease provisions prohibiting serious misconduct or criminal acts, except as provided by this section;

(4) the tenant holds over after giving notice of termination or intent to vacate;

(5) the tenant holds over after the landlord gives notice of termination at the end of the rental term and the tenant does not take action under Section 92.331 until after the landlord gives notice of termination; or

(6) the tenant holds over and the landlord's notice of termination is motivated by a good faith belief that the tenant, a member of the tenant's family, or a guest or invitee of the tenant might:

(A) adversely affect the quiet enjoyment by other tenants or neighbors;

(B) materially affect the health or safety of the landlord, other tenants, or neighbors; or

(C) damage the property of the landlord, other tenants, or neighbors.

§ 92.333. Tenant Remedies
In addition to other remedies provided by law, if a landlord retaliates against a tenant under this subchapter, the tenant may recover from the landlord a civil penalty of one month's rent plus $500, actual damages, court costs, and reasonable attorney's fees in an action for recovery of property damages, moving costs, actual expenses, civil penalties, or declaratory or injunctive relief, less any delinquent rents or other sums for which the tenant is liable to the landlord. If the tenant's rent payment to the landlord is subsidized in whole or in part by a governmental entity, the civil penalty granted under this section shall reflect the fair market rent of the dwelling plus $500.

§ 92.334. Invalid Complaints
(a) If a tenant files or prosecutes a suit for retaliatory action based on a complaint asserted under Section 92.331(a)(3), and the government building or housing inspector or utility company representative visits the premises and determines in writing that a violation of a building or housing code does not exist or that a utility problem does not exist, there is a rebuttable presumption that the tenant acted in bad faith.

(b) If a tenant files or prosecutes a suit under this subchapter in bad faith, the landlord may recover possession of the dwelling unit and may recover from the tenant a civil penalty of one month's rent plus $500, court costs, and reasonable attorney's fees. If the tenant's rent payment to the landlord is subsidized in whole or in part by a governmental entity, the civil penalty granted under this section shall reflect the fair market rent of the dwelling plus $500.

§ 92.335. Eviction Suits

In an eviction suit, retaliation by the landlord under Section 92.331 is a defense and a rent deduction lawfully made by the tenant under this chapter is a defense for nonpayment of the rent to the extent allowed by this chapter. Other judicial actions under this chapter may not be joined with an eviction suit or asserted as a defense or crossclaim in an eviction suit.

SUBCHAPTER I. RENTAL APPLICATION DEPOSITS

§ 92.351. Definitions

For purposes of this subchapter:

(1) "Application deposit" means a sum of money that is given to the landlord in connection with a rental application and that is refundable to the applicant if the applicant is rejected as a tenant.

(2) "Applicant" or "rental applicant" means a person who makes an application to a landlord for rental of a dwelling.

(3) "Co-applicant" means a person who makes an application for rental of a dwelling with other applicants and who plans to live in the dwelling with other applicants.

(4) "Deposited" means deposited in an account of the landlord or the landlord's agent in a bank or other financial institution.

(5) "Landlord" means a prospective landlord to whom a person makes application for rental of a dwelling.

(6) "Required date" means the required date for any acceptance of the applicant under Section 92.352.

§ 92.352. Rejection of Applicant

(a) The applicant is deemed rejected by the landlord if the landlord does not give notice of acceptance of the applicant on or before the seventh day after the:

(1) date the applicant submits a completed rental application to the landlord on an application form furnished by the landlord; or

(2) date the landlord accepts an application deposit if the landlord does not furnish the applicant an application form.

(b) A landlord's rejection of one co-applicant shall be deemed as a rejection of all co-applicants.

§ 92.353. Procedures for Notice or Refund

(a) Except as provided in Subsection (b), a landlord is presumed to have given notice of an applicant's acceptance or rejection if the notice is by:

(1) telephone to the applicant, co-applicant, or a person living with the applicant or co-applicant on or before the required date; or

(2) United States mail, addressed to the applicant and postmarked on or before the required date.

(b) If a rental applicant requests that any acceptance of the applicant or any refund of the applicant's application deposit be mailed to the applicant, the landlord must mail the refund check to the applicant at the address furnished by the applicant.

(c) If the date of required notice of acceptance or required refund of an application deposit is a Saturday, Sunday, or state or federal holiday, the required date shall be extended to the end of the next day following the Saturday, Sunday, or holiday.

§ 92.354. Liability of Landlord

A landlord who in bad faith fails to refund an application deposit in violation of this subchapter is liable for an amount equal to the sum of $100, three times the amount of the application deposit, and the applicant's reasonable attorney's fees in a suit to recover the deposit.

CHAPTER 93. COMMERCIAL TENANCIES

§ 93.001. Applicability of Chapter

(a) This chapter applies only to the relationship between landlords and tenants of commercial rental property.

(b) For purposes of this chapter, "commercial rental property" means rental property that is not covered by Chapter 92.

§ 93.002. Interruption of Utilities, Removal of Property, and Exclusion of Commercial Tenant

(a) A landlord or a landlord's agent may not interrupt or cause the interruption of utility service paid for directly to the utility company by a tenant unless the interruption results from bona fide repairs, construction, or an emergency.

(b) A landlord may not remove a door, window, or attic hatchway cover or a lock, latch, hinge, hinge pin, doorknob, or other mechanism connected to a door, window, or attic hatchway cover from premises leased to a tenant or remove furniture, fixtures, or appliances furnished by the landlord from premises leased to a tenant unless the landlord removes the item for a bona fide repair or replacement. If a landlord removes any of the items listed in this subsection for a bona fide repair or replacement, the repair or replacement must be promptly performed.

(c) A landlord may not intentionally prevent a tenant from entering the leased premises except by judicial process unless the exclusion results from:

(1) bona fide repairs, construction, or an emergency;

(2) removing the contents of premises abandoned by a tenant; or

(3) changing the door locks of a tenant who is delinquent in paying at least part of the rent.

(d) A tenant is presumed to have abandoned the premises if goods, equipment, or other property, in an amount substantial enough to indicate a probable intent to abandon the premises, is being or has been removed from the premises and the removal is not within the normal course of the tenant's business.

(e) A landlord may remove and store any property of a tenant that remains on premises that are abandoned. In addition to the landlord's other rights, the landlord may dispose of the stored property if the tenant does not claim the property within 60 days after the date the property is stored. The landlord shall deliver by certified mail to the tenant at the tenant's last known address a notice stating that the landlord may dispose of the tenant's property if the tenant does not claim the property within 60 days after the date the property is stored.

(f) If a landlord or a landlord's agent changes the door lock of a tenant who is delinquent in paying rent, the landlord or agent must place a written notice on the tenant's front door stating the name and the address or telephone number of the individual or company from which the new key may be obtained. The new key is required to be provided only during the tenant's regular business hours and only if the tenant pays the delinquent rent.

(g) If a landlord or a landlord's agent violates this section, the tenant may:

(1) either recover possession of the premises or terminate the lease; and

(2) recover from the landlord an amount equal to the sum of the tenant's actual damages, one month's rent or $500, whichever is greater, reasonable attorney's fees, and court costs, less any delinquent rents or other sums for which the tenant is liable to the landlord.

(h) A lease supersedes this section to the extent of any conflict.

§ 93.003. Commercial Tenant's Right of Reentry After Unlawful Lockout

(a) If a landlord has locked a tenant out of leased premises in violation of Section 93.002, the tenant may recover possession of the premises as provided by this section.

(b) The tenant must file with the justice court in the precinct in which the rental premises are located a sworn complaint for reentry, specifying the facts of the alleged unlawful lockout by the landlord or the landlord's agent. The tenant must also state orally under oath to the justice the facts of the alleged unlawful lockout.

(c) If the tenant has complied with Subsection (b) and if the justice reasonably believes an unlawful lockout has likely occurred, the justice may issue, ex parte, a writ of reentry that entitles the tenant to immediate and temporary possession of the premises, pending a final hearing on the tenant's sworn complaint for reentry.

(d) The writ of reentry must be served on either the landlord or the landlord's management company, on-premises manager, or rent collector in the same manner as a writ of possession in a forcible detainer action. A sheriff or constable may use reasonable force in executing a writ of reentry under this section.

(e) The landlord is entitled to a hearing on the tenant's sworn complaint for reentry. The writ of reentry must notify the landlord of the right to a hearing. The hearing shall be held not earlier than the first day and not later than the seventh day after the date the landlord requests a hearing.

(f) If the landlord fails to request a hearing on the tenant's sworn complaint for reentry before the eighth day after the date of service of the writ of reentry on the landlord under Subsection (d), a judgment for court costs may be rendered against the landlord.

(g) A party may appeal from the court's judgment at the hearing on the sworn complaint for reentry in the same manner as a party may appeal a judgment in a forcible detainer suit.

(h) If a writ of possession is issued, it supersedes a writ of reentry.

(i) If the landlord or the person on whom a writ of reentry is served fails to immediately comply with the writ or later disobeys the writ, the failure is grounds for contempt of court against the landlord or the person on whom the writ was served, under Section 21.002, Government Code. If the writ is disobeyed, the tenant or the tenant's attorney may file in the court in which the reentry action is pending an affidavit stating the name of the person who has disobeyed the writ and describing the acts or omissions constituting the disobedience. On receipt of an affidavit, the justice shall issue a show cause order, directing the person to appear on a designated date and show cause why he should not be adjudged

in contempt of court. If the justice finds, after considering the evidence at the hearing, that the person has directly or indirectly disobeyed the writ, the justice may commit the person to jail without bail until the person purges himself of the contempt in a manner and form as the justice may direct. If the person disobeyed the writ before receiving the show cause order but has complied with the writ after receiving the order, the justice may find the person in contempt and assess punishment under Section 21.002(c), Government Code.

(j) This section does not affect a tenant's right to pursue a separate cause of action under Section 93.002.

(k) If a tenant in bad faith files a sworn complaint for reentry resulting in a writ of reentry being served on the landlord or landlord's agent, the landlord may in a separate cause of action recover from the tenant an amount equal to actual damages, one month's rent or $500, whichever is greater, reasonable attorney's fees, and costs of court, less any sums for which the landlord is liable to the tenant.

(l) The fee for filing a sworn complaint for reentry is the same as that for filing a civil action in justice court. The fee for service of a writ of reentry is the same as that for service of a writ of possession. The fee for service of a show cause order is the same as that for service of a civil citation. The justice may defer payment of the tenant's filing fees and service costs for the sworn complaint for reentry and writ of reentry. Court costs may be waived only if the tenant executes a pauper's affidavit.

(m) This section does not affect the rights of a landlord or tenant in a forcible detainer or forcible entry and detainer action.

§ 93.006. Retention of Security Deposit; Accounting

(a) Before returning a security deposit, the landlord may deduct from the deposit damages and charges for which the tenant is legally liable under the lease or damages and charges that result from a breach of the lease.

(b) The landlord may not retain any portion of a security deposit to cover normal wear and tear. In this subsection, "normal wear and tear" means deterioration that results from the intended use of the commercial premises, including breakage or malfunction due to age or deteriorated condition, but the term does not include deterioration that results from negligence, carelessness, accident, or abuse of the premises, equipment, or chattels by the tenant or by a guest or invitee of the tenant.

(c) If the landlord retains all or part of a security deposit under this section, the landlord shall give to the tenant the balance of the security deposit, if any, together with a written description and itemized list of all deductions. The landlord is not required to give the tenant a description and itemized list of deductions if:

(1) the tenant owes rent when the tenant surrenders possession of the premises; and

(2) no controversy exists concerning the amount of rent owed.

§ 93.007. Cessation of Owner's Interest

(a) If the owner's interest in the premises is terminated by sale, assignment, death, appointment of a receiver, bankruptcy, or otherwise, the new owner is liable for the return of the security deposit according to this chapter from the date title to the premises is acquired, regardless of whether an acknowledgement is given to the tenant under Subsection (b).

(b) The person who no longer owns an interest in the rental premises remains liable for a security deposit received while the person was the owner until the new owner delivers to the tenant a signed statement acknowledging that the new owner has received and is responsible for the tenant's security deposit and specifying the exact dollar amount of the deposit. The amount of the security deposit is the greater of:

(1) the amount provided in the tenant's lease; or

(2) the amount provided in an estoppel certificate prepared by the owner at the time the lease was executed or prepared by the new owner at the time the commercial property is transferred.

(c) Subsection (a) does not apply to a real estate mortgage lienholder who acquires title by foreclosure.

§ 93.008. Records

The landlord shall keep accurate records of all security deposits.

§ 93.009. Tenant's Forwarding Address

(a) The landlord is not obligated to return a tenant's security deposit or give the tenant a written description of damages and charges until the tenant gives the landlord a written statement of the tenant's forwarding address for the purpose of refunding the security deposit.

(b) The tenant does not forfeit the right to a refund of the security deposit or the right to receive a description of damages and charges for failing to give a forwarding address to the landlord.

§ 93.010. Liability for Withholding Last Month's Rent

(a) The tenant may not withhold payment of any portion of the last month's rent on grounds that the security deposit is security for unpaid rent.

(b) A tenant who violates this section is presumed to have acted in bad faith. A tenant who in bad faith violates this section is liable to the landlord for an amount equal to three times the rent wrongfully withheld and the landlord's reasonable attorney's fees in a suit to recover the rent.

§ 93.011. Liability of Landlord

(a) A landlord who in bad faith retains a security deposit in violation of this chapter is liable for an amount equal to the sum of $100, three times the portion of the deposit wrongfully withheld, and the tenant's reasonable attorney's fees incurred in a suit to recover the deposit after the period prescribed for returning the deposit expires.

(b) A landlord who in bad faith does not provide a written description and itemized list of damages and charges in violation of this chapter:

(1) forfeits the right to withhold any portion of the security deposit or to bring suit against the tenant for damages to the premises; and

(2) is liable for the tenant's reasonable attorney's fees in a suit to recover the deposit.

(c) In a suit brought by a tenant under this chapter, the landlord has the burden of proving that the retention of any portion of the security deposit was reasonable.

(d) A landlord who fails to return a security deposit or to provide a written description and itemized list of deductions on or before the 30th day after the date the tenant surrenders possession is presumed to have acted in bad faith.

CHAPTER 94. MANUFACTURED HOME TENANCIES
SUBCHAPTER A. GENERAL PROVISIONS

§ 94.001. Definitions

In this chapter:

(1) "Landlord" means the owner or manager of a manufactured home community and includes an employee or agent of the landlord.

(2) "Lease agreement" means a written agreement between a landlord and a tenant that establishes the terms, conditions, and other provisions for placing a manufactured home on the premises of a manufactured home community.

(3) "Manufactured home" has the meaning assigned by Section 3, Texas Manufactured Housing Standards Act (Article 5221f, Vernon's Texas Civil Statutes), and for purposes of this chapter, a reference to a manufactured home includes a recreational vehicle.

(4) "Manufactured home community" means a parcel of land on which four or more lots are offered for lease for installing and occupying manufactured homes.

(5) "Manufactured home community rules" means the rules provided in a written document that establish the policies and regulations of the manufactured home community, including regulations relating to the use, occupancy, and quiet enjoyment of and the health, safety, and welfare of tenants of the manufactured home community.

(6) "Manufactured home lot" means the space allocated in the lease agreement for the placement of the tenant's manufactured home and the area adjacent to that space designated in the lease agreement for the tenant's exclusive use.

(7) "Normal wear and tear" means deterioration that results from intended use of the premises, including breakage or malfunction due to age or deteriorated condition, but the term does not include deterioration that results from negligence, carelessness, accident, or abuse of the premises, equipment, or chattels by the tenant, a member of the tenant's household, or a guest or invitee of the tenant.

(8) "Premises" means a tenant's manufactured home lot, any area or facility the lease authorizes the tenant to use, and the appurtenances, grounds, and facilities held out for the use of tenants generally.

(9) "Recreational vehicle" means a motor vehicle primarily designed as a temporary living quarters for recreational camping or travel use.

(10) "Tenant" means a person who is:

(A) authorized by a lease agreement to occupy a lot to the exclusion of others in a manufactured home community; and

(B) obligated under the lease agreement to pay rent, fees, and other charges.

§ 94.002. Applicability

(a) This chapter applies only to the relationship between a landlord who leases property in a manufactured home community and a tenant leasing property in the manufactured home community for the purpose of situating a manufactured home or a recreational vehicle on the property.

(b) This chapter does not apply to the relationship between:

(1) a landlord who owns a manufactured home and a tenant who leases the manufactured home from the landlord;

(2) a landlord who leases property in a manufactured home community and a tenant leasing property in the manufactured home community for the placement of personal property to be used for human habitation, excluding a manufactured home or a recreational vehicle; or

(3) a landlord and an employee or an agent of the landlord.

§ 94.003. Waiver of Rights and Duties

A provision in a lease agreement or a manufactured home community rule that purports to waive a right or to exempt a landlord or a tenant from a duty or from liability under this chapter is void.

§ 94.004. Landlord's Right of Entry

(a) Except as provided by this chapter, the landlord may not enter a tenant's manufactured home unless:

(1) the tenant is present and gives consent; or

(2) the tenant has previously given written consent.

(b) The written consent under Subsection (a)(2) must specify the date and time entry is permitted and is valid only for the date and time specified. The tenant may revoke the consent without penalty at any time by notifying the landlord in writing that the consent has been revoked.

(c) The landlord may enter the tenant's manufactured home in a reasonable manner and at a reasonable time if:

(1) an emergency exists; or

(2) the tenant abandons the manufactured home.

§ 94.005. Common Area Facilities

Each common area facility, if any, must be open or available to tenants. The landlord shall post the hours of operation or availability of the facility in a conspicuous place at the facility.

§ 94.006. Tenant Meetings

(a) Except as provided by Subsection (b), a landlord may not interfere with meetings by tenants of the manufactured home community related to manufactured home living.

(b) Any limitations on meetings by tenants in the common area facilities must be included in the manufactured home community rules.

§ 94.007. Cash Rental Payments

(a) A landlord shall accept a tenant's cash rental payment unless the lease agreement requires the tenant to make rental payments by check, money order, or other traceable or negotiable instrument.

(b) A landlord who receives a cash rental payment shall:2

(1) provide the tenant with a written receipt; and

(2) enter the payment date and amount in a record book maintained by the landlord.

(c) A tenant or a governmental entity or civic association acting on the tenant's behalf may file suit against a landlord to enjoin a violation of this section.

§ 94.008. Manufactured Home Community Rules

(a) A landlord may adopt manufactured home community rules that are not arbitrary or capricious.

(b) Manufactured home community rules are considered part of the lease agreement.

(c) The landlord may add to or amend manufactured home community rules. If the landlord adds or amends a rule:

(1) the rule is not effective until the 30th day after the date each tenant is provided with a written copy of the added or amended rule; and

(2) if a tenant is required to take any action that requires the expenditure of funds in excess of $25 to comply with the rule, the landlord shall give the tenant at least 90 days after the date each tenant is provided with a written copy of the added or amended rule to comply with the rule.

§ 94.009. Notice to Tenant at Primary Residence

(a) If, at the time of signing a lease agreement or lease renewal, a tenant gives written notice to the tenant's landlord that the tenant does not occupy the manufactured home lot as a primary residence and requests in writing that the landlord send notices to the tenant at the tenant's primary residence and provides to the landlord the address of the tenant's primary residence, the landlord shall mail to the tenant's primary residence all notices required by the lease agreement, by this chapter, or by Chapter 24.

(b) The tenant shall notify the landlord in writing of any change in the tenant's primary residence address. Oral notices of change are insufficient.

(c) A notice to a tenant's primary residence under Subsection (a) may be sent by regular United States mail and is considered as having been given on the date of postmark of the notice.

(d) If there is more than one tenant on a lease agreement, the landlord is not required under this section to send notices to the primary residence of more than one tenant.

(e) This section does not apply if notice is actually hand delivered to and received by a person 16 years of age or older occupying the leased premises.

§ 94.010. Disclosure of Ownership and Management

(a) A landlord shall disclose to a tenant, or to any governmental official or employee acting in an official capacity, according to this section:

(1) the name and either a street or post office box address of the holder of record title, according to the deed records in the county clerk's office, of the premises leased by the tenant or inquired about by the governmental official or employee acting in an official capacity; and

(2) if an entity located off-site from the manufactured home community is primarily responsible for managing the leased premises, the name and street address of that entity.

(b) Disclosure to a tenant under Subsection (a) must be made by:

(1) giving the information in writing to the tenant on or before the seventh day after the date the landlord receives the tenant's written request for the information;

(2) continuously posting the information in a conspicuous place in the manufactured home community or the office of the on-site manager or on the outside of the entry door to the office of the on-site manager on or before the seventh day after the date the landlord receives the tenant's written request for the information; or

(3) including the information in a copy of the tenant's lease or in written manufactured home community rules given to the tenant before the tenant requests the information.

(c) Disclosure of information to a tenant may be made under Subsection (b)(1) or (2) before the tenant requests the information.

(d) Disclosure of information to a governmental official or employee must be made by giving the information in writing to the official or employee on or before the seventh day after the date the landlord receives a written request for the information from the official or employee.

(e) A correction to the information may be made by any of the methods authorized and must be made within the period prescribed by this section for providing the information.

(f) For the purposes of this section, an owner or property manager may disclose either an actual name or an assumed name if an assumed name certificate has been recorded with the county clerk.

(g) A landlord who provides information under this section violates this section if:

(1) the information becomes incorrect because a name or address changes; and

(2) the landlord fails to correct the information given to a tenant on or before the 15th day after the date the information becomes incorrect.

§ 94.011. Landlord's Agent for Service of Process

(a) In a lawsuit by a tenant to enforce a legal obligation of the owner as landlord of the manufactured home community, the owner's agent for service of process is determined according to this section.

(b) The owner's management company, on-site manager, or rent collector for the manufactured home community is the owner's authorized agent for service of process unless the owner's name and business street address have been furnished in writing to the tenant.

§ 94.012. Venue

Venue for an action under this chapter is governed by Section 15.0115, Civil Practice and Remedies Code.

LEASE AGREEMENT

§ 94.051. Information to be Provided to Prospective Tenant

At the time the landlord receives an application from a prospective tenant, the landlord shall give the tenant a copy of:

(1) the proposed lease agreement for the manufactured home community;

(2) any manufactured home community rules; and

(3) a separate disclosure statement with the following prominently printed in at least 10-point type:

"You have the legal right to an initial lease term of six months. If you prefer a different lease period, you and your landlord may negotiate a shorter or longer lease period. After the initial lease period expires, you and your landlord may negotiate a new lease term by mutual agreement. Regardless of the term of the lease, the landlord must give you at least 60 days' notice if the landlord will not renew your lease and will require that you relocate your manufactured home or recreational vehicle. During the 60-day period, you must continue to pay all rent and other amounts due under the lease agreement, including late charges, if any."

§ 94.052. Term of Lease

(a) A landlord shall offer the tenant a lease agreement with an initial lease term of at least six months. If the tenant requests a lease agreement with a different lease period, the landlord and the tenant may mutually agree to a shorter or longer lease period. The landlord and the tenant may mutually agree to subsequent lease periods of any length for each renewal of the lease agreement.

(b) Regardless of the term of the lease, the landlord must provide notice to the tenant not later than the 60th day before the date of the expiration of the lease if the landlord does not renew the lease. During the 60-day period, the tenant must pay all rent and other amounts due under the lease agreement, including late charges, if any.

§ 94.053. Lease Requirements and Disclosures

(a) A lease agreement must be:

(1) typed or printed in legible handwriting; and

(2) signed by the landlord and the tenant.

(b) The landlord shall provide the tenant with a copy of the lease agreement and a current copy of the manufactured home community rules after the lease has been signed.

(c) A lease agreement must contain the following information:

(1) the address or number of the manufactured home lot and the number and location of any accompanying parking spaces;

(2) the lease term;

(3) the rental amount;

(4) the interval at which rent must be paid and the date on which periodic rental payments are due;

(5) any late charge or fee or charge for any service or facility;

(6) the amount of any security deposit;

(7) a description of the landlord's maintenance responsibilities;

(8) the telephone number of the person who may be contacted for emergency maintenance;

(9) the name and address of the person designated to accept official notices for the landlord;

(10) the penalty the landlord may impose for the tenant's early termination as provided by Section 94.201;

(11) the grounds for eviction as provided by Subchapter E;

(12) a disclosure of the landlord's right to terminate the lease agreement if there is a change in the land use of the manufactured home community during the lease term as provided by Section 94.204;

(13) a disclosure of any incorporation by reference of an addendum relating to submetering of utility services;

(14) a prominent disclosure informing the tenant that Chapter 94, Property Code, governs certain rights granted to the tenant and obligations imposed on the landlord by law;

(15) if there is a temporary zoning permit for the land use of the manufactured home community, the date the zoning permit expires; and

(16) any other terms or conditions of occupancy not expressly included in the manufactured home community rules.

(d) A lease provision requiring an increase in rent or in fees or charges during the lease term must be initialed by the tenant or the provision is void.

(e) Any illegal or unconscionable provision in a lease is void. If a lease provision is determined void, the invalidity of the provision does not affect other provisions of the lease that can be given effect without reference to the invalid provision.

§ 94.054. Disclosure by Tenant Required

A tenant shall disclose to the landlord before the lease agreement is signed the name and address of any person who holds a lien on the tenant's manufactured home.

§ 94.055. Notice of Lease Renewal

(a) The landlord shall provide a tenant a notice to vacate the leased premises or an offer of lease renewal:

(1) not later than the 60th day before the date the current lease term expires; or

(2) if the lease is a month-to-month lease, not later than the 60th day before the date the landlord intends to terminate the current term of the lease.

(b) If the landlord offers to renew the lease, the landlord shall notify the tenant of the proposed rent amount and any change in the lease terms. The notice must also include a statement informing the tenant that the tenant's failure to reject the landlord's offer to renew the lease within the 30-day period prescribed by Subsection (c) will result in the renewal of the lease under the modified terms as provided by Subsection (c).

(c) If the landlord offers to renew the lease, the tenant must notify the landlord not later than the 30th day before the date the current lease expires whether the tenant rejects the terms of the offer and intends to vacate the leased premises on the date the current lease term expires. If the tenant fails to provide the notice within the period prescribed by this subsection, the lease is renewed under the modified terms beginning on the first day after the date of the expiration of the current lease term.

(d) Notwithstanding Subsection (a), the landlord may request a tenant to vacate the leased premises before the end of the notice period prescribed by Subsection (a) only if the landlord compensates the tenant in advance for relocation expenses, including the cost of moving and installing the manufactured home at a new location.

§ 94.056. Penalty for Late Payment

A landlord may assess a penalty for late payment of rent or another fee or charge if the payment is not remitted on or before the date stipulated in the lease agreement.

§ 94.057. Assignment of Lease and Sublease

(a) A landlord may prohibit a tenant from assigning a lease agreement or subleasing the leased premises if the prohibition is included in the lease agreement.

(b) If the landlord permits a tenant to assign a lease agreement or sublease the leased premises, the lease agreement must specify the conditions under which the tenant may enter into an assignment or sublease agreement.

SECURITY DEPOSIT

§ 94.101. Security Deposit

In this chapter, "security deposit" means any advance of money, other than a rental application deposit or an advance payment of rent, that is intended primarily to secure performance under a lease of a lot in a manufactured home community that has been entered into by a landlord and a tenant.

§ 94.102. Security Deposit Permitted

(a) At the time the tenant executes the initial lease agreement, the landlord may require a security deposit.

(b) The landlord shall keep accurate records relating to security deposits.

§ 94.103. Obligation to Refund

(a) Except as provided by this subchapter, the landlord shall refund the security deposit not later than the 30th day after the date the tenant surrenders the manufactured home lot.

(b) A requirement that a tenant give advance notice of surrender as a condition for refunding the security deposit is effective only if the requirement is underlined or is printed in conspicuous bold print in the lease.

(c) The tenant's claim to the security deposit takes priority over the claim of any creditor of the landlord, including a trustee in bankruptcy.

§ 94.104. Conditions for Retention of Security Deposit or Rent Prepayment

(a) Except as provided by Subsection (b), a landlord who receives a security deposit or rent prepayment for a manufactured home lot from a tenant who fails to occupy the lot according to a lease agreement between the landlord and the tenant may not retain the security deposit or rent prepayment if:

(1) the tenant secures a replacement tenant satisfactory to the landlord and the replacement tenant occupies the lot on or before the commencement date of the lease; or

(2) the landlord secures a replacement tenant satisfactory to the landlord and the replacement tenant occupies the lot on or before the commencement date of the lease.

(b) If the landlord secures the replacement tenant, the landlord may retain and deduct from the security deposit or rent prepayment either:

(1) an amount agreed to in the lease agreement as a lease cancellation fee; or

(2) actual expenses incurred by the landlord in securing the replacement tenant, including a reasonable amount for the time spent by the landlord in securing the replacement tenant.

§ 94.105. Retention of Security Deposit; Accounting

(a) Before returning a security deposit, the landlord may deduct from the deposit damages and charges for which the tenant is legally liable under the lease agreement or as a result of breaching the lease.

(b) The landlord may not retain any portion of a security deposit to cover normal wear and tear.

(c) If the landlord retains all or part of a security deposit under this section, the landlord shall give to the tenant the balance of the security deposit, if any, together with a written description and itemized list of all deductions. The landlord is not required to give the tenant a description and itemized list of deductions if:

(1) the tenant owes rent when the tenant surrenders possession of the manufactured home lot; and

(2) no controversy exists concerning the amount of rent owed.

§ 94.106. Cessation of Owner's Interest

(a) If the owner's interest in the premises is terminated by sale, assignment, death, appointment of a receiver, bankruptcy, or otherwise, the new owner is liable for the return of security deposits according to this subchapter from the date title to the premises is acquired, regardless of whether notice is given to the tenant under Subsection (b).

(b) The person who no longer owns an interest in the leased premises remains liable for a security deposit received while the person was the owner until the new owner delivers to the tenant a signed statement acknowledging that the new owner has received and is responsible for the tenant's security deposit and specifying the exact dollar amount of the deposit.

(c) Subsection (a) does not apply to a real estate mortgage lienholder who acquires title by foreclosure.

§ 94.107. Tenant's Forwarding Address

(a) A landlord is not obligated to return a tenant's security deposit or give the tenant a written description of damages and charges until the tenant gives the landlord a written statement of the tenant's forwarding address for the purpose of refunding the security deposit.

(b) The tenant does not forfeit the right to a refund of the security deposit or the right to receive a description of damages and charges merely for failing to give a forwarding address to the landlord.

§ 94.108. Liability for Withholding Last Month's Rent

(a) A tenant may not withhold payment of any portion of the last month's rent on grounds that the security deposit is security for unpaid rent.

(b) A tenant who violates this section is presumed to have acted in bad faith. A tenant who in bad faith violates this section is liable to the landlord for an amount equal to three times the rent wrongfully withheld and the landlord's reasonable attorney's fees in a suit to recover the rent.

§ 94.109. Liability of Landlord

(a) A landlord who in bad faith retains a security deposit in violation of this subchapter is liable for an amount equal to the sum of $100, three times the portion of the deposit wrongfully withheld, and the tenant's reasonable attorney's fees in a suit to recover the deposit.

(b) A landlord who in bad faith does not provide a written description and itemized list of damages and charges in violation of this subchapter:

(1) forfeits the right to withhold any portion of the security deposit or to bring suit against the tenant for damages to the premises; and

(2) is liable for the tenant's reasonable attorney's fees in a suit to recover the deposit.

(c) In an action brought by a tenant under this subchapter, the landlord has the burden of proving that the retention of any portion of the security deposit was reasonable.

(d) A landlord who fails either to return a security deposit or to provide a written description and itemization of deductions on or before the 30th day after the date the tenant surrenders possession is presumed to have acted in bad faith.

PREMISES CONDITION, MAINTENANCE, AND REPAIRS

§ 94.151. Warranty of Suitability

By executing a lease agreement, the landlord warrants that the manufactured home lot is suitable for the installation of a manufactured home during the term of the lease agreement.

§ 94.152. Landlord's Maintenance Obligations

The landlord shall:

(1) comply with any code, statute, ordinance, and administrative rule applicable to the manufactured home community;

(2) maintain all common areas, if any, of the manufactured home community in a clean and useable condition;

(3) maintain all utility lines installed in the manufactured home community by the landlord unless the utility lines are maintained by a public utility or political subdivision, including a municipality;

(4) maintain individual mailboxes for the tenants in accordance with United States Postal Service regulations unless mailboxes are permitted to be located on the tenant's manufactured home lot;

(5) maintain roads in the manufactured home community to the extent necessary to provide access to each tenant's manufactured home lot;

(6) provide services for the common collection and removal of garbage and solid waste from within the manufactured home community; and

(7) repair or remedy conditions on the premises that materially affect the physical health or safety of an ordinary tenant of the manufactured home community.

§ 94.153. Landlord's Repair Obligations

(a) This section does not apply to a condition present in or on a tenant's manufactured home.

(b) A landlord shall make a diligent effort to repair or remedy a condition if:

(1) the tenant specifies the condition in a notice to the person to whom or to the place at which rent is normally paid;

(2) the tenant is not delinquent in the payment of rent at the time notice is given; and

(3) the condition materially affects the physical health or safety of an ordinary tenant.

(c) Unless the condition was caused by normal wear and tear, the landlord does not have a duty during the lease term or a renewal or extension to repair or remedy a condition caused by:

(1) the tenant;

(2) a lawful occupant of the tenant's manufactured home lot;

(3) a member of the tenant's family; or

(4) a guest or invitee of the tenant.

(d) This subchapter does not require the landlord:

(1) to furnish utilities from a utility company if as a practical matter the utility lines of the company are not reasonably available; or

(2) to furnish security guards.

§ 94.154. Burden of Proof

(a) Except as provided by this section, the tenant has the burden of proof in a judicial action to enforce a right resulting from the landlord's failure to repair or remedy a condition under Section 94.153.

(b) If the landlord does not provide a written explanation for delay in performing a duty to repair or remedy on or before the fifth day after receiving from the tenant a written demand for an explanation, the landlord has the burden of proving that the landlord made a diligent effort to repair and that a reasonable time for repair did not elapse.

§ 94.155. Casualty Loss

(a) If a condition results from an insured casualty loss, such as fire, smoke, hail, explosion, or a similar cause, the period for repair does not begin until the landlord receives the insurance proceeds.

(b) If after a casualty loss the leased premises are as a practical matter totally unusable for the purposes for which the premises were leased and if the casualty loss is not caused by the negligence or fault of the tenant, a member of the tenant's family, or a guest or invitee of the tenant, either the landlord or the tenant may terminate the lease by giving written notice to the other any time before repairs are completed. If the lease is terminated, the tenant is entitled only to a pro rata refund of rent from the date the tenant moves out and to a refund of any security deposit otherwise required by law.

(c) If after a casualty loss the leased premises are partially unusable for the purposes for which the premises were leased and if the casualty loss is not caused by the negligence or fault of the tenant, a member of the tenant's family, or a guest or invitee of the tenant, the tenant is entitled to reduction in the rent in an amount proportionate to the extent the premises are unusable because of the casualty, but only on judgment of a county or district court. A landlord and tenant may agree otherwise in a written lease.

§ 94.156. Landlord Liability and Tenant Remedies; Notice and Time for Repair

(a) A landlord's liability under this section is subject to Section 94.153(c) regarding conditions that are caused by a tenant.

(b) A landlord is liable to a tenant as provided by this subchapter if:

(1) the tenant has given the landlord notice to repair or remedy a condition by giving that notice to the person to whom or to the place where the tenant's rent is normally paid;

(2) the condition materially affects the physical health or safety of an ordinary tenant;

(3) the tenant has given the landlord a subsequent written notice to repair or remedy the condition after a reasonable time to repair or remedy the condition following the notice given under Subdivision (1) or the tenant has given the notice under Subdivision (1) by sending that notice by certified mail, return receipt requested, or by registered mail;

(4) the landlord has had a reasonable time to repair or remedy the condition after the landlord received the tenant's notice under Subdivision (1) and, if applicable, the tenant's subsequent notice under Subdivision (3);

(5) the landlord has not made a diligent effort to repair or remedy the condition after the landlord received the tenant's notice under Subdivision (1) and, if applicable, the tenant's notice under Subdivision (3); and

(6) the tenant was not delinquent in the payment of rent at the time any notice required by this subsection was given.

(c) For purposes of Subsection (b)(4) or (5), a landlord is considered to have received the tenant's notice when the landlord or the landlord's agent or employee has actually received the notice or when the United States Postal Service has attempted to deliver the notice to the landlord.

(d) For purposes of Subsection (b)(3) or (4), in determining whether a period of time is a reasonable time to repair or remedy a condition, there is a rebuttable presumption that seven days is a reasonable time. To rebut that presumption, the date on which the landlord received the tenant's notice, the severity and nature of the condition, and the reasonable availability of materials and labor and of utilities from a utility company must be considered.

(e) Except as provided by Subsection (f), a tenant to whom a landlord is liable under Subsection (b) may:

(1) terminate the lease;

(2) have the condition repaired or remedied according to Section 94.157;

(3) deduct from the tenant's rent, without necessity of judicial action, the cost of the repair or remedy according to Section 94.157; and

(4) obtain judicial remedies according to Section 94.159.

(f) A tenant who elects to terminate the lease under Subsection (e) is:

(1) entitled to a pro rata refund of rent from the date of termination or the date the tenant moves out, whichever is later;

(2) entitled to deduct the tenant's security deposit from the tenant's rent without necessity of lawsuit or to obtain a refund of the tenant's security deposit according to law; and

(3) not entitled to the other repair and deduct remedies under Section 94.157 or the judicial remedies under Sections 94.159(a)(1) and (2).

§ 94.157. Tenant's Repair and Deduct Remedies

(a) If the landlord is liable to the tenant under Section 94.156(b), the tenant may have the condition repaired or remedied and may deduct the cost from a subsequent rent payment as provided by this section.

(b) Except as provided by this subsection, the tenant's deduction for the cost of the repair or remedy may not exceed the amount of one month's rent under the lease agreement or $500, whichever is greater. If the tenant's rent is subsidized in whole or in part by a governmental agency, the deduction limitation of one month's rent means the fair market rent for the manufactured home lot and not the rent that the tenant pays. The governmental agency subsidizing the rent shall determine the fair market rent. If the governmental agency does not make a determination, the fair market rent means a reasonable amount of rent under the circumstances.

(c) Repairs and deductions under this section may be made as often as necessary provided that the total repairs and deductions in any one month may not exceed one month's rent or $500, whichever is greater.

(d) Repairs under this section may be made only if all of the following requirements are met:

(1) the landlord has a duty to repair or remedy the condition under Section 94.153;

(2) the tenant has given notice to the landlord in the same manner as prescribed by Section 92.056(b)(1) and, if required under Section 92.056(b)(3), a subsequent notice in the same manner as prescribed by that subsection; and

(3) any one of the following events has occurred:

(A) the landlord has failed to remedy the backup or overflow of raw sewage inside the tenant's manufactured home that results from a condition in the utility lines installed in the manufactured home community by the landlord;

(B) the landlord has expressly or impliedly agreed in the lease agreement to furnish potable water to the tenant's manufactured home lot and the water service to the lot has totally ceased; or

(C) the landlord has been notified in writing by the appropriate local housing, building, or health official or other official having jurisdiction that a condition existing on the manufactured home lot materially affects the health or safety of an ordinary tenant.

(e) At least one of the notices given under Subsection (d)(2) must state that the tenant intends to repair or remedy the condition. The notice must also contain a reasonable description of the intended repair or remedy.

(f) If the requirements prescribed by Subsections (d) and (e) are met, a tenant may:

(1) have the condition repaired or remedied immediately following the tenant's notice of intent to repair if the condition involves the backup or overflow of sewage;

(2) have the condition repaired or remedied if the condition involves a cessation of potable water if the landlord has failed to repair or remedy the condition before the fourth day after the date the tenant delivers a notice of intent to repair; or

(3) have the condition repaired or remedied if the condition is not covered by Subsection (d)(3)(A) or (B) and involves a condition affecting the physical health or safety of the ordinary tenant if the landlord has failed to repair or remedy the condition before the eighth day after the date the tenant delivers a notice of intent to repair.

(g) Repairs made based on a tenant's notice must be made by a company, contractor, or repairman listed at the time of the tenant's notice of intent to repair in the yellow or business pages of the telephone directory or in the classified advertising section of a newspaper of the municipality or county in which the manufactured home community is located or in an adjacent county. Unless the landlord and tenant agree otherwise under Subsection (i), repairs may not be made by the tenant, the tenant's immediate family, the tenant's employer or employees, or a company in which the tenant has an ownership interest. Repairs may not be made to the foundation or load-bearing structural elements of the manufactured home lot.

(h) Repairs made based on a tenant's notice must comply with applicable building codes, including any required building permit.

(i) A landlord and a tenant may mutually agree for the tenant to repair or remedy, at the landlord's expense, any condition on the manufactured home lot regardless of whether it materially affects the health or safety of an ordinary tenant.

(j) The tenant may not contract for labor or materials in excess of the amount the tenant may deduct under this section. The landlord is not liable to repairmen, contractors, or material suppliers who furnish labor or materials to repair or remedy the condition. A repairman or supplier does not have a lien for materials or services arising out of repairs contracted for by the tenant under this section.

(k) When deducting the cost of repairs from the rent payment, the tenant shall furnish the landlord, along with payment of the balance of the rent, a copy of the repair bill and the receipt for its payment. A repair bill and receipt may be the same document.

(l) If the landlord repairs or remedies the condition after the tenant has contacted a repairman but before the repairman commences work, the landlord is liable for the cost incurred by the tenant for the repairman's charge for traveling to the premises, and the tenant may deduct the charge from the tenant's rent as if it were a repair cost.

§ 94.158. Landlord Affidavit for Delay

(a) The tenant must delay contracting for repairs under Section 94.157 if, before the tenant contracts for the repairs, the landlord delivers to the tenant an affidavit signed and sworn to under oath by the landlord or the landlord's authorized agent and complying with this section.

(b) The affidavit must summarize the reasons for the delay and the diligent efforts made by the landlord up to the date of the affidavit to get the repairs done. The affidavit must state facts showing that the landlord has made and is making diligent efforts to repair the condition, and it must contain dates, names, addresses, and telephone numbers of contractors, suppliers, and repairers contacted by the owner.

(c) Affidavits under this section may delay repair by the tenant for:

(1) 15 days if the landlord's failure to repair is caused by a delay in obtaining necessary parts for which the landlord is not at fault; or

(2) 30 days if the landlord's failure to repair is caused by a general shortage of labor or materials for repair following a natural disaster such as a hurricane, tornado, flood, extended freeze, or widespread windstorm.

(d) Affidavits for delay based on grounds other than those listed in Subsection (c) are unlawful and, if used, are of no effect. The landlord may file subsequent affidavits, provided that the total delay of the repair or remedy extends no longer than six months from the date the landlord delivers the first affidavit to the tenant.

(e) The affidavit must be delivered to the tenant by any of the following methods:

(1) personal delivery to the tenant;

(2) certified mail, return receipt requested, to the tenant; or

(3) leaving the notice securely fixed on the outside of the main entry door of the manufactured home if notice in that manner is authorized in a written lease.

(f) Affidavits for delay by a landlord under this section must be submitted in good faith. Following delivery of the affidavit, the landlord must continue diligent efforts to repair or remedy the condition. There shall be a rebuttable presumption that the landlord acted in good faith and with continued diligence for the first affidavit for delay the landlord delivers to the tenant. The landlord shall have the burden of pleading and proving good faith and continued diligence for subsequent affidavits for delay. A landlord who violates this section shall be liable to the tenant for all judicial remedies under Section 94.159, except that the civil penalty under Section 94.159(a)(3) shall be one month's rent plus $1,000.

(g) If the landlord is liable to the tenant under Section 94.156 and if a new landlord, in good faith and without knowledge of the tenant's notice of intent to repair, has acquired title to the tenant's dwelling by foreclosure, deed in lieu of foreclosure, or general warranty deed in a bona fide purchase, then the following shall apply:

(1) The tenant's right to terminate the lease under this subchapter shall not be affected, and the tenant shall have no duty to give additional notice to the new landlord.

(2) The tenant's right to repair and deduct for conditions involving sewage backup or overflow or a cutoff of potable water under Section 94.157(f) shall not be affected, and the tenant shall have no duty to give additional notice to the new landlord.

(3) For conditions other than those specified in Subdivision (2), if the new landlord acquires title as described by this subsection and has notified the tenant of the name and address of the new landlord or the new landlord's authorized agent and if the tenant has not already contracted for the repair or remedy at the time the tenant is so notified, the tenant must deliver to the new landlord a written notice of intent to repair or remedy the condition, and the new landlord shall have a reasonable time to complete the repair before the tenant may repair or remedy the condition. No further notice from the tenant is necessary in order for the tenant to repair or remedy the condition after a reasonable time has elapsed.

(4) The tenant's judicial remedies under Section 94.159 shall be limited to recovery against the landlord to whom the tenant gave the required notices until the tenant has given the new landlord the notices required by this section and otherwise complied with Section 94.156 as to the new landlord.

(5) If the new landlord violates this subsection, the new landlord is liable to the tenant for a civil penalty of one month's rent plus $2,000, actual damages, and attorney's fees.

(6) No provision of this section shall affect any right of a foreclosing superior lienholder to terminate, according to law, any interest in the premises held by the holders of subordinate liens, encumbrances, leases, or other interests and shall not affect any right of the tenant to terminate the lease according to law.

§ 94.159. Tenant's Judicial Remedies2

(a) A tenant's judicial remedies under Section 94.156 shall include:

(1) an order directing the landlord to take reasonable action to repair or remedy the condition;

(2) an order reducing the tenant's rent, from the date of the first repair notice, in proportion to the reduced rental value resulting from the condition until the condition is repaired or remedied;

(3) a judgment against the landlord for a civil penalty of one month's rent plus $500;

(4) a judgment against the landlord for the amount of the tenant's actual damages; and

(5) court costs and attorney's fees, excluding any attorney's fees for a cause of action for damages relating to a personal injury.

(b) A landlord who knowingly violates Section 94.003 by contracting with a tenant to waive the landlord's duty to repair under this subchapter shall be liable to the tenant for actual damages, a civil penalty of one month's rent plus $2,000, and reasonable attorney's fees. For purposes of this subsection, there shall be a rebuttable presumption that the landlord acted without knowledge of the violation. The tenant shall have the burden of pleading and proving a knowing violation. If the lease is not in violation of Section 94.003, the tenant's proof of a knowing violation must be clear and convincing. A mutual agreement for tenant repair under Section 94.157(i) is not a violation of Section 94.003.

(c) The justice, county, and district courts have concurrent jurisdiction of an action under Subsection (a), except that the justice court may not order repairs under Subsection (a)(1).

§ 94.160. Landlord Remedy for Tenant Violation

(a) If a tenant withholds rent, causes repairs to be performed, or makes rent deductions for repairs in violation of this subchapter, the landlord may recover actual damages from the tenant. If, after a landlord has notified a tenant in writing of the illegality of the tenant's rent withholding or the tenant's proposed repair and the penalties of this subchapter, the tenant withholds rent, causes repairs to be performed, or makes rent deductions for repairs in bad faith violation of this subchapter, the landlord may recover from the tenant a civil penalty of one month's rent plus $500.

(b) Notice under this section must be in writing and may be given in person, by mail, or by delivery to the premises.

(c) The landlord has the burden of pleading and proving, by clear and convincing evidence, that the landlord gave the tenant the required notice of the illegality and the penalties and that the tenant's violation was done in bad faith. In any litigation under this subsection, the prevailing party shall recover reasonable attorney's fees from the nonprevailing party.

§ 94.161. Agents for Delivery of Notice

A managing agent, leasing agent, or resident manager is the agent of the landlord for purposes of notice and other communications required or permitted by this subchapter.

§ 94.162. Effect on Other Rights

The duties of a landlord and the remedies of a tenant under this subchapter are in lieu of existing common law and other statutory law warranties and duties of landlords for maintenance, repair, security, suitability, and nonretaliation, and remedies of tenants for a violation of those warranties and duties. Otherwise, this subchapter does not affect any other right of a landlord or tenant under contract, statutory law, or common law that is consistent with the purposes of this subchapter or any right a landlord or tenant may have to bring an action for personal injury or property damage under the law of this state. This subchapter does not impose obligations on a landlord or tenant other than those expressly stated in this subchapter.

TERMINATION, EVICTION, AND FORECLOSURE

§ 94.201. Landlord's Remedy for Early Termination

(a) Except as provided by Subsection (b), the maximum amount a landlord may recover as damages for a tenant's early termination of a lease agreement is an amount equal to the amount of rent that remains outstanding for the term of the lease and any other amounts owed for the remainder of the lease under the terms of the lease.

(b) If the tenant's manufactured home lot is reoccupied before the 21st day after the date the tenant surrenders the lot, the maximum amount the landlord may obtain as damages is an amount equal to one month's rent.

§ 94.202. Landlord's Duty to Mitigate Damages

(a) A landlord has a duty to mitigate damages if a tenant vacates the manufactured home lot before the end of the lease term.

(b) A provision of a lease agreement that purports to waive a right or to exempt a landlord from a liability or duty under this section is void.

§ 94.203. Eviction Procedures Generally

(a) A landlord may prevent a tenant from entering the manufactured home lot, evict a tenant, or require the removal of a manufactured home from the manufactured home lot only after obtaining a writ of possession under Chapter 24.

(b) If the tenant has disclosed the name of a lienholder as provided by Section 94.054, the landlord shall give written notice of eviction proceedings to the lienholder of the manufactured home not later than the third day after the date the landlord files an application or petition for a judgment for possession.

(c) If the court finds that the landlord initiated the eviction proceeding to retaliate against the tenant in violation of Section 94.251, the court may not approve the eviction of the tenant.

(d) Notwithstanding other law, a court may not issue a writ of possession in favor of a landlord before the 30th day after the date the judgment for possession is rendered if the tenant has paid the rent amount due under the lease for that 30-day period.

(e) The court shall notify a tenant in writing of a default judgment for possession by sending a copy of the judgment to the leased premises by first class mail not later than 48 hours after the entry of the judgment. In addition, the court shall send a copy of the judgment to the owner of the manufactured home if the tenant is not the owner and to any person who holds a lien on the manufactured home if the court has been notified in writing of the name and address of the owner and lienholder.

(f) If, after executing a writ of possession for the manufactured home lot, the landlord removes the manufactured home from the lot, the landlord not later than the 10th day after the date the manufactured home is removed shall send a written notice regarding the location of the manufactured home to the tenant at the tenant's most recent mailing address as reflected in the landlord's records and, if different, to the owner if the landlord is given written notice of the owner's name and address.

§ 94.204. Termination for Change in Land Use

(a) A landlord may terminate a lease agreement to change the manufactured home community's land use only if:

(1) not later than the 120th day before the date the land use changes, the landlord sends notice to the tenant, to the owner of the manufactured home if the owner is not the tenant, and to the holder of any lien on the manufactured home:

(A) specifying the date that the land use will change; and

(B) informing the tenant, owner, and lienholder, if any, that the owner must relocate the manufactured home; and

(2) not later than the 120th day before the date the land use changes, the landlord posts in a conspicuous place in the manufactured home community a notice stating that the land use will change and specifying the date that the land use will change.

(b) The landlord is required to give the owner and lienholder, if any, of the manufactured home notice under Subsection

(a)(1) only if the landlord is given written notice of the name and address of the owner and lienholder.

§ 94.205. Termination and Eviction for Violation of Lease

A landlord may terminate the lease agreement and evict a tenant for a violation of a lease provision, including a manufactured home community rule incorporated in the lease.

§ 94.206. Termination and Eviction for Nonpayment of Rent

A landlord may terminate the lease agreement and evict a tenant if:

(1) the tenant fails to timely pay rent or other amounts due under the lease that in the aggregate equal the amount of at least one month's rent;

(2) the landlord notifies the tenant in writing that the payment is delinquent; and

(3) the tenant has not tendered the delinquent payment in full to the landlord before the 10th day after the date the tenant receives the notice.

PROHIBITED ACTS

§ 94.251. Retaliation by Landlord

(a) A landlord may not retaliate against a tenant by taking an action described by Subsection (b) because the tenant:

(1) in good faith exercises or attempts to exercise against a landlord a right or remedy granted to the tenant by the lease agreement, a municipal ordinance, or a federal or state statute;

(2) gives the landlord a notice to repair or exercise a remedy under this chapter; or

(3) complains to a governmental entity responsible for enforcing building or housing codes, a public utility, or a civic or nonprofit agency, and the tenant:

(A) claims a building or housing code violation or utility problem; and

(B) believes in good faith that the complaint is valid and that the violation or problem occurred.

(b) A landlord may not, within six months after the date of the tenant's action under Subsection (a), retaliate against the tenant by:

(1) filing an eviction proceeding, except for the grounds stated by Subchapter E;

(2) depriving the tenant of the use of the premises, except for reasons authorized by law;

(3) decreasing services to the tenant;

(4) increasing the tenant's rent;

(5) terminating the tenant's lease agreement; or

(6) engaging, in bad faith, in a course of conduct that materially interferes with the tenant's rights under the tenant's lease agreement.

§ 94.252. Restriction on Sale of Manufactured Home

(a) The owner of a manufactured home may sell a home located on the leased premises if:

(1) the purchaser is approved in writing by the landlord; and

(2) a lease agreement is signed by the purchaser.

(b) Unless the owner of a manufactured home has agreed in writing, the landlord may not:

(1) require the owner to contract with the landlord to act as an agent or broker in selling the home; or

(2) require the owner to pay a commission or fee from the sale of the home.

§ 94.253. Nonretaliation

(a) A landlord is not liable for retaliation under this subchapter if the landlord proves that the action was not made for purposes of retaliation, nor is the landlord liable, unless the action violates a prior court order under Section 94.159, for:

(1) increasing rent under an escalation clause in a written lease for utilities, taxes, or insurance; or

(2) increasing rent or reducing services as part of a pattern of rent increases or service reductions for an entire manufactured home community.

(b) An eviction or lease termination based on the following circumstances, which are valid grounds for eviction or lease termination in any event, does not constitute retaliation:

(1) the tenant is delinquent in rent or other amounts due under the lease that in the aggregate equal the amount of at least one month's rent when the landlord gives notice to vacate or files an eviction action;

(2) the tenant, a member of the tenant's family, or a guest or invitee of the tenant intentionally damages property on the premises or by word or conduct threatens the personal safety of the landlord, the landlord's employees, or another tenant;

(3) the tenant has materially breached the lease, other than by holding over, by an action such as violating written lease provisions prohibiting serious misconduct or criminal acts, except as provided by this section;

(4) the tenant holds over after giving notice of termination or intent to vacate;

(5) the tenant holds over after the landlord gives notice of termination at the end of the rental term and the tenant does not take action under Section 94.251 until after the landlord gives notice of termination; or

(6) the tenant holds over and the landlord's notice of termination is motivated by a good faith belief that the tenant, a member of the tenant's family, or a guest or invitee of the tenant might:

(A) adversely affect the quiet enjoyment by other tenants or neighbors;

(B) materially affect the health or safety of the landlord, other tenants, or neighbors; or

(C) damage the property of the landlord, other tenants, or neighbors.

§ 94.254. Tenant Remedies

In addition to other remedies provided by law, if a landlord retaliates against a tenant under this subchapter, the tenant may recover from the landlord a civil penalty of one month's rent plus $500, actual damages, court costs, and reasonable attorney's fees in an action for recovery of property damages, moving costs, actual expenses, civil penalties, or declaratory or injunctive relief, less any delinquent rents or other sums for which the tenant is liable to the landlord. If the tenant's rent payment to the landlord is subsidized in whole or in part by a governmental entity, the civil penalty granted under this section shall reflect the fair market rent of the leased premises plus $500.

§ 94.255. Invalid Complaints

(a) If a tenant files or prosecutes a suit for retaliatory action based on a complaint asserted under Section 94.251(a)(3), and a government building or housing inspector or utility company representative visits the manufactured home community and determines in writing that a violation of a building or housing code does not exist or that a utility problem does not exist, there is a rebuttable presumption that the tenant acted in bad faith.

(b) If a tenant files or prosecutes a suit under this subchapter in bad faith, the landlord may recover possession of the leased premises and may recover from the tenant a civil penalty of one month's rent plus $500, court costs, and reasonable attorney's fees. If the tenant's rent payment to the landlord is subsidized in whole or in part by a governmental entity, the civil penalty granted under this subsection shall reflect the fair market rent of the leased premises plus $500.

§ 94.256. Eviction Suits

In an eviction suit, retaliation by the landlord under Section 94.251 is a defense and a rent deduction lawfully made by the tenant under this chapter is a defense for nonpayment of the rent to the extent allowed by this chapter. Other judicial actions under this chapter, excluding an action that would be permitted under Chapter 24, may not be joined with an eviction suit or asserted as a defense or cross-claim in an eviction suit.

REMEDIES

§ 94.301. Tenant's Remedies

A person may recover from a landlord who violates this chapter:

(1) actual damages;

(2) a civil penalty in an amount equal to two months' rent and $500; and

(3) reasonable attorney's fees and costs.

§ 94.302. Landlord's Remedies

If the court finds that a tenant filed or prosecuted a suit under this chapter in bad faith or for purposes of harassment, the court shall award the landlord:

(1) an amount equal to two months' rent and $500; and

(2) reasonable attorney's fees and costs.

§ 94.303. Cumulative Remedies

(a) The provisions of this chapter are not exclusive and are in addition to any other remedy provided by other law.

(b) A specific remedy provided by this chapter supersedes the general remedy provided by this subchapter and is in addition to any other remedy provided by other law.

Appendix B:
Texas Forcible Entry
and Detainer Statutes

Title 4. ACTIONS AND REMEDIES

Chapter 24. FORCIBLE ENTRY AND DETAINER

§ 24.0061. Writ of Possession.

(a) A landlord who prevails in an eviction suit is entitled to a judgment for possession of the premises and a writ of possession. In this chapter, "premises" means the unit that is occupied or rented and any outside area or facility that the tenant is entitled to use under a written lease or oral rental agreement, or that is held out for the use of tenants generally.

(b) A writ of possession may not be issued before the sixth day after the date on which the judgment for possession is rendered unless a possession bond has been filed and approved under the Texas Rules of Civil Procedure and judgment for possession is thereafter granted by default.

(c) The court shall notify a tenant in writing of a default judgment for possession by sending a copy of the judgment to the premises by first class mail not later than 48 hours after the entry of the judgment.

(d) The writ of possession shall order the officer executing the writ to:

(1) post a written warning of at least 8 1/2 by 11 inches on the exterior of the front door of the rental unit notifying the tenant that the writ has been issued

and that the writ will be executed on or after a specific date and time stated in the warning not sooner than 24 hours after the warning is posted; and

(2) when the writ is executed:

(A) deliver possession of the premises to the landlord;

(B) instruct the tenant and all persons claiming under the tenant to leave the premises immediately, and, if the persons fail to comply, physically remove them;

(C) instruct the tenant to remove or to allow the landlord, the landlord's representatives, or other persons acting under the officer's supervision to remove all personal property from the rental unit other than personal property claimed to be owned by the landlord; and,

(D) place, or have an authorized person place, the removed personal property outside the rental unit at a nearby location, but not blocking a public sidewalk, passageway, or street and not while it is raining, sleeting, or snowing.

(e) The writ of possession shall authorize the officer, at the officer's discretion, to engage the services of a bonded or insured warehouseman to remove and store, subject to applicable law, part or all of the property at no cost to the landlord or the officer executing the writ.

(f) The officer may not require the landlord to store the property.

(g) The writ of possession shall contain notice to the officer that under Section 7.003, Civil Practice and Remedies Code, the officer is not liable for damages resulting from the execution of the writ if the officer executes the writ in good faith and with reasonable diligence.

(h) A sheriff or constable may use reasonable force in executing a writ under this section.

§ 24.0062. Warehouseman's Lien.

(a) If personal property is removed from a tenant's premises as the result of an action brought under this chapter and stored in a bonded or insured public warehouse, the warehouseman has a lien on the property to the extent of any reasonable storage and moving charges incurred by the warehouseman. The lien does not attach to any property until the property has been stored by the warehouseman.

(b) If property is to be removed and stored in a public warehouse under a writ of possession, the officer executing the writ shall, at the time of execution, deliver in person to the tenant, or by first class mail to the tenant's last known address not later than 72 hours after execution of the writ if the tenant is not present, a written notice stating the complete address and telephone number of the location at which the property may be redeemed and stating that:

(1) the tenant's property is to be removed and stored by a public warehouseman under Section 24.0062 of the Property Code;

(2) the tenant may redeem any of the property, without payment of moving or storage charges, on demand during the time the warehouseman is removing the property from the tenant's premises and before the warehouseman permanently leaves the tenant's premises;

(3) within 30 days from the date of storage, the tenant may redeem any of the property described by Section 24.0062(e), Property Code, on demand by the tenant and on payment of the moving and storage charges reasonably attributable to the items being redeemed;

(4) after the 30-day period and before sale, the tenant may redeem the property on demand by the tenant and on payment of all moving and storage charges; and,

(5) subject to the previously stated conditions, the warehouseman has a lien on the property to secure payment of moving and storage charges and may sell all the property to satisfy reasonable moving and storage charges after 30 days, subject to the requirements of Section 24.0062(j) of the Property Code.

(c) The statement required by Subsection (b)(2) must be underlined or in boldfaced print.

(d) On demand by the tenant during the time the warehouseman is removing the property from the tenant's premises and before the warehouseman permanently leaves the tenant's premises, the warehouseman shall return to the tenant all property requested by the tenant, without charge.

(e) On demand by the tenant within 30 days after the date the property is stored by the warehouseman and on payment by the tenant of the moving and storage charges reasonably attributable to the items being redeemed, the warehouseman shall return to the tenant at the warehouse the following property:

(1) wearing apparel;

(2) tools, apparatus, and books of a trade or profession;

(3) school books;

(4) a family library;

(5) family portraits and pictures;

(6) one couch, two living room chairs, and a dining table and chairs;

(7) beds and bedding;

(8) kitchen furniture and utensils;

(9) food and foodstuffs;

(10) medicine and medical supplies;

(11) one automobile and one truck;

(12) agricultural implements;

(13) children's toys not commonly used by adults;

(14) goods that the warehouseman or the warehouseman's agent knows are owned by a person other than the tenant or an occupant of the residence;

(15) goods that the warehouseman or the warehouseman's agent knows are subject to a recorded chattel mortgage or financing agreement; and,

(16) cash.

(f) During the first 30 days after the date of storage, the warehouseman may not require payment of removal or storage charges for other items as a condition for redeeming the items described by Subsection (e).

(g) On demand by the tenant to the warehouseman after the 30-day period and before sale and on payment by the tenant of all unpaid moving and storage charges on all the property, the warehouseman shall return all the previously unredeemed property to the tenant at the warehouse.

(h) A warehouseman may not recover any moving or storage charges if the court determines under Subsection (i) that the warehouseman's moving or storage charges are not reasonable.

(i) Before the sale of the property by the warehouseman, the tenant may file suit in the justice court in which the eviction judgment was rendered, or in another court of competent jurisdiction in the county in which the rental premises are located, to recover the property described by Subsection (e) on the ground that the landlord failed to return the property after timely demand and payment by the tenant, as provided by this section. Before sale, the tenant may also file suit to recover all property moved or stored by the warehouseman on the ground that the amount of the warehouseman's moving or storage charges is not reasonable. All proceedings under this subsection have precedence over other matters on the court's docket. The justice court that issued the writ of possession has jurisdiction under this section regardless of the amount in controversy.

(j) Any sale of property that is subject to a lien under this section shall be conducted in accordance with Section 7.210 and Subchapters D and F, Chapter 9, Business & Commerce Code.

(k) In a proceeding under this section, the prevailing party is entitled to recover actual damages, reasonable attorney's fees, court costs, and, if appropriate, any property withheld in violation of this section or the value of that property if it has been sold.

Appendix C:
Texas Rules of Civil Procedure Relating to Forcible Entry and Detainer

TEXAS RULES OF CIVIL PROCEDURE
PART VII RULES RELATING TO SPECIAL PROCEEDINGS
SECTION 3 Forcible Entry and Detainer

Rule 738 May Sue for Rent

A suit for rent may be joined with an action of forcible entry and detainer, wherever the suit for rent is within the jurisdiction of the justice court. In such case the court in rendering judgment in the action of forcible entry and detainer, may at the same time render judgment for any rent due the landlord by the renter; provided the amount thereof is within the jurisdiction of the justice court.

Rule 739 Citation

When the party aggrieved or his authorized agent shall file his written sworn complaint with such justice, the justice shall immediately issue citation directed to the defendant or defendants commanding him to appear before such justice at a time and place named in such citation, such time being not more than ten days nor less than six days from the date of service of the citation. The citation shall inform the parties that, upon timely request and payment of a jury fee no later than five days after the defendant is served with citation, the case shall be heard by a jury.

Rule 740 Complainant May Have Possession

The party aggrieved may, at the time of filing his complaint, or thereafter prior to final judgment in the justice court, execute and file a possession bond to be approved by the justice in such amount as the justice may fix as the probable amount of costs of suit and damages which may result to defendant in the event that the suit has been improperly instituted, and conditioned that the plaintiff will pay defendant all such costs and damages as shall be adjudged against plaintiff. The defendant shall be notified by the justice court that plaintiff has filed a possession bond. Such notice shall be served in the same manner as service of citation and shall inform the defendant of all of the following rules and procedures: (a) Defendant may remain in possession if defendant executes and files a counterbond prior to the expiration of six days from the date defendant is served with notice of the filing of plaintiff's bond. Said counterbond shall be approved by the justice and shall be in such amount as the justice may fix as the probable amount of costs of suit and damages which may result to plaintiff in the event possession has been improperly withheld by defendant; (b) Defendant is entitled to demand and he shall be granted a trial to be held prior to the expiration of six days from the date defendant is served with notice of the filing of plaintiff's possession bond; (c) If defendant does not file a counterbond and if defendant does not demand that trial be held prior to the expiration of said six-day period, the constable of the precinct or the sheriff of the county where the property is situated, shall place the plaintiff in possession of the property promptly after the expiration of six days from the date defendant is served with notice of the filing of plaintiff's possession bond; and (d) If, in lieu of a counterbond, defendant demands trial within said six-day period, and if the justice of the peace rules after trial that plaintiff is entitled to possession of the property, the constable or sheriff shall place the plaintiff in possession of the property five days after such determination by the justice of the peace.

Rule 741 Requisites of Complaint

The complaint shall describe the lands, tenements or premises, the possession of which is claimed, with sufficient certainty to identify the same, and it shall also state the facts which entitled the complainant to the possession and authorize the action under Sections 24.001-24.004, Texas Property Code.

Rule 742 Service of Citation

The officer receiving such citation shall execute the same by delivering a copy of it to the defendant, or by leaving a copy thereof with some person over the age of sixteen years, at his usual place of abode, at least six days before the return day thereof; and on or before the day assigned for trial he shall return such citation, with his action written thereon, to the justice who issued the same.

Rule 742a Service by Delivery to Premises

If the sworn complaint lists all home and work addresses of the defendant which are known to the person filing the sworn complaint and if it states that such person knows of no other home or work addresses of the defendant in the county where the premises are located, service of citation may be by delivery to the premises in question as follows: If the officer receiving such citation is unsuccessful in serving such citation under Rule 742, the officer shall no later than five days after receiving such citation execute a sworn statement that the officer has made diligent efforts to serve such citation on at least two occasions at all addresses of the defendant in the county where the premises are located as may be shown on the sworn complaint, stating the times and places of attempted service. Such sworn statement shall be filed by the officer with the justice who shall promptly consider the sworn statement of the officer. The justice may then authorize service according to the following: (a) The officer shall place the citation inside the premises by placing it through a door mail chute or by slipping it under the front door; and if neither method is possible or practical, the officer shall securely affix the citation to the front door or main entry to the premises. (b) The officer shall that same day or the next day deposit in the mail a true copy of such citation with a copy of the sworn complaint attached thereto, addressed to defendant at the premises in question and sent by first class mail; (c) The officer shall note on the return of such citation the date of delivery under (a) above and the date of mailing under (b) above; and (d) Such delivery and mailing to the premises shall occur at least six days before the return day of the citation; and on or before the day assigned for trial he shall return such citation with his action written thereon, to the justice who issued the same. It shall not be necessary for the aggrieved party or his authorized agent to make request for or motion for alternative service pursuant to this rule.

Rule 743 Docketed

The cause shall be docketed and tried as other cases. If the defendant shall fail to enter an appearance upon the docket in the justice court or file answer before the case is called for trial, the allegations of the complaint may be taken as admitted and judgment by default entered accordingly. The justice shall have authority to issue subpoenas for witnesses to enforce their attendance, and to punish for contempt.

Rule 744 Demanding Jury

Any party shall have the right of trial by jury, by making a request to the court on or before five days from the date the defendant is served with citation, and by paying a jury fee of five dollars. Upon such request, a jury shall be summoned as in other cases in justice court.

Rule 745 Trial Postponed

For good cause shown, supported by affidavit of either party, the trial may be postponed not exceeding six days.

Rule 746 Only Issue

In case of forcible entry or of forcible detainer under Sections 24.001-24.008, Texas Property Code, the only issue shall be as to the right to actual possession; and the merits of the title shall not be adjudicated.

Rule 747 Trial

If no jury is demanded by either party, the justice shall try the case. If a jury is demanded by either party, the jury shall be empaneled and sworn as in other cases; and after hearing the evidence it shall return its verdict in favor of the plaintiff or the defendant as it shall find.

Rule 747a Representation by Agents

In forcible entry and detainer cases for non-payment of rent or holding over beyond the rental term, the parties may represent themselves or be represented by their authorized agents in justice court.

Rule 748 Judgment and Writ

If the judgment or verdict be in favor of the plaintiff, the justice shall give judgment for plaintiff for possession of the premises, costs, and damages; and he shall award his writ of possession. If the judgment or verdict be in favor of the defendant, the justice shall give judgment for defendant against the plaintiff for costs and any damages. No writ of possession shall issue until the expiration of five days from the time the judgment is signed.

Rule 749 May Appeal

In appeals in forcible entry and detainer cases, no motion for new trial shall be filed. Either party may appeal from a final judgment in such case, to the county court of the county in which the judgment is rendered by filing with the justice within five days after the judgment is signed, a bond to be approved by said justice, and payable to the adverse party, conditioned that he will prosecute his appeal with effect, or pay all costs and damages which may be adjudged against him. The justice shall set the amount of the bond to include the items enumerated in Rule 752. Within five days following the filing of such bond, the party appealing shall give notice as provided in Rule 21a of the filing of such bond to the adverse party. No judgment shall be taken by default against the adverse party in the court to which the cause has been appealed without first showing substantial compliance with this rule.

Rule 749a Pauper's Affidavit

If appellant is unable to pay the costs of appeal, or file a bond as required by Rule 749, he shall nevertheless be entitled to appeal by making strict proof of such inability within five days after the judgment is signed, which shall consist of his affidavit filed with the justice of the peace stating his inability to pay such costs, or any part thereof, or to give security, which may be contested within five days after the filing of such affidavit and notice thereof to the opposite party or his attorney of record by any officer of the court or party to the suit, whereupon it shall be the duty of the justice of the peace in whose court the suit is pending to hear evidence and determine the right of the party to appeal, and he shall enter his finding on the docket as a part of the record. Upon the filing of a pauper's affidavit the justice of the peace or clerk of the court shall notice the opposing party of the filing of the affidavit of inability within one working day of its filing by written notification accomplished through first class mail. It will be presumed prima facie that the affidavit speaks the truth, and, unless contested within five days after the filing and notice thereof, the presumption shall be deemed conclusive; but if a contest is filed, the burden shall then be on the appellant to prove his alleged inability by competent evidence other than by the affidavit above referred to. When a pauper's affidavit is timely contested by the appellee, the justice shall hold a hearing and rule on the matter within five days. If the justice of the peace disapproves the pauper's affidavit, appellant may, within five days thereafter bring the matter before the county judge for a final decision, and, on request, the justice shall certify to the county judge appellant's affidavit, the contest thereof, and all documents, and papers thereto. The county judge shall set a day for hearing, not later than five days, and shall hear the contest de novo. If the pauper's affidavit is approved by the county judge, he shall direct the justice to transmit to the clerk of the county court, the transcript, records and papers of the case. A pauper's affidavit will be considered approved upon one of the following occurrences: (1) the pauper's affidavit is not contested by the other party; (2) the pauper's affidavit is contested by the other party and upon a hearing the justice determines that the pauper's affidavit is approved; or (3) upon a hearing by the justice disapproving of the pauper's affidavit the appellant appeals to the county judge who then, after a hearing, approves the pauper's affidavit. No writ of possession may issue pending the hearing by the county judge of the appellant's right to appeal on a pauper's affidavit. If the county judge disapproves the pauper's affidavit, appellant may perfect his appeal by filing an appeal bond in the amount as required by Rule 749 within five days thereafter. If no appeal bond is filed within five days, a writ of possession may issue.

Rule 749b Pauper's Affidavit in Nonpayment of Rent Appeals

In a nonpayment of rent forcible detainer case a tenant/appellant who has appealed by filing a pauper's affidavit under these rules shall be entitled to stay in possession of the premises during the pendency of the appeal, by complying with the following procedure: (1) Within five days of the date that the tenant/appellant files his pauper's affidavit, he must pay into the justice court registry one rental period's rent under the terms of the rental agreement. (2) During the appeal process as rent becomes due under the rental agreement, the tenant/appellant shall pay the rent into the county court registry within five days of the due date under the terms of the rental agreement. (3) If the tenant/appellant fails to pay the rent into the court registry within the time limits prescribed by these rules, the appellee may file a notice of default in county court. Upon sworn motion by the appellee and a showing of default to the judge, the court shall issue a writ of restitution. (4) Landlord/appellee may withdraw any or all rent in the county court registry upon a) sworn motion and hearing, prior to final determination of the case, showing just cause, b) dismissal of the appeal, or c) order of the court upon final hearing. (5) All hearings and motions under this rule shall be entitled to precedence in the county court.

Rule 749c Appeal Perfected

When an appeal bond has been timely filed in conformity with Rule 749 or a pauper's affidavit approved in conformity with Rule 749a, the appeal shall be perfected. Change by amendment effective August 15, 1982: This rule is amended so that one month's rent need not be paid when an appeal bond is made. Change by amendment effective September 1, 1990: To dispense with the appellate requirement of payment of any rent into the court registry.

Rule 750 Form of Appeal Bond

The appeal bond authorized in the preceding article may be substantially as follows: "The State of Texas, "County of _____ "Whereas, upon a writ of forcible entry (or forcible detainer) in favor of A.B., and against C.D., tried before _____, a justice of the peace of _____ county, a judgment was rendered in favor of the said A.B. on the _____ day of _____, A.D. _____, and against the said C.D., from which the said C.D. has appealed to the county court; now, therefore, the said C.D. and _____ his sureties, covenant that he will prosecute his said appeal with effect and pay all costs and damages which may be adjudged against him, provided the sureties shall not be liable in an amount greater than $ _____, said amount being the amount of the bond herein. "Given under our hands this _____ day of _____, A.D. _____."

Rule 751 Transcript

When an appeal has been perfected, the justice shall stay all further proceedings on the judgment, and immediately make out a transcript of all the entries made on his docket of the proceedings had in the case; and he shall immediately file the same, together with the original papers and any money in the court registry, including sums tendered pursuant to Rule 749b(1), with the clerk of the county court of the county in which the trial was had, or other court having jurisdiction of such appeal. The clerk shall docket the cause, and the trial shall be de novo. The clerk shall immediately notify both appellant and the adverse party of the date of receipt of the transcript and the docket number of the cause. Such notice shall advise the defendant of the necessity for filing a written answer in the county court when the defendant has pleaded orally in the justice court. The trial, as well as all hearings and motions, shall be entitled to precedence in the county court.

Rule 752 Damages

On the trial of the cause in the county court the appellant or appellee shall be permitted to plead, prove and recover his damages, if any, suffered for withholding or defending possession of the premises during the pendency of the appeal. Damages may include but are not limited to loss of rentals during the pendency of the appeal and reasonable attorney fees in the justice and country courts provided, as to attorney fees, that the requirements of Section 24.006 of the Texas Property Code have been met. Only the party prevailing in the county court shall be entitled to recover damages against the adverse party. He shall also be entitled to recover court costs. He shall be entitled to recover against the sureties on the appeal bond in cases where the adverse party has executed such bond.

Rule 753 Judgment by Default

Said cause shall be subject to trial at any time after the expiration of eight full days after the date the transcript is filed in the county court. If the defendant has filed a written answer in the justice court, the same shall be taken to constitute his appearance and answer in the county court, and such answer may be amended as in other cases. If the defendant made no answer in writing in the justice court, and if he fails to file a written answer within eight full days after the transcript is filed in the county court, the allegations of the complaint may be taken as admitted and judgment by default may be entered accordingly.

Rule 754 [Rule Not Adopted]

Rule 755 Writ of Possession

The writ of possession, or execution, or both, shall be issued by the clerk of the county court according to the judgment rendered, and the same shall be executed by the sheriff or constable, as in other cases; and such writ of possession shall not be suspended or superseded in any case by appeal from such final judgment in the county court, unless the premises in question are being used as the principal residence of a party.

APPENDIX D
BLANK FORMS

Table of Forms

Tenant Application

Name _____

Date of Birth: _____

Driver's License No. _____

Social Security Number: _____

Name: _____

Date of Birth _____

Driver's License No. _____

Social Security No. _____

Children:
Names and dates of birth: _____

Present address: _____

Length of time at that address: _____

Name, address, and phone number of present landlord: _____

_____

Previous address: _____

Length of time at that address: _____

Name, address, and phone number of that landlord: _____

_____

Name, address, and phone number of any landlords in previous seven years: _____

_____

Name, address, phone number, and name of contact person for each applicant's employer:

_____

List any pets: _____

Name, address, and phone number of nearest relative: _____

_____

List all banks with whom you have accounts, and provide account numbers:

_____

Have you ever been evicted? _____

Have you ever been in litigation with a landlord? _____

If your answer to either of the above 2 questions is yes, please describe the circumstances. If any legal proceedings were filed, please list the county, state, and case number of each of them

_____

By signing this application, each applicant hereby authorizes landlord or landlord's representative to obtain and/or verify credit, employment, and rental history and information. Each applicant who signs this application attests that the information provided in the application is true.

_____   _____
Applicant   Applicant

_____   _____
Date signed   Date signed

Residential Lease

This lease agreement is made and entered into on _____, by and between _____ and _____ (hereinafter referred to as "tenant") and _____ (hereinafter referred to as "landlord").

The term of the lease shall be for a period of one year, beginning on _____ and ending on _____. Tenant shall have an option, so long as tenant is not in default of any provision of this lease, to renew the lease for an additional period of _____, on the same terms and conditions contained in this lease, except that the rental may, at landlord's option, be increased to $_____ per month. The option to renew shall be exercised by tenant by the tenant's delivery to the landlord written notice of his or her election to renew on or before the first day of the final month of the lease term.

The leased premises are _____.

Tenant agrees to pay to landlord as rent for the leased premises the sum of $_____ per month, in advance, with the payments being due on the first day of each month, beginning on _____, 20__, and continuing on the first day of each month thereafter during the term of this lease. If the rent is not paid in full by the fifth day of the month in which it is due, tenant shall pay a late fee of $_____. Rental payments must be by check or money order. Cash payments will not be accepted.

In the event eviction proceedings have been instituted against tenant or a notice to vacate has been delivered to tenant, landlord may accept full or partial payments of unpaid rent. Acceptance of such payments does not waive landlord's right to proceed with eviction of tenant.

Tenant shall pay all utilities charges related to the leased premises. The only exceptions to this requirement are: _____.

Landlord acknowledges the receipt of $_____ as the first and last month's rent under this lease as well as $_____ as a security deposit. In the event tenant terminates the lease prior to its expiration date, these amounts are non–refundable. In addition, landlord reserves the right to seek additional damages if the damages suffered by landlord are in excess of the above amounts. In the event tenant defaults or is in breach of any of the terms of this lease, landlord may recover possession as provided by law and seek monetary damages.

Tenant stipulates that tenant has examined the leased premises as well as all buildings and improvements located on the premises and they are all, as of the date of this lease, in good order and repair and in a safe and clean condition. Tenant agrees, at tenant's own cost and expense, to maintain the leased premises and the buildings and improvements on the leased premises during the lease in as good order, repair, and condition as they were in on the date of this lease. Any repairs to the leased premises or the buildings and improvements on the leased premises which exceed $_____ in cost shall be performed by landlord at landlord's sole cost and expense. TENANT SHALL REPAIR THE FOLLOWING, REGARDLESS OF COST, UNLESS CAUSED BY LANDLORD'S NEGLIGENCE: WASTE WATER STOPPAGE CAUSED BY FOREIGN OR IMPROPER OBJECTS IN PLUMBING LINES, DAMAGE TO DOORS AND WINDOWS, DAMAGE CAUSED BY DOORS AND WINDOWS BEING LEFT OPEN. TENANT SHALL GIVE LANDLORD WRITTEN NOTICE OF ANY CONDITION IN OR AN THE LEASED PREMISES TENANT BELIEVES AFFECTS TENANT'S HEALTH OR PHYSICAL SAFETY.

Tenant stipulates that Tenant has examined and inspected all smoke detectors, that smoke detectors are installed, and that the smoke detectors are in working order.

TENANT SHALL PAY FOR ALL REPAIR AND REPLACEMENT OF SECURITY DEVICES IF THE DAMAGE IS CAUSED BY THE TENANT. TENANT ACKNOWLEDGES THAT IT IS UNLAWFUL TO DISCONNECT OR DISABLE OR INTENTIONALLY DAMAGE A SMOKE DETECTOR OR REMOVE THE BATTERY WITHOUT IMMEDIATELY REPLACING IT WITH A WORKING BATTERY. FAILURE TO COMPLY WITH THIS NOTICE IS SUBJECT TO PENALTIES IMPOSED BY LAW AS WELL AS DAMAGES AND ATTORNEY'S FEES ASSESSED AGAINST TENANT IN A COURT OF LAW PURSUANT TO CHAPTER 92 OF THE TEXAS PROPERTY CODE.

Tenant shall not make any alterations, changes, or improvements to the leased premises without the written consent of the landlord. Any alterations, changes, or improvements, other than movable personal property, shall become the property of the landlord and remain on the leased premises after the termination of this lease unless the parties agree otherwise in writing.

Tenant shall not assign this lease or sublet the leased premises or any interest in the premises without the prior written consent of the landlord. An assignment or subletting by tenant in violation of this provision shall be void and shall, at the landlord's option, terminate this lease.

Landlord and landlord's agents have the right at all reasonable times to enter the leased premises for the purpose of inspecting them and all buildings and improvements on the premises and for the purpose of showing the premises to prospective purchasers.

In the event tenant remains in possession of the leased premises with the consent of landlord after the expiration of this lease, a new tenancy from month to month will be created and shall be subject to the same conditions and terms of this lease. This tenancy shall be terminable upon thirty days written notice to the other party.

All notices or other communications required or permitted by this lease to be given to either party by the other party shall be in writing and shall be deemed served or delivered when personally delivered to the party or deposited in the United States mail, postage prepaid, to the tenant at the tenant's last known mailing address and to the landlord at _____. Unless otherwise changed by written notice, all rent due and payable under this lease shall be paid to landlord at the above address.

No pets are allowed in or on the leased premises unless a separate written pet agreement is signed by the parties and any required pet deposit paid. Support dogs for the disabled are not subject to this restriction.

Should any litigation be commenced between the parties concerning the leased premises, this lease, or the rights and duties of either party in relation to the lease or the leased premises, the prevailing party shall be entitled to have the other party pay the prevailing party's reasonable attorney's fees in addition to any other relief to which the prevailing party may be entitled.

If the tenant changes the locks or adds locks on the leased premises, tenant shall promptly deliver a copy of each key to landlord.

Tenant shall be responsible to any and all damages to tenant's property and agrees to hold landlord harmless for any such damages.

The leased premises shall not be occupied by more than _____ adults and _____ children. Guests of tenants staying in the leased premises for more than thirty consecutive days shall be deemed to be occupying the leased premises for purposes of this clause.

In the event tenant abandons the leased premises prior to the expiration of the lease term, landlord may relet the premises and tenant shall be liable to landlord for any costs, lost rent, or damage to the leased premises. Landlord may dispose of any property abandoned by tenant and shall not be responsible to tenant for any such property.

At the expiration of the lease term, tenant shall immediately surrender the leased premises, in as good a condition as at the beginning of the lease term.

Tenant shall not use the leased premises for any illegal purpose or any purpose that will increase the rate of insurance or create a nuisance for landlord or any neighbors. Tenant shall not do any acts to harass landlord, other tenants, or neighbors.

Time is expressly declared to be of the essence in this agreement.

This lease shall be construed under and in accordance with the laws of the State of Texas, and all obligations of the parties created under this lease are performable in _____ County, Texas. If any provision of this lease shall for any reason be held to be invalid, illegal, or unenforceable in any respect, the invalidity, illegality, or unenforceability shall not effect any other provisions of this lease and all provisions not declared invalid, illegal, or unenforceable shall remain in full force and effect.

The waiver by either party of any breach of any provision of this lease shall not constitute a continuing waiver or waiver of any subsequent breach of the same or a different provision of this lease.

This lease contains the entire agreement between the parties and may not be modified except by written agreement which is signed by both parties. Any prior agreements or understandings between the parties, whether written or oral, are superceded by this lease.

TENANT GRANTS TO LANDLORD A CONTRACTUAL LIEN ON ALL NONEX-EMPT PROPERTY IN, ON, OR ABOUT THE LEASED PREMISES. LANDLORD MAY SEIZE AND SELL SUCH PROPERTY TO SATISFY TENANT'S OBLIGATIONS UNDER THIS LEASE BY PROCEEDING IN ACCORDANCE WITH CHAPTER 54 OF THE TEXAS PROPERTY CODE. LANDLORD IS ENTITLED TO COLLECT FROM THE PROCEEDS OF ANY SALE OR FROM TENANT THE COST OF PACKING, REMOVING, AND STORING ANY PROPERTY SEIZED UNDER THIS PROVISION OF THE LEASE.

In witness whereof, the undersigned tenant and landlord execute this agreement as of the date set out above as the date of this lease.

_____   _____
Tenant   Landlord

Periodic Tenancy Lease

This lease agreement is made and entered into on _____, by and between
_____ and _____ (hereinafter referred to as "tenant")
and _____ (hereinafter referred to as "landlord").

This lease shall create a periodic tenancy of one month, beginning on the first day of
_____, 200__ and ending on the last day of that month. In the event that timely
makes the rental period for the month following the expiration of the periodic tenancy and is not in
default of any of the provisions of this agreement, the lease shall be automatically renewed for the
additional one month period under the same terms and conditions as the original lease.

The leased premises are _____.

Tenant agrees to pay to landlord as rent for the leased premises the sum of $_____
per month, in advance, with the payments being due on the first day of each month, beginning on
_____, 20__, and continuing on the first day of each month thereafter during the term
of this lease. If the rent is not paid in full by the fifth day of the month in which it is due, tenant shall
pay a late fee of $_____. Rental payments must be by check or money order. Cash pay-
ments will not be accepted.

In the event eviction proceedings have been instituted against tenant or a notice to vacate has
been delivered to tenant, landlord may accept full or partial payments of unpaid rent. Acceptance of
such payments does not waive landlord's right to proceed with eviction of tenant.

Tenant shall pay all utilities charges related to the leased premises. The only exceptions to this
requirement are: _____.

Landlord acknowledges the receipt of $_____ as the first and last month's
rent under this lease as well as $_____ as a security deposit. In the event tenant ter-
minates the lease prior to its expiration date, these amounts are non–refundable. In addition, landlord
reserves the right to seek additional damages if the damages suffered by landlord are in excess of the
above amounts. In the event tenant defaults or is in breach of any of the terms of this lease, landlord
may recover possession as provided by law and seek monetary damages.

Tenant stipulates that tenant has examined the leased premises as well as all buildings and
improvements located on the premises and they are all, as of the date of this lease, in good order and
repair and in a safe and clean condition. Tenant agrees, at tenant's own cost and expense, to maintain
the leased premises and the buildings and improvements on the leased premises during the lease in as
good order, repair, and condition as they were in on the date of this lease. Any repairs to the leased

premises or the buildings and improvements on the leased premises which exceed $_____ in cost shall be performed by landlord at landlord's sole cost and expense. TENANT SHALL REPAIR THE FOLLOWING, REGARDLESS OF COST, UNLESS CAUSED BY LANDLORD'S NEGLIGENCE: WASTE WATER STOPPAGE CAUSED BY FOREIGN OR IMPROPER OBJECTS IN PLUMBING LINES, DAMAGE TO DOORS AND WINDOWS, DAMAGE CAUSED BY DOORS AND WINDOWS BEING LEFT OPEN. TENANT SHALL GIVE LANDLORD WRITTEN NOTICE OF ANY CONDITION IN OR AN THE LEASED PREMISES TENANT BELIEVES AFFECTS TENANT'S HEALTH OR PHYSICAL SAFETY.

Tenant stipulates that Tenant has examined and inspected all smoke detectors, that smoke detectors are installed, and that the smoke detectors are in working order.

TENANT SHALL PAY FOR ALL REPAIR AND REPLACEMENT OF SECURITY DEVICES IF THE DAMAGE IS CAUSED BY THE TENANT. TENANT ACKNOWLEDGES THAT IT IS UNLAWFUL TO DISCONNECT OR DISABLE OR INTENTIONALLY DAMAGE A SMOKE DETECTOR OR REMOVE THE BATTERY WITHOUT IMMEDIATELY REPLACING IT WITH A WORKING BATTERY. FAILURE TO COMPLY WITH THIS NOTICE IS SUBJECT TO PENALTIES IMPOSED BY LAW AS WELL AS DAMAGES AND ATTORNEY'S FEES ASSESSED AGAINST TENANT IN A COURT OF LAW PURSUANT TO CHAPTER 92 OF THE TEXAS PROPERTY CODE.

Tenant shall not make any alterations, changes, or improvements to the leased premises without the written consent of the landlord. Any alterations, changes, or improvements, other than movable personal property, shall become the property of the landlord and remain on the leased premises after the termination of this lease unless the parties agree otherwise in writing.

Tenant shall not assign this lease or sublet the leased premises or any interest in the premises without the prior written consent of the landlord. An assignment or subletting by tenant in violation of this provision shall be void and shall, at the landlord's option, terminate this lease.

Landlord and landlord's agents have the right at all reasonable times to enter the leased premises for the purpose of inspecting them and all buildings and improvements on the premises and for the purpose of showing the premises to prospective purchasers.

In the event tenant remains in possession of the leased premises with the consent of landlord after the expiration of this lease, a new tenancy from month to month will be created and shall be subject to the same conditions and terms of this lease. This tenancy shall be terminable upon thirty days written notice to the other party.

All notices or other communications required or permitted by this lease to be given to either party by the other party shall be in writing and shall be deemed served or delivered when personally delivered to the party or deposited in the United States mail, postage prepaid, to the tenant at the tenant's last known mailing address and to the landlord at _____. Unless otherwise changed by written notice, all rent due and payable under this lease shall be paid to landlord at the above address.

No pets are allowed in or on the leased premises unless a separate written pet agreement is signed by the parties and any required pet deposit paid. Support dogs for the disabled are not subject to this restriction.

Should any litigation be commenced between the parties concerning the leased premises, this lease, or the rights and duties of either party in relation to the lease or the leased premises, the prevailing party shall be entitled to have the other party pay the prevailing party's reasonable attorney's fees in addition to any other relief to which the prevailing party may be entitled.

If the tenant changes the locks or adds locks on the leased premises, tenant shall promptly deliver a copy of each key to landlord.

Tenant shall be responsible to any and all damages to tenant's property and agrees to hold landlord harmless for any such damages.

The leased premises shall not be occupied by more than _____ adults and _____ children. Guests of tenants staying in the leased premises for more than thirty consecutive days shall be deemed to be occupying the leased premises for purposes of this clause.

In the event tenant abandons the leased premises prior to the expiration of the lease term, landlord may relet the premises and tenant shall be liable to landlord for any costs, lost rent, or damage to the leased premises. Landlord may dispose of any property abandoned by tenant and shall not be responsible to tenant for any such property.

At the expiration of the lease term, tenant shall immediately surrender the leased premises, in as good a condition as at the beginning of the lease term.

Tenant shall not use the leased premises for any illegal purpose or any purpose that will increase the rate of insurance or create a nuisance for landlord or any neighbors. Tenant shall not do any acts to harass landlord, other tenants, or neighbors.

Time is expressly declared to be of the essence in this agreement.

This lease shall be construed under and in accordance with the laws of the State of Texas, and all obligations of the parties created under this lease are performable in _____ County, Texas. If any provision of this lease shall for any reason be held to be invalid, illegal, or unenforceable in any respect, the invalidity, illegality, or unenforceability shall not effect any other provisions of this lease and all provisions not declared invalid, illegal, or unenforceable shall remain in full force and effect.

The waiver by either party of any breach of any provision of this lease shall not constitute a continuing waiver or waiver of any subsequent breach of the same or a different provision of this lease.

This lease contains the entire agreement between the parties and may not be modified except by written agreement which is signed by both parties. Any prior agreements or understandings between the parties, whether written or oral, are superceded by this lease.

TENANT GRANTS TO LANDLORD A CONTRACTUAL LIEN ON ALL NONEX-EMPT PROPERTY IN, ON, OR ABOUT THE LEASED PREMISES. LANDLORD MAY SEIZE AND SELL SUCH PROPERTY TO SATISFY TENANT'S OBLIGATIONS UNDER THIS LEASE BY PROCEEDING IN ACCORDANCE WITH CHAPTER 54 OF THE TEXAS PROP-ERTY CODE. LANDLORD IS ENTITLED TO COLLECT FROM THE PROCEEDS OF ANY SALE OR FROM TENANT THE COST OF PACKING, REMOVING, AND STORING ANY PROPERTY SEIZED UNDER THIS PROVISION OF THE LEASE.

In witness whereof, the undersigned tenant and landlord execute this agreement as of the date set out above as the date of this lease.

_____   _____
Tenant   Landlord

Landlord's Notice to Terminate Lease

Name of Tenant: _____

Leased Premises: _____

Date of Notice: _____

You are hereby notified that, effective as of the end of your current lease period, your lease will not be renewed. We are requesting that you return the premises to us no later than that date, which is _____, 200___. Please consider this your formal notice to vacate.

Signed: _____

Lead Paint Disclosure

Disclosure of Information on Lead–Based Paint and/or Lead–Based Paint Hazards:

Lead Warning Statement:

Housing built before 1978 may contain lead–based paint. Lead from paint, paint chips, and dust can pose health hazards if not managed properly. Lead exposure is especially harmful to young children and pregnant women. Before renting pre–1978 housing, lessors must disclose the presence of known lead–based paint and/or lead–based paint hazards in the dwelling. Lessees must also receive a federally–approved pamphlet on lead poisoning prevention.

Lessor's Disclosure:

(a)Presence of lead–based paint and/or lead–based paint hazards : (check (i) or (ii) below):

(i) _____ Known lead–based paint and/or lead–based paint hazards are present in the housing (explain): _____

(ii)_____ Lessor has no knowledge of lead–based paint and/or lead–based paint hazards in the housing.

(B) Records and reports available to the lessor (check (i) or (ii) below):

(i) _____ Lessor has provided lessee with all available records and reports pertaining to the lead–based paint and/or lead–based paint hazards in the housing: List documents:

_____

(ii) _____Lessor has no reports or records pertaining to lead–based paint or lead–based paint hazards in the housing.

Lessee's acknowledgment: (initial)

(C) _____ Lessee has received copies of all the information listed above.

(D) _____ Lessee has received the pamphlet Protect Your Family from Lead in Your Home.

Agent's acknowledgment: (initial)

(E) _____ Agent has informed lessor of the lessor's obligations under 42 U.S.C. 4821 (d) and is aware of his/her responsibility to ensure compliance.

Certification of accuracy:

    The following parties have reviewed the information above and certify, to the best of their knowledge, that the information they have provided is accurate.

_____

Lessor   Dated

_____

Lessee   Dated

_____

Agent   Dated

Pet Addendum

This agreement is by and between _____(hereinafter referred to as tenant) and _____ (hereinafter referred to as landlord) and is an addendum to the lease agreement between the parties dated _____.

For and in consideration of the sum of $_____ which has this day been paid to landlord by tenant as a pet deposit, tenant is authorized to have in and on the leased premises the following pets: no more than _____ dogs and no more than _____ cats. Tenant shall also pay to landlord at the time of signing of this pet addendum the sum of $_____ as a nonrefundable cleaning deposit. The security deposit shall be refundable under the same terms and conditions as the remainder of the security deposit. Tenant may not keep any additional pets in, on, or about the leased premises without the additional written consent of landlord. However, if any of tenant's authorized pets produce a litter, tenant may keep the litter at the premises for up to forty–five days after weaning. Tenant shall not engage in any commercial breeding activities on the leased premises without the written consent of landlord. If, at any time, the pet causes damage to or destruction of the leased premises or becomes a nuisance, the landlord may require the tenant to either terminate the lease or remove the pets from the leased premises within thirty days; this notification must be given to tenant in writing. If tenant otherwise violates any term of this agreement, landlord shall have the right to terminate the lease agreement under the same terms and conditions as the breach of any other provision of the lease.

_____   _____
Tenant   Landlord

Landlord's Notice to Tenant of Retention of Security Deposit

Name of Tenant: _____

Forwarding address provided by Tenant: _____

Address of Leased Premises: _____

Date of This Notice: _____

Date of End of Tenancy: _____

As of the date of this notice, there is $_____ in unpaid rent due and owing.

The following items had to be repaired or replaced because they were either damaged or missing Note: No item on this list was repaired or replaced as a result of normal wear and tear.

Item: Repair made or replacement made   Cost

The following costs were incurred to restore the premises to the condition as of date of initial occupancy by tenant:

Cleaning:

Items cleaned	Cost

Painting:

Items painted	Cost

Other deductions:

Reason for deduction	Amount of Deduction

Total deductions:$_____

Total amount of security deposit: $_____

Amount Refunded to Tenant:$_____

Amount Due From Tenant: $_____

Property Report

Date: _____

Property Address: _____

_____

Condition of Property on (circle one) Move–in/Move–out

Signature of Inspecting Person: _____

Describe condition of the following areas:

Area of Property   Condition

Living Room

Dining Room

Halls

Bedrooms

Bathrooms

Kitchen

Yard/garden

Driveway

Patio/porch

Exterior

Entry

Floors/carpets

Walls/ceilings

Doors/locks

Fixtures/lights

Outlets/switches

Faucets

Toilet

Sinks

Bathtub

Shower

Refrigerator

Range

Oven

Dishwasher

Garbage Disposal

Cabinets/counters

Closets

Pantry

Garage

Keys

Smoke Detector

Landlord's Notice of Intent to Enter Premises

To: _____

Date: _____

Address of Leased Premises: _____

Please be advised that we intend to enter your residence on _____ between the hours of _____ and _____. The reason for this entry is _____ _____ _____.

If you need to reschedule this entry for any reason, please contact the following person:

Name: _____

Address: _____

_____

Phone number: _____

Thank you for your cooperation.

Signed: _____

Tenant's Repair Notice to Landlord

To: _____

From: _____

Date of Notice: _____

Address of Leased Premises: _____

The following items in or on the leased premises need repair or replacement:

You are hereby placed on notice pursuant to the Texas Property Code that these repairs must be made in a timely manner according to Texas law.

Signed: _____

Landlord's Notice to Tenant For Repairs

To: _____

Date: _____

Address of Leased Premises: _____

The following items required repair or replacement as a result of damages caused by you or one or more of your guests. Pursuant to the written lease agreement and Texas law, you are responsible for payment for these repair and replacement costs. Please remit this amount to the address below.

Item   Cost for Repair or Replacement

Signed: _____

Address for Payment: _____

Landlord's Notice to Tenant for Wrongfully Withholding Rent

To: _____

Date of Notice: _____

Address of Leased Premises: _____

Your rent for the following rental periods has not been paid: _____.
The total amount of rent now due and owing is $_____.

If you are withholding rent based on a landlord's alleged failure to make repairs or remedy a condition on or in the leased premises, please consider this your formal notice that the withholding of rent by a tenant on these grounds is a violation of Texas law. §92.058 of the Texas Property Code allows the landlord to sue a tenant who wrongfully withholds rent in violation of Chapter 92 of the Texas Property Code for a civil penalty of one month's rent plus the landlord's reasonable attorney's fees. In addition, please consider this your formal notice of the landlord's intention to pursue all other available legal remedies available as a result of your actions, including but not limited to filing a suit to evict you from the leased premises and a suit for damages.

If you have any complaints or concerns regarding the condition of the leased premises, please contact the following person:

Name: _____

Address: _____

Phone number: _____

Signed: _____

Printed name: _____

Address: _____

Phone number: _____

Landlord/Authorized representative

Tenant's Request for Compliance with Security Device Requirements

To: _____

From: _____

Date of Notice: _____

Address of Leased Premises: _____

Please consider this your formal notice of my request that you comply with the legal requirements of the Texas Property Code regarding security devices as follows:

_____

If this action has not been taken within the time allowed by law, you are hereby notified that I will remedy this problem and deduct the costs of labor, material, taxes, and additional keys (if applicable) from my rent.

Signed: _____

Landlord's Notice to Tenant Regarding Smoke Detector

To: _____

Date: _____

Address of Leased Premises: _____

It has come to our attention that you have either disabled or disconnected one or more of the smoke detectors in the leased premises. Pursuant to the written lease and Texas law, you are hereby notified that you must return all smoke detectors in the leased premises to working order within seven days of your receipt of this notice. If you fail to reconnect, repair, or replace the smoke detector within the time allowed, you are notified that the landlord will exercise all legal remedies available, including but not limited to filing suit for damages, court costs, and attorney's fees. In addition, you can be assessed a civil penalty of one month's rent plus $100.

Signed: _____

Printed name: _____

Address: _____

_____

Phone number: _____

Tenant's Notice of Termination—Utility Cutoff

To : _____

From: _____

Date of Notice: _____

Address of Leased Premises: _____

Please consider this your formal notice of my intent to terminate the lease agreement based on your violation of §92.301 of the Texas Property Code. On _____, I received notice from _____ that electricity to my leased premises would be terminated on _____. Our written lease agreement requires you to provide electricity for the premises at your expense. Please be advised that I will be moving out on _____ which is within the thirty days from the date of the notice of termination.

Signed: _____

Landlord's Notice to Tenant of Entry of Premises and Seizure of Property

To: _____

Date: _____

Address of Leased Premises: _____

You are hereby notified that the landlord or a representative or agent of the landlord has entered your residence for the purpose of exercising the landlord's lien established in the written lease agreement dated _____.

The lease requires you to make rental payments of $_____ per month. Your payments are due and payable on the first day of each month, beginning on _____. You have failed to make the rental payments due on the following dates: _____. The total amount of rent now due and owing is $_____. You should contact the following person regarding payment arrangement for the delinquent rental payments:

Name: _____

Address: _____

_____

Phone number: _____

In addition to the unpaid rental amounts, the lease agreement allows the landlord to charge you for packing, removing, and storing the seized property.

The following items of your property were taken:

_____

_____

_____

Your property will be returned to you promptly upon payment in full of the delinquent rent. If you do not make payment in full, your property will be sold in accordance with Chapter 54 of the Texas Property Code.

Signed: _____

Printed name: _____

Address: _____

_____

Phone number: _____

Notice of Sale of Seized Property

To: _____

Date: _____

Address of Leased Premises: _____

Tenant's Last Known Address: _____

You are hereby notified that your property, which was seized on _____ to satisfy the contractual lien established in the written lease agreement dated _____ will be sold at public sale on _____ at _____o'clock ___.m. at the following address: _____. You may contact the following person in regard to this sale:

Name: _____

Address: _____

_____

Phone number: _____

The following is an itemized list of the amounts you now owe:

Unpaid rent: $_____

Unpaid Rent dates: _____

Packing and Removal Costs:$_____

Storage Costs: _____ days @ $_____ per day for a total of $_____

Landlord's Demand for Unpaid Rent

To: _____

From: _____

Date of Notice: _____

Address of Leased Premises: _____

Amount of Monthly Rent: _____

Please be advised that on the following dates, rental payments were due from you under the lease agreement. These payments have not been made and demand is hereby made upon you for payment of those amounts, in the total sum of $_____.

Dates due: _____   Date of Payment: _____

If payment is not received within thirty days, we may file suit against you in court to collect the unpaid rent.

THIS IS AN ATTEMPT TO COLLECT A DEBT AND ANY INFORMATION OBTAINED MAY BE USED FOR THIS PURPOSE.

Signed: _____

Original Petition to Collect Unpaid Rent

Cause No. _____

Landlord's name,	§	**IN THE JUSTICE COURT**
PLAINTIFF	§	
	§	
I.	§	**PRECINCT___, PLACE____**
	§	
Tenant's name,	§	_____ **COUNTY, TEXAS**
DEFENDANT	§	

ORIGINAL PETITION TO COLLECT UNPAID RENT

COMES NOW _____, hereinafter referred to as Plaintiff, complaining of _____, hereinafter referred to as Defendant, and shows the Court as follows:

I.

Plaintiff is an (individual, partnership, corporation) and is the owner of the property located at _____. Defendant is an individual whose last known home address is _____ and whose last known work address is _____. Process may be served at those addresses.

II.

On or about _____, Plaintiff and Defendant entered into a written lease whereby Defendant agreed to lease the property located at _____. As a part of the lease, Defendant agreed to pay rent in the amount of $_____ per month, beginning on _____. On the following dates, rental payments became due and owing and were not paid by Defendant: _____. As of this date, none of those amounts have been paid to Plaintiff by Defendant.

III.

Defendant's failure to make the rental payments when due constitutes a breach of the written lease agreement and a forfeiture by Defendant of his right to possession of the premises. On _____, Plaintiff made demand for payment to Defendant, by certified mail, return receipt requested, and regular mail, on _____. Defendant has failed to comply with this demand. Plaintiff sues for the unpaid rent in the amount of $_____ and for all costs of court.

WHEREFORE, PREMISES CONSIDERED, Plaintiff prays that the Defendant be cited to appear and answer, and that a judgment be entered against Defendant in the amount of $_____ for the unpaid rent and for all costs of court.

Respectfully submitted,

_____

Landlord's name

Address

Phone number

Fax number if any

BEFORE ME, the undersigned authority, on this day personally appeared _____, who after being duly sworn, stated as follows:

My name is _____. I am the Plaintiff in the above cause and I swear that the allegations in this petition are true and correct and within my personal knowledge.

_____

SWORN TO AND SUBSCRIBED before me this _____ day of _____, 200_.

_____

Notary Public in and for the State of Texas

You may redeem your property by paying in full all delinquent rent plus the packing, removal, and storage costs. You may exercise this right at any time prior to the sale of the property. The property will be sold to the highest cash bidder and proceeds will be applied in the following order: any recorded mortgage or financing statement, unpaid rent, and then packing, removal, and storage costs. Any proceeds remaining after the payment of these amounts will be mailed to you at your last known address not later than the 30th day after the date of the sale.

Signed: _____

Printed name: _____

Address: _____

_____

Phone number: _____

Landlord's Notice to Tenant Regarding Disposal of Abandoned Property

To: _____   Date: _____

Address of Leased Premises: _____

Tenant's Last Known Address: _____

Date of Storage: _____

You are hereby notified that the following items of property which were abandoned by you have been removed from the leased premises and stored.

_____

_____

_____

_____

You have the right to reclaim this property by contacting the following person:

Name: _____

Address: _____

_____

Phone number: _____

If you have not claimed this property within sixty days, the property will be sold.

Signed: _____

Printed name: _____

Address: _____

_____

Phone number: _____

Notice of Changing of Lock to Commercial Tenant

To: _____

Date: _____

Address of Leased Premises: _____

You are hereby notified that you have failed to pay your rent as due as follows:

Amount of monthly payment: _____

Due dates of unpaid rent: _____

Amount of rent now due and owing: _____

Based on the failure to pay your rent, you are notified that the landlord has changed the locks controlling access to the leased premises. A new key may be obtained by paying all delinquent rents. The key will be supplied during normal business hours and may be obtained by contacting the following person:

Name: _____

Address: _____

_____

Phone number: _____

Signed: _____

Printed name: _____

Address: _____

_____

Phone number: _____

Eviction Notice

To: _____

Date: _____

Address of Leased Premises: _____

You are hereby notified that you have failed to pay your rent as due as follows:

Amount of monthly payment: _____

Due dates of unpaid rent: _____

Amount of rent now due and owing: _____

Because you are in default of your obligation under the lease to make all rental payments, please consider this your formal notice to vacate the leased premises listed above within _____ days of your receipt of this notice.

If you fail to vacate the premises within the time allowed, the landlord will file an eviction suit to have you removed from the leased premises as well as a suit to recover the unpaid rent and any damages. You could be ordered to make court costs and attorney's fees as a result of these court actions.

Signed: _____

Printed name: _____

Address: _____

_____

Phone number: _____

Eviction Petition

Cause No. _____

Landlord's name,	§	**IN THE JUSTICE COURT**
PLAINTIFF	§	
	§	
I.	§	**PRECINCT___, PLACE____**
	§	
Tenant's name,	§	**_____ COUNTY, TEXAS**
DEFENDANT	§	

ORIGINAL PETITION

COMES NOW _____, hereinafter referred to as Plaintiff, complaining of _____, hereinafter referred to as Defendant, and shows the Court as follows:

I.

Plaintiff is an (individual, partnership, corporation) and is the owner of the property located at _____. Defendant is an individual whose last known home address is _____ and whose last known work address is _____. Process may be served at those addresses.

II.

On or about _____, Plaintiff and Defendant entered into a written lease whereby Defendant agreed to lease the property located at _____. As a part of the lease, Defendant agreed to pay rent in the amount of $_____ per month, beginning on _____. On the following dates, rental payments became due and owing and were not paid by Defendant: _____. As of this date, none of those amounts have been paid to Plaintiff by Defendant.

III.

Defendant's failure to make the rental payments when due constitutes a breach of the written lease agreement and a forfeiture by Defendant of his right to possession of the premises. On _____, Plaintiff gave notice to Defendant, by certified mail, return receipt requested, and regular mail, notice to vacate the premises. Defendant has failed to comply with this demand and Plaintiff is entitled to immediate possession of the premises, for which Plaintiff now sues. In addition, Plaintiff sues for the unpaid rent in the amount of $_____ and for all costs of court.

WHEREFORE, PREMISES CONSIDERED, Plaintiff prays that the Defendant be cited to appear and answer, that the Court award Plaintiff immediate possession of the premises, and that a judgment be entered against Defendant in the amount of $_____ for the unpaid rent and for all costs of court.

Respectfully submitted,

_____

Landlord's name: _____

Address: _____

Phone number: _____

Fax number if any: _____

BEFORE ME, the undersigned authority, on this day personally appeared _____, who after being duly sworn, stated as follows:

My name is _____. I am the Plaintiff in the above cause and I swear that the allegations in this petition are true and correct and within my personal knowledge.

SWORN TO AND SUBSCRIBED before me this _____ day of _____, 200_.

_____

Notary Public in and for the State of Texas

Landlord's Notice to Tenant Regarding Storage of Property after Writ of Possession

To: _____

Date: _____

Address of Leased Premises: _____

Tenant's Last Known Address: _____

Date Writ Executed and Property Removed: _____

You are hereby notified that the property have been removed from the leased premises pursuant to a Writ of Possession and stored.

_____

_____

You have the right to reclaim this property by contacting the following person:

Name: _____

Address: _____

_____

Phone number: _____

If you have not claimed this property within thirty days, the property will be sold.

Notice: You may redeem your property without the payment of moving and storage costs if you do so prior to the time the warehouseman leaves the leased premises for the last time while in the process of removing your property.

Signed: _____

Printed name: _____

Address: _____

_____

Phone number: _____

Release of Judgment

NO. _____

_____	§	**IN THE JUSTICE COURT**
	§	
I.	§	**PCT. __, PLACE ____**
	§	
_____	§	_____ **COUNTY, TEXAS**

RELEASE OF JUDGMENT

STATE OF TEXAS

COUNTY OF _____

      WHEREAS, on _____, 200__, Plaintiff _____ recovered a judgment against Defendant _____ in the Justice Court, Precinct __, Place ___ of _____ County, Texas, in which the presiding judge in case no. _____ on the docket of that court entered a judgment for Plaintiff _____ in the sum of $_____ together with post judgment interest at _____ % from _____ ;

      WHEREAS Plaintiff and Defendant have fully resolved and settled this judgement for a sum that constitutes payment in full of all amounts due and owing pursuant to the judgment;

      NOW, THEREFORE, for good and valuable consideration, the parties to the above described judgment have resolved the dispute, Plaintiff does forever discharge and release the Defendant, _____, for the payment of any and all claims, damages, costs of court, including attorney's allegedly due and owing pursuant to the judgment in the above described cause of action. It is further agreed that no further action of execution or for collection of any additional sums recited in the judgement be taken.

      This agreement shall constitute a full release of any and all claims or judgement liens of Plaintiff, _____, against _____, Defendant, and shall be binding upon Plaintiff, its heirs and assigns and agents forever.

This agreement is executed this day by Plaintiff.

Signed_____

_____

SUBSCRIBED AND SWORN TO BEFORE ME on _____.

_____

Notary Public in and for the
State of Texas

INDEX

Your #1 Source for Real World Legal Information...

SPHINX® PUBLISHING
An Imprint of Sourcebooks, Inc.®

- Written by lawyers
- Simple English explanation of the law
- Forms and instructions included

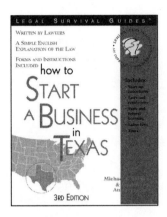

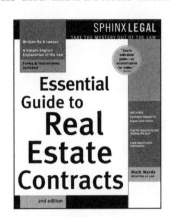

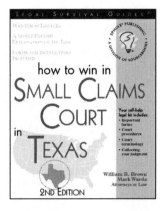

HOW TO START A
BUSINESS IN TEXAS, 3RD ED.

This book simplifies the start-up process while saving you time and money. It uses an easy-to-understand approach to business regulations for anyone considering opening a business in Texas.

264 pages; $18.95;
ISBN 1-57248-228-1

ESSENTIAL GUIDE TO
REAL ESTATE CONTRACTS, 2ND ED.

Maximize your real estate investment by learning to understand the ins and outs of real estate contracts. This book includes sample contrats and is your personal manual to developing the contract you want and getting the deal that is in your best interest.

232 pages; $18.95;
ISBN 1-57248-346-6

HOW TO WIN IN SMALL CLAIMS
COURT IN TEXAS, 2ND ED.

Small claims court can be very complicated unless you know the process and language of the courts. This book makes filing or defending suits in small claims court inexpensive and hassle-free.

258 pages; $16.95;
ISBN 1-57248-111-0

See the following order form for books written specifically for California, the District of Columbia, Florida, Georgia, Illinois, Maryland, Massachusetts, Michigan, Minnesota, New Jersey, New York, North Carolina, Ohio, Pennsylvania, Texas, and Virginia!

What our customers say about our books:

"It couldn't be more clear for the lay person." —R.D.

"I want you to know I really appreciate your book. It has saved me a lot of time and money." —L.T.

"Your real estate contracts book has saved me nearly $12,000.00 in closing costs over the past year." —A.B.

"...many of the legal questions that I have had over the years were answered clearly and concisely through your plain English interpretation of the law." —C.E.H.

"If there weren't people out there like you I'd be lost. You have the best books of this type out there." —S.B.

"...your forms and directions are easy to follow." —C.V.M.

Sphinx Publishing's Legal Survival Guides
are directly available from Sourcebooks, Inc., or from your local bookstores.

For credit card orders call 1–800–432–7444, write P.O. Box 4410, Naperville, IL 60567-4410,
or fax 630-961-2168
Find more legal information at: www.SphinxLegal.com

SPHINX® PUBLISHING'S NATIONAL TITLES
Valid in All 50 States

LEGAL SURVIVAL IN BUSINESS

The Complete Book of Corporate Forms	$24.95
The Complete Patent Book	$26.95
The Entrepreneur's Internet Handbook	$21.95
How to Form a Limited Liability Company (2E)	$24.95
Incorporate in Delaware from Any State	$24.95
Incorporate in Nevada from Any State	$24.95
How to Form a Nonprofit Corporation (2E)	$24.95
How to Form Your Own Corporation (4E)	$26.95
How to Form Your Own Partnership (2E)	$24.95
How to Register Your Own Copyright (4E)	$24.95
How to Register Your Own Trademark (3E)	$21.95
Most Valuable Business Legal Forms You'll Ever Need (3E)	$21.95
Profit from Intellectual Property	$28.95
Protect Your Patent	$24.95
The Small Business Owner's Guide to Bankruptcy	$21.95

LEGAL SURVIVAL IN COURT

Crime Victim's Guide to Justice (2E)	$21.95
Grandparents' Rights (3E)	$24.95
Help Your Lawyer Win Your Case (2E)	$14.95
Jurors' Rights (2E)	$12.95
Legal Research Made Easy (3E)	$21.95
Winning Your Personal Injury Claim (2E)	$24.95
Your Rights When You Owe Too Much	$16.95

LEGAL SURVIVAL IN REAL ESTATE

Essential Guide to Real Estate Contracts (2E)	$18.95
Essential Guide to Real Estate Leases	$18.95
How to Buy a Condominium or Townhome (2E)	$19.95
How to Buy Your First Home	$18.95
Working with Your Homeowners Association	$19.95

LEGAL SURVIVAL IN PERSONAL AFFAIRS

The 529 College Savings Plan	$16.95
The Antique and Art Collector's Legal Guide	$24.95
Cómo Hacer su Propio Testamento	$16.95
Cómo Restablecer su propio Crédito y Renegociar sus Deudas	$21.95
Cómo Solicitar su Propio Divorcio	$24.95
The Complete Legal Guide to Senior Care	$21.95
Family Limited Partnership	$26.95
Gay & Lesbian Rights	$26.95
Guía de Inmigración a Estados Unidos (3E)	$24.95
Guía de Justicia para Víctimas del Crimen	$21.95
How to File Your Own Bankruptcy (5E)	$21.95
How to File Your Own Divorce (5E)	$26.95
How to Make Your Own Simple Will (3E)	$18.95
How to Write Your Own Living Will (3E)	$18.95
How to Write Your Own Premarital Agreement (3E)	$24.95
Inmigración a los EE. UU. Paso a Paso	$22.95
Living Trusts and Other Ways to Avoid Probate (3E)	$24.95
Manual de Beneficios para el Seguro Social	$18.95
Mastering the MBE	$16.95
Most Valuable Personal Legal Forms You'll Ever Need (2E)	$26.95
Neighbor v. Neighbor (2E)	$16.95
The Nanny and Domestic Help Legal Kit	$22.95
The Power of Attorney Handbook (4E)	$19.95
Repair Your Own Credit and Deal with Debt (2E)	$18.95
El Seguro Social Preguntas y Respuestas	$14.95
Sexual Harassment:Your Guide to Legal Action	$18.95
The Social Security Benefits Handbook (3E)	$18.95
Social Security Q&A	$12.95
Teen Rights	$22.95
Traveler's Rights	$21.95
Unmarried Parents' Rights (2E)	$19.95
U.S. Immigration Step by Step	$21.95
U.S.A. Immigration Guide (4E)	$24.95
The Visitation Handbook	$18.95
The Wills, Estate Planning and Trusts Legal Kit	&26.95
Win Your Unemployment Compensation Claim (2E)	$21.95
Your Right to Child Custody, Visitation and Support (2E)	$24.95

Legal Survival Guides are directly available from Sourcebooks, Inc., or from your local bookstores.

SPHINX® PUBLISHING ORDER FORM

BILL TO:	SHIP TO:

Phone #	Terms	F.O.B. Chicago, IL	Ship Date

Charge my: ☐ VISA   ☐ MasterCard   ☐ American Express

☐ **Money Order or Personal Check**

Credit Card Number   Expiration Date

Qty	ISBN	Title	Retail	Ext.	Qty	ISBN	Title	Retail	Ext.
		SPHINX PUBLISHING NATIONAL TITLES				1-57248-169-2	The Power of Attorney Handbook (4E)	$19.95	
	1-57248-238-9	The 529 College Savings Plan	$16.95			1-57248-332-6	Profit from Intellectual Property	$28.95	
	1-57248-349-0	The Antique and Art Collector's Legal Guide	$24.95			1-57248-329-6	Protect Your Patent	$24.95	
	1-57248-148-X	Cómo Hacer su Propio Testamento	$16.95			1-57248-344-X	Repair Your Own Credit and Deal with Debt (2E)	$18.95	
	1-57248-226-5	Cómo Restablecer su propio Crédito y Renegociar sus Deudas	$21.95			1-57248-350-4	El Seguro Social Preguntas y Respuestas	$14.95	
	1-57248-147-1	Cómo Solicitar su Propio Divorcio	$24.95			1-57248-217-6	Sexual Harassment: Your Guide to Legal Action	$18.95	
	1-57248-166-8	The Complete Book of Corporate Forms	$24.95			1-57248-219-2	The Small Business Owner's Guide to Bankruptcy	$21.95	
	1-57248-229-X	The Complete Legal Guide to Senior Care	$21.95			1-57248-168-4	The Social Security Benefits Handbook (3E)	$18.95	
	1-57248-201-X	The Complete Patent Book	$26.95			1-57248-216-8	Social Security Q&A	$12.95	
	1-57248-163-3	Crime Victim's Guide to Justice (2E)	$21.95			1-57248-221-4	Teen Rights	$22.95	
	1-57248-251-6	The Entrepreneur's Internet Handbook	$21.95			1-57248-335-0	Traveler's Rights	$21.95	
	1-57248-346-6	Essential Guide to Real Estate Contracts (2E)	$18.95			1-57248-236-2	Unmarried Parents' Rights (2E)	$19.95	
	1-57248-160-9	Essential Guide to Real Estate Leases	$18.95			1-57248-218-4	U.S. Immigration Step by Step	$21.95	
	1-57248-254-0	Family Limited Partnership	$26.95			1-57248-161-7	U.S.A. Immigration Guide (4E)	$24.95	
	1-57248-331-8	Gay & Lesbian Rights	$26.95			1-57248-192-7	The Visitation Handbook	$18.95	
	1-57248-139-0	Grandparents' Rights (3E)	$24.95			1-57248-225-7	Win Your Unemployment Compensation Claim (2E)	$21.95	
	1-57248-188-9	Guía de Inmigración a Estados Unidos (3E)	$24.95			1-57248-330-X	The Wills, Estate Planning and Trusts Legal Kit	&26.95	
	1-57248-187-0	Guía de Justicia para Víctimas del Crimen	$21.95			1-57248-138-2	Winning Your Personal Injury Claim (2E)	$24.95	
	1-57248-103-X	Help Your Lawyer Win Your Case (2E)	$14.95			1-57248-333-4	Working with Your Homeowners Association	$19.95	
	1-57248-164-1	How to Buy a Condominium or Townhome (2E)	$19.95			1-57248-162-5	Your Right to Child Custody, Visitation and Support (2E)	$24.95	
	1-57248-328-8	How to Buy Your First Home	$18.95			1-57248-157-9	Your Rights When You Owe Too Much	$16.95	
	1-57248-191-9	How to File Your Own Bankruptcy (5E)	$21.95				**CALIFORNIA TITLES**		
	1-57248-343-1	How to File Your Own Divorce (5E)	$26.95			1-57248-150-1	CA Power of Attorney Handbook (2E)	$18.95	
	1-57248-222-2	How to Form a Limited Liability Company (2E)	$24.95			1-57248-337-7	How to File for Divorce in CA (4E)	$26.95	
	1-57248-231-1	How to Form a Nonprofit Corporation (2E)	$24.95			1-57248-145-5	How to Probate and Settle an Estate in CA	$26.95	
	1-57248-345-8	How to Form Your Own Corporation (4E)	$26.95			1-57248-336-9	How to Start a Business in CA (2E)	$21.95	
	1-57248-224-9	How to Form Your Own Partnership (2E)	$24.95			1-57248-194-3	How to Win in Small Claims Court in CA (2E)	$18.95	
	1-57248-232-X	How to Make Your Own Simple Will (3E)	$18.95			1-57248-246-X	Make Your Own CA Will	$18.95	
	1-57248-200-1	How to Register Your Own Copyright (4E)	$24.95			1-57248-196-X	The Landlord's Legal Guide in CA	$24.95	
	1-57248-104-8	How to Register Your Own Trademark (3E)	$21.95			1-57248-241-9	Tenants' Rights in CA	$21.95	
	1-57248-233-8	How to Write Your Own Living Will (3E)	$18.95				**FLORIDA TITLES**		
	1-57248-156-0	How to Write Your Own Premarital Agreement (3E)	$24.95			1-57071-363-4	Florida Power of Attorney Handbook (2E)	$16.95	
	1-57248-230-3	Incorporate in Delaware from Any State	$24.95			1-57248-176-5	How to File for Divorce in FL (7E)	$26.95	
	1-57248-158-7	Incorporate in Nevada from Any State	$24.95			1-57248-356-3	How to Form a Corporation in FL (6E)	$24.95	
	1-57248-250-8	Inmigración a los EE.UU. Paso a Paso	$22.95			1-57248-203-6	How to Form a Limited Liability Co. in FL (2E)	$24.95	
	1-57071-333-2	Jurors' Rights (2E)	$12.95			1-57071-401-0	How to Form a Partnership in FL	$22.95	
	1-57248-223-0	Legal Research Made Easy (3E)	$21.95			1-57248-113-7	How to Make a FL Will (6E)	$16.95	
	1-57248-165-X	Living Trusts and Other Ways to Avoid Probate (3E)	$24.95			1-57248-088-2	•How to Modify Your FL Divorce Judgment (4E)	$24.95	
	1-57248-186-2	Manual de Beneficios para el Seguro Social	$18.95			1-57248-144-7	How to Probate and Settle an Estate in FL (4E)	$26.95	
	1-57248-220-6	Mastering the MBE	$16.95			1-57248-339-3	How to Start a Business in FL (7E)	$21.95	
	1-57248-167-6	Most Val. Business Legal Forms You'll Ever Need (3E)	$21.95			1-57248-204-4	How to Win in Small Claims Court in FL (7E)	$18.95	
	1-57248-360-1	Most Val. Personal Legal Forms You'll Ever Need (2E)	$26.95			1-57248-202-8	Land Trusts in Florida (6E)	$29.95	
	1-57248-098-X	The Nanny and Domestic Help Legal Kit	$22.95			1-57248-338-5	Landlords' Rights and Duties in FL (9E)	$22.95	
	1-57248-089-0	Neighbor v. Neighbor (2E)	$16.95			***Form Continued on Following Page***		**SUBTOTAL**	

To order, call Sourcebooks at 1-800-432-7444 or FAX (630) 961-2168 (Bookstores, libraries, wholesalers—please call for discount)

Prices are subject to change without notice.

Find more legal information at: **www.SphinxLegal.com**

SPHINX® PUBLISHING ORDER FORM

Qty	ISBN	Title	Retail	Ext.
		GEORGIA TITLES		
_____	1-57248-340-7	How to File for Divorce in GA (5E)	$21.95	_____
_____	1-57248-180-3	How to Make a GA Will (4E)	$21.95	_____
_____	1-57248-341-5	How to Start a Business in Georgia (3E)	$21.95	_____
		ILLINOIS TITLES		
_____	1-57248-244-3	Child Custody, Visitation, and Support in IL	$24.95	_____
_____	1-57248-206-0	How to File for Divorce in IL (3E)	$24.95	_____
_____	1-57248-170-6	How to Make an IL Will (3E)	$16.95	_____
_____	1-57248-247-8	How to Start a Business in IL (3E)	$21.95	_____
_____	1-57248-252-4	The Landlord's Legal Guide in IL	$24.95	_____
		MARYLAND, VIRGINIA AND THE DISTRICT OF COLUMBIA		
_____	1-57248-240-0	How to File for Divorce in MD, VA and DC	$28.95	_____
		MASSACHUSETTS TITLES		
_____	1-57248-128-5	How to File for Divorce in MA (3E)	$24.95	_____
_____	1-57248-115-3	How to Form a Corporation in MA	$24.95	_____
_____	1-57248-108-0	How to Make a MA Will (2E)	$16.95	_____
_____	1-57248-248-6	How to Start a Business in MA (3E)	$21.95	_____
_____	1-57248-209-5	The Landlord's Legal Guide in MA	$24.95	_____
		MICHIGAN TITLES		
_____	1-57248-215-X	How to File for Divorce in MI (3E)	$24.95	_____
_____	1-57248-182-X	How to Make a MI Will (3E)	$16.95	_____
_____	1-57248-183-8	How to Start a Business in MI (3E)	$18.95	_____
		MINNESOTA TITLES		
_____	1-57248-142-0	How to File for Divorce in MN	$21.95	_____
_____	1-57248-179-X	How to Form a Corporation in MN	$24.95	_____
_____	1-57248-178-1	How to Make a MN Will (2E)	$16.95	_____
		NEW JERSEY TITLES		
_____	1-57248-239-7	How to File for Divorce in NJ	$24.95	_____
		NEW YORK TITLES		
_____	1-57248-193-5	Child Custody, Visitation and Support in NY	$26.95	_____
_____	1-57248-351-2	File for Divorce in NY	$26.95	_____
_____	1-57248-249-4	How to Form a Corporation in NY (2E)	$24.95	_____
_____	1-57248-095-5	How to Make a NY Will (2E)	$16.95	_____
_____	1-57248-199-4	How to Start a Business in NY (2E)	$18.95	_____
_____	1-57248-198-6	How to Win in Small Claims Court in NY (2E)	$18.95	_____
_____	1-57248-197-8	Landlords' Legal Guide in NY	$24.95	_____
_____	1-57071-188-7	New York Power of Attorney Handbook	$19.95	_____
_____	1-57248-122-6	Tenants' Rights in NY	$21.95	_____

Qty	ISBN	Title	Retail	Ext.
		NORTH CAROLINA TITLES		
_____	1-57248-185-4	How to File for Divorce in NC (3E)	$22.95	_____
_____	1-57248-129-3	How to Make a NC Will (3E)	$16.95	_____
_____	1-57248-184-6	How to Start a Business in NC (3E)	$18.95	_____
_____	1-57248-091-2	Landlords' Rights & Duties in NC	$21.95	_____
		OHIO TITLES		
_____	1-57248-190-0	How to File for Divorce in OH (2E)	$24.95	_____
_____	1-57248-174-9	How to Form a Corporation in OH	$24.95	_____
_____	1-57248-173-0	How to Make an OH Will	$16.95	_____
		PENNSYLVANIA TITLES		
_____	1-57248-242-7	Child Custody, Visitation and Support in PA	$26.95	_____
_____	1-57248-211-7	How to File for Divorce in PA (3E)	$26.95	_____
_____	1-57248-094-7	How to Make a PA Will (2E)	$16.95	_____
_____	1-57248-357-1	How to Start a Business in PA (3E)	$21.95	_____
_____	1-57248-245-1	The Landlord's Legal Guide in PA	$24.95	_____
		TEXAS TITLES		
_____	1-57248-171-4	Child Custody, Visitation, and Support in TX	$22.95	_____
_____	1-57248-172-2	How to File for Divorce in TX (3E)	$24.95	_____
_____	1-57248-114-5	How to Form a Corporation in TX (2E)	$24.95	_____
_____	1-57248-255-9	How to Make a TX Will (3E)	$16.95	_____
_____	1-57248-214-1	How to Probate and Settle an Estate in TX (3E)	$26.95	_____
_____	1-57248-228-1	How to Start a Business in TX (3E)	$18.95	_____
_____	1-57248-111-0	How to Win in Small Claims Court in TX (2E)	$16.95	_____
_____	1-57248-355-5	the Landlord's Legal Guide in TX	$24.95	_____

SUBTOTAL THIS PAGE _____

SUBTOTAL PREVIOUS PAGE _____

Shipping — $5.00 for 1st book, $1.00 each additional _____

Illinois residents add 6.75% sales tax _____

Connecticut residents add 6.00% sales tax _____

TOTAL _____

To order, call Sourcebooks at 1-800-432-7444 or FAX (630) 961-2168 (Bookstores, libraries, wholesalers—please call for discount)
Prices are subject to change without notice.
Find more legal information at: **www.SphinxLegal.com**